François Laruelle's
Philosophies of Difference

François Laruelle's
Philosophies of Difference
A Critical Introduction and Guide

ROCCO GANGLE

EDINBURGH
University Press

Edinburgh University Press Ltd
22 George Square, Edinburgh EH8 9LF

www.euppublishing.com

Typeset in 11/13pt Monotype Ehrhardt by
Servis Filmsetting Ltd, Stockport, Cheshire, and
printed and bound in Great Britain by
CPI Group (UK) Ltd, Croydon CR0 4YY

A CIP record for this book is available from the British Library

ISBN 978 0 7486 6812 0 (hardback)
ISBN 978 0 7486 6813 7 (paperback)
ISBN 978 0 7486 6814 4 (webready PDF)
ISBN 978 0 7486 6815 1 (epub)

Contents

Acknowledgements

I would like to thank first my philosophical brethren, those close friends who have shaped my own thinking at its very roots: Micah Murphy for Marx, anarchy and uncompromising resistance, Jason Smick for phenomenology, time and the God of the philosophers, Joshua Ramey for Deleuze, divination and the next Renaissance. Special appreciation as well to Willie Young and Gitte Butin for taking the time to read and comment helpfully on an early, not-so-pretty draft. Sundry and disparate thanks to Tom Higgins, Matthew Haar Farris, Dan Barber, Anthony Paul Smith, Tim Titus, Ryan Wingert, Gianluca Caterina, Fernando Tohme, Betsy Mesard, Creston Davis, Tony Baker, Willis Jenkins, Brian Sholl, Trent Pomplun and the whole Virginia crew. Long-due recognition is owed my academic mentors, especially Peter Ochs, Eleanor Kaufman, John Milbank and Larry Bouchard. Immeasurable gratitude to those closest: Margaret Young and Quentin Gangle. Much appreciation to Endicott College for two semesters of research support on this project and to the Department of Humanities for providing an exceptionally collegial environment for pursuing such work. Thanks to Carol MacDonald, Jenny Daly and James Dale at Edinburgh University Press – your initiative, assistance and patience made this book possible. Heartfelt gratitude to Albana Meta and the baristas at the Gusto Café in downtown Beverly – your superb espresso made it real. Gratefulness penultimately to François Laruelle for thinking it first and thinking it through. Finally to my parents Eugene and Sandra for everything over the years, this book is dedicated to you.

1

Situating Philosophies of Difference

What has philosophy done for you lately? Has it challenged you? Has it saved you? Has it become an instrument in your hands for challenging and saving others? Or has it used you merely to propagate itself? Has it tricked you? In this dance or friendship or war between you and philosophy, who leads and who follows? Are you philosophy's subject or its object, its mirror or its image? Are you Master or Slave here; maker, tool or half-finished product? To be sure, such images and relations are just metaphors and not concepts, yet we cannot help but ask what metaphor or image would be appropriate to such questions. Are *kosmos*, *physis*, *polis* meta-phors? For whom exactly and to what ends? In such matters, the choice of metaphor largely determines the stakes. What are the stakes between you and philosophy? Are these stakes themselves philosophical? Who decides this? Do you?

But perhaps it is not about you. Perhaps the world and its scattered Others need philosophy. Certainly there is the undeniable call of suffering, individual and collective, personal and historical. It is not difficult today to recite a litany of contemporary disaster and imminent catastrophe at global and not only global scales. This has been true for some time now, perhaps as long as human memory. To the real suffering of those who live and have lived in the world, philosophy promises justice or at least suggests intelligent compromise. Unavoidably, we pose again and again a naive and yet sophisticated question to philosophy: What can be done? Is this question itself already philosophical? The world seems at times to be missing philosophy in the way a problem misses its solution, lacks its essential completion. But philosophy is also a problem and its historical effects a real source of suffering. Even in principle, what would the world's philosophical completion mean if not the closure of the Whole and the loss of what still remains humanly and humanely real? Perhaps it would be better simply to work toward the weakening of philosophy, to turn philosophy against itself in order to restrain its own worst tendencies and to hope for the best.

In question here is the authoritative status of philosophy. From this derives philosophy's problematic nature as well as its salutary promise. The ultimate stakes of philosophical authority are set according to the question: Can philosophy be both *general* and *rigorous*? It seems clear that philosophy is at times one or the other. Can it be both at once? Can it cover *everything exactly*? Can it cover itself while doing so?

On the one hand, *generality* is evident everywhere in philosophy, but it is surely most evident and most general in ontology and metaphysics, the branches (or roots?) of philosophy that purport to examine Being as such, its structures and first principles. Everything, that is to say, *all* things are ultimately subsumed under these headings (however metaphysics and ontology themselves might be distinguished). 'Everything' includes much. It is a category at least general enough to include all the objects of other domains of inquiry, in particular those of the various sciences. Yet when it comes to theoretical rigour, it is not at all clear that much has been achieved at this most general level. No doubt there are theoretically rich systems, but are there really determinate *results* in ontology or metaphysics that can compare to rigorous proofs in mathematics, for instance, or to experimental progress in physics? Does Being submit to rigorous conception? Is there a perfectly general science of the Real?

Conversely, *rigour* is no doubt found throughout philosophy to varying degrees, but it tends to be maximised only in its more specialised subdivisions, such as formal logic. Indeed, logic provides an interesting case. Logicians might well argue that their discipline marks precisely the intersection of generality and rigour. Yet generality here must mean *real* generality, not just hypothetical or abstract generality. Formal logic is rigorous in the sense of being fully determined and calculable, while in general the logic of philosophical arguments is not. But rather than a weakness, this is in fact the strength of philosophical reasoning as manifest especially through the poetic depths and rhetorical flexibility of socially embedded texts. Words spoken and written in natural language best (perhaps exclusively) express the affective movement and power of the concept.

At least since Hegel, philosophy has recognised the danger of logic's false and misleading appearance of rigorous generality. In particular, formal rigour reveals its limits as soon as it is forced to confront life's ordinary messiness. It is not just that the actual world is too complex and varied to be modelled by systems of formal logic, although this may in fact be the case. It is that *our* reality, human reality – incidentally the only one we have, even if we inevitably misjudge its limits – is so often caught up in stupidity, opaqueness, ambiguity and sheer wrongness (not to mention the transports of beauty and ecstatic joy). Real generality, if such a thing is truly possible for thought, must include such mixed, non-rigorous and failing (as well as sublime) human experiences. If these are rejected and excluded *a priori* or treated as mere epiphenomena, then rigour trumps generality and the Real is *decided upon* rather than respected as such. The world itself is not a representation or a decision. How could any representation or decision be adequate to it?

Philosophical authority seems to work somewhat like a human eye. As it takes in more and more, it tends to lose details. And it focuses at the expense of breadth and range. Are such trade-offs inevitable? Does generality of scope necessarily imply laxity of rigour? And does theoretical rigour always entail narrowness of purview? Does rigour in this way lead inevitably to forms of theoretical ideology, if not ethical and political authoritarianism? At any rate, it seems doubtful whether any philosophy in the contemporary scene would claim to be both *perfectly general* and *perfectly rigorous*, with good reason.

Laruelle's non-philosophy breaks with the philosophical images of generality and rigour in order to make evident the possibility and reality of a new mode of thought. This non-philosophical thinking is conceived on the one hand as *perfectly generic* in that it excludes no domains of thought, experience, being or non-being and thus cannot be determined through any Other or limit. In this way, it claims like science to involve no ideological particularity, while it claims like the best of continental philosophy to escape the traps of representation and like the best of analytic philosophy to dissolve the webs of hand-waving conceptual obscurity. On the other hand, it is also conceived as *perfectly exact* in that it does not depend on any slippage or difference, however minimal, between thought and what thought would think, between form and content, *noesis* and *noema* or any of the other multifarious dyads and differences of which philosophy makes extensive use. It stays true to the Real not by picturing it correctly, but by thinking according to its exact indivisibility. And it claims that this exactness according to the Real is thoroughly humane.

This latter claim is key. Non-philosophy attains a rigour that acknowledges the human Real in the only way it can be rightly acknowledged: in person. It directly instantiates a human thought that does not subsume those who think (and those for whom they might think) under one or another regime of inhuman determination (through Life, History, Power, Text, God, Being and so on).

Philosophies of Difference, one of Laruelle's most important books, applies this mode of non-philosophical thinking directly to philosophy itself and in particular to the contemporary continental philosophies of Difference. After the valuable critical interventions in philosophy since Nietzsche that reject thought's historical closure and aim at opening real possibilities for resistance and creation, it looks to realise these critical and constructive tendencies with alternate means that are no longer themselves philosophical and thus no longer subject to the interminable oscillation between a thought that needs the Real and a Real that calls for thinking. Need and call: these terms may very well harbour servile affections and authoritarian impulses, as may well their deployments in every species of philosophical idealism and anti-idealism. Non-philosophy is neither idealist nor realist. Instead, it marks a new way to think the philosophical problem of ideality and reality in view of the dangers and concrete effects of thought's authoritarian attractions.

The success of Laruelle's non-philosophical critique of philosophy will depend upon the discovery or invention of a *form of critique* that is not itself philosophically structured. In his preparatory 'Instructions for Use', Laruelle states that he aims to mount

> a critique that would no longer be a complement, a rectification, a deconstruction, a supplement, one of these innumerable 'experiences' (through Being, Text, Power, Desire, Politics, Ethics) that the Occident has invented in order to cleanse itself of its congenital defect – to think through unifying duality, through the synthesis of contraries, through the One as All or as unity of contraries, through dialectic and difference – and through which it would be content to re-infect the wound.[1]

With this passage before us, we note at the outset three questions that will govern the analysis as a whole:

1. In what sense is the synthesis or unity of contraries understood to be a philosophical 'defect'?
2. Why do philosophy's critical attempts to rectify, supplement or deconstruct this 'defect' repeatedly and inevitably fail?
3. What sort of critique does Laruelle propose instead?

LARUELLE AMONG HIS CONTEMPORARIES

Philosophies of Difference, Laruelle's eighth book, was published by Presses Universitaires de France in 1986, nearly 100 years after Nietzsche's last gloriously productive year of 1888, over a half century after the publication of *Being and Time* and ten years after Heidegger's death, and almost two decades after the tumultuous events of the late 1960s, the same years in which, in the French philosophical arena, Derrida published several of his most definitive works and gave his seminal talk on *différance* before the *Société française de philosophie* at the Sorbonne, while Deleuze released the great trio of *Spinoza: Expressionism in Philosophy*, *Difference and Repetition* and *The Logic of Sense*. Nietzsche, Heidegger, Derrida, Deleuze – although these four thinkers mark out the primary coordinates of Laruelle's book, the orientation they provide is essentially structural and not historical. Laruelle's concern is to elaborate a critical exposition of a determinate although highly general philosophical concept – Difference. He does so not in terms of a historical narrative or conceptual genealogy but rather as a transcendental analysis of a new, non-Kantian and non-phenomenological type.

This analysis – even where it directly engages the thought of Nietzsche, Heidegger, Derrida and Deleuze – is 'situated' in a highly unusual fashion both with respect to these thinkers themselves and to the complex textual and conceptual arenas in which their philosophies are composed and staged. Laruelle's analysis will merge with these complex objects and their conditions almost to the point of indiscernibility *while nonetheless* remaining entirely 'separate' in principle. Separation in thinking need not be a matter of distance. In general, we fall much too easily into spatial metaphors when abstract relations are at issue: concepts are said to be 'far' from one another; thinkers are brought into 'proximity'. Laruelle pushes his readers to abandon the residual spatiality still at work in even the most sophisticated, critical and post-representational modes of philosophy. In consequence, the stakes of his analysis will be those of the relationality of thought *per se*, namely the twofold problem of thought's relations (1) to itself and (2) to its other(s).

In the introductory chapter of *Philosophies of Difference* Laruelle writes of the object of his critical exposition – the general structure of philosophical Difference – that on the one hand it 'appears to arise fully armed on the philosophical scene, like a figure at once new and unengendered, lacking sufficient cause in its historical vicinities.' Yet he specifies on the other hand that, 'from another perspective, more sober but not necessarily any more truthful, Difference is seen to be situated on an empirical and historical terrain, in the midst of certain vicinities or neighborhoods that determine it without really engendering it'.[2] In other words, Difference cannot be accounted for simply by reducing it to its historical context, but neither should it be understood entirely independently of that context. Indeed, this dialectic or, better, 'amphibology' of creative upsurge and historical conditioning will come to define Difference itself.

Two sets of claims present themselves. While each must be affirmed separately on its own terms, their coexistence and integral coherence cannot. On the one hand, (A) Difference is absolute, ahistorical, *ex nihilo* or *causa sui*; on the other, (B) Difference is relative, historical, engendered, exteriorly determined. A similar pair of claims can and must be made about Laruelle's own project. It consists, on its own account, (A') of a radically new form of thought that remains irreducible to the core assumptions and methods of philosophy. In fact, its theoretical aim is to elicit a purely scientific perspective on philosophy that would avoid such dialectics and amphibologies that arise inherently within philosophy. Above all, Laruelle's analysis will aim to instantiate a non-philosophical form of thought subsisting prior to any structure of division or opposition whatsoever yet which does not thereby resolve itself into an *a priori* synthesis of differences or 'unity of contraries'. It thus works to generalise thinking as such outside of philosophy's own circumscription of itself as distinct from and reflexively dominant with respect to other modes of thought and experience. In this way, non-philosophy should not be understood as sharing either continuity or discontinuity with the philosophical tradition. It is neither a new kind of philosophy nor a 'break' with philosophy. Rather, as a real generalisation of philosophical thought, it is strictly 'other than' philosophical.

Even at a superficial level, Laruelle's own textual procedures tend to bear this out: he eschews the standard scholarly apparatus of citation and textual warrant, and frequently his arguments proceed simply on their own terms, without positioning themselves with respect to a given ongoing scholarly conversation. This is, in part, why the present work – ostensibly a 'critical introduction to a critical introduction' – is perhaps warranted. Although *Philosophies of Difference* is subtitled in French '*une introduction critique*', the book is certainly not what Anglophone readers have come to expect as anything like a 'critical introduction' to the thought of Nietzsche, Heidegger, Deleuze and Derrida, the main figures Laruelle addresses therein.[3] There is no textual exegesis (or almost none) and very little in the way of summary overviews of the 'positions' or 'views' of these thinkers. What *Philosophies of Difference* introduces is not the more or less familiar terrain of late-twentieth-century continental philosophy and its determinative problematics but instead a radically new conception of thought – at once a critique and a generalisation of philosophy – that goes by the name 'non-philosophy'. 'Non-philosophy' designates a mode of thinking for which the fundamental and seemingly unsurpassable categories and horizons of thought – Being, World, History, Logic, Language, Politics – are thrown into relief as projections and symptoms of philosophy's own self-constituting structures. Non-philosophy introduces a stance of thinking

6

'in-One' in which such horizons and categories are no longer operative but are transformed instead into data for analysis and experimentation. From within the stance of non-philosophy, the various ways distinct philosophies correlate thought, being and entities with respect to one another are identified as belonging to a common schema, the most general of philosophical structures: Difference.

At the same time, (B') Laruelle's work itself undoubtedly takes place in the world and in history, in the sphere of philosophical effectivity which that work will nonetheless critique as falsely all-englobing. Whatever the status of its theoretical accomplishments, the concrete origins of non-philosophy in a specific social, historical and political context and its initial development relative to a specific set of philosophical influences and problematics are more or less definite and traceable. Crucially, it is through this side of non-philosophy (the mixed and relative aspect that it critiques on its own terms as philosophical) that any reader new to Laruelle must inevitably approach his work. There is in this way a distinctive 'pedagogical' or 'initiatory' problem built into the very fabric of non-philosophy to which perhaps *Philosophies of Difference* remains the best answer provided by Laruelle so far. The present introduction and guide is intended largely to unfold this important initiatory or expository dimension of the text.

In this regard, one of the primary advantages of *Philosophies of Difference* is that it engages with more familiar thinkers from the philosophical tradition in greater detail than any other of Laruelle's non-philosophical works. It thus serves as a natural point of entry into an often forbidding terrain of technical terminology and hermetic style. Laruelle's difficult syntax puts his work at an immediate remove from the casual reader. However, Laruelle's style is part and parcel of the strangeness, power and truth of what non-philosophy aims to instantiate. Accessibility seems to mark an inevitable trade-off with a form of thought that makes the very logic of trade-offs the object of its uncompromising critique. Yet if Laruelle is right, no such trade-off is able to touch the essence of non-philosophy in the first place. At any rate, the Real 'object' of non-philosophy – the One-in-One – is in no way threatened by what is not it. This notion of inviolability should be kept in mind.

The very form of Laruelle's project is highly unusual. He aims at a kind of thinking that would no longer be characterised or characterisable by its position relative to other views, problematics, approaches and so on. Thus, what becomes non-philosophy is not only a singular project but a new *kind* of singularity, one which cannot be put into relation with other singularities. To get a handle on what Laruelle is doing, however, it is helpful to sketch some of the main features of the intellectual context from within which Laruelle's project originally emerges. This context is first of all that of late-twentieth-century French philosophy. Laruelle's first books appear in the late 1970s in a highly charged French intellectual scene dominated by a newly ascendant set of figures: Lacan had been prominent for some time; Althusser's authority held sway on the Rue d'Ulm; and the relatively new names of Derrida, Deleuze and Foucault were making a significant impact. Much of this history will already be familiar to those who work in continental philosophy and are at home among Kant, Hegel, Nietzsche, Heidegger, Derrida and Deleuze (the usual suspects who will be the *dramatis personae* in PD).[4] Such readers are welcome to skip ahead. In any case, we will only touch upon a few key points of orientation.

Laruelle's generation was brought up in the wake of a highly destabilised and creative philosophical scene. After the Second World War, French philosophy had been revitalised by an influx of German phenomenology, while a dominant Neo-Kantianism (associated especially with the philosophy of Brunschvicg) continued to exert its influence. Husserl's methods of phenomenological reduction and eidetic analysis became central points of reference as a new generation of philosophers aimed to bring philosophy into more immediate contact with the complexities of lived experience. At the same time, Heidegger's existential critique of Husserl emerged more or less simultaneously with the translations and dissemination of Husserl's work in France.[5]

Laruelle's thought, especially in *Philosophies of Difference*, is structured in key ways by the debates between Kantianism and phenomenology. As we will see, the problem of Kant's thing-in-itself in particular is one of the main points of contention between Nietzsche and Heidegger on Laruelle's reading. From a Husserlian phenomenological perspective, Kant's recourse to the thing-in-itself, like his conception of sensibility, remains still too metaphysical in essence. Heidegger in turn will critique the idealist assumptions of Husserl, and in his turn to existential facticity will mark something of a return to Kant, although on ontological rather than subjective terrain. This broad problem of idealism and realism as structured through the role of a withdrawn in-itself will be one of the major themes of *Philosophies of Difference*.

Besides the debates between Neo-Kantian and phenomenological method (and within phenomenology between transcendental and existential orientations), one of the common *topoi* that links an otherwise diverse group of philosophers in France in the second half of the twentieth century is that of structuralism and the critique of structuralism.[6] In the 1950s and '60s both structuralism and then post-structuralism remained in a complex relation to the Kantian tradition and especially to the Kantian notion of critique on the one hand and to phenomenology on the other. Structuralism in philosophy – imported largely from linguistics and anthropology –

offered both intriguing parallels with phenomenological method as well as a sharp critical edge with respect to the phenomenological emphasis on lived experience.

The rise of post-structuralism (a somewhat vague term often applied indiscriminately to Derrida, Deleuze and Foucault, among others) advanced this critical aspect of structuralism and turned it against structuralism itself. The framework for Laruelle's project emerges especially in this milieu of recursive critique. If structuralism tended to displace the categories of experience and subjectivity in favour of systems of differential opposition underlying society and language, and if post-structuralism deepened this displacement by bringing the dynamics of displacement and violence into the inner conflict constituting such systems themselves, rendering them untotalisable, Laruelle will aim through non-philosophical critique to uncover an irreducible 'structure' of a new type that organises philosophy as such.

In general, the various issues at stake in the structuralist and post-structuralist interventions in philosophy may be grouped together under the common heading of the *critique of representation*. If one philosophical concern links philosophers as otherwise divergent as Bataille, Levinas, Derrida, Foucault, Lyotard and Deleuze it is the desire to shift philosophy away from the many variants and avatars of representationalism. What becomes of thought when it no longer aims to picture the world correctly or to render the Real propositionally? In posing this question, all of these thinkers find themselves standing in an uneasy relation to Hegel, whose critique of Kantian representation had in many ways laid the groundwork for a dynamic conception of thought as Real and as historically effective/effected. Alexandre Kojève's lectures on Hegel have since taken on an almost mythic status in this regard, and Kojève's perhaps excessive focus on the Master-Slave dialectic in the *Phenomenology* helped to put the concept of *desire* at the centre of the emerging problematic of Difference.[7] Equally influential for this generation was the work of Hyppolite, whose *Genesis and Structure of Hegel's Phenomenology of Spirit* and *Logic and Existence* opened anew the question of the relation between Hegel's *Phenomenology* and his *Science of Logic*. On the one hand, the systematic and totalising aspects of Hegel's thought were viewed generally with deep suspicion, while on the other hand his ultimate identification of thought with the Real appealed to the post-war, post-Sartre generation's desire for philosophy's direct contact with the world and its resistance to the abstraction of representation. The highly charged political conjuncture of French thought in the years stretching especially from the Algerian war through the aftermath of the 1968 revolts made this philosophical issue – and indeed all the guiding questions indicated here – far from merely theoretical. The political stakes of philosophy were universally recognised, if quite variously conceived and interpreted.

The break between structuralism and post-structuralism is in this respect strongly associated with the resurgence of interest in Nietzsche in the late 1960s.[8] Nietzschean 'total critique' (the term is drawn from Deleuze's influential *Nietzsche and Philosophy*) was advanced against a perceived residual Kantianism in structuralist method. In opposition to any ahistorical and aprioristic investigation into structural conditions of possibility, against every static or consummated systematisation of phenomena, Nietzsche's emphasis on an immanent play of active and reactive forces placed philosophy itself into immediate and irreducibly polemical contact with its various objects. In particular, renewed engagement with Nietzsche's concept of Will opened points of contact between philosophy and psychoanalysis (especially Lacan), deepening but also qualifying the Kojève-Hegelian emphasis on desire and the historical effectivity of thought. Importantly, Nietzschean Will to Power expresses itself non-dialectically: it is essentially creative and discontinuous, not historical and synthetic. As we will see, the influence of Nietzsche on Laruelle's early work was immense. Indeed, the broadly political problematic that opposes Nietzschean immanence and power to Kantian (and structuralist) transcendentalism on the one hand and Hegelian closure on the other – with these latter interpreted largely in terms of Heidegger's thought – may be taken to constitute the most basic framework for Laruelle's thought up to the emergence of non-philosophy.

Furthermore, as new technologies transformed the social and political arenas and various modes of critique challenged models of modern rationality and objective knowledge production, the problem of the *relation between philosophy and science* for this generation took on a new urgency. This particular concern becomes one of the central issues in its own way for Laruelle. On one side, this problem can be seen as yet another component of the reception of phenomenology. The question of the scientific character of phenomenology – both in its methodology and in its ultimate aims – was one of the most important points of contention between Husserlian and Heideggerean phenomenological strains. On another side, the writings and personality of Louis Althusser, who taught at the *Ecole Normale Supérieure*, were a common touchstone both politically and philosophically for this entire generation of thinkers, and one of the key concerns for Althusser was how within a broadly Marxist political framework to guarantee a scientific analysis of society and economy as well as a scientific critique of ideology.[9] For Althusser, philosophy plays a highly ambiguous role in this context as both a positive, critical instrument for making visible the contradictions and theoretical gaps within the human and social sciences as well as a conservative, ideological construct for reproducing and rationalising the dominant social relations of production under capitalism. Laruelle's own insistence on the scientific character of non-philosophy – precisely the shift from a meta-philosophical 'philosophy of philosophy' to a non-philosophical 'science (of) philosophy' – may be approached at least initially from this broad Althusserian problematic. In particular (to jump past *Philosophies of Difference* to our own current philosophical conjuncture), it is in relation to this Althusserian problematic that the contemporary engagement of Laruelle and Badiou may perhaps most clearly be formulated.[10] Among other things, Laruelle's appropriation of Marx's notion of 'determination in the last instance' draws upon Althusser while nonetheless diverging from his overall view.

All of these diverse issues – the debates cutting between and across phenomenology and Neo-Kantianism, the rise of structuralism and the general critique of representation, the resurgence of Nietzschean thought *against* structuralism, the problem of the relation between science and philosophy, the immediately political context of philosophy – converge on the question of humanism and anti-humanism.[11] Both structuralism and post-structuralism tended toward the dissolution of the transcendental subject and the anthropocentrism it entailed. Yet in the generally 'anti-humanist' atmosphere of post-Heideggerean French philosophy, the status of the dispossessed, minoritarian, excluded segments of capitalist modernity came to the fore as perhaps the most plausible ultimate 'reason' for the various modalities of the critique of representation and of Reason. What remains of philosophy's critical and polemical functions after both Truth and Humanity have dissolved? How is anti-humanism anything other than merely *inhuman*?

In fact, the issue of humanism and anti-humanism as it emerged within the French philosophical context just sketched probably provides the best point of entry for understanding Laruelle's intervention into this philosophical history. Alongside thinkers such as Levinas and Adorno, Laruelle remains acutely aware of the authoritarian, oppressive and ultimately totalitarian tendencies woven into the very fabric of Western rationality and philosophy, even when and where these latter are explicitly placed at the service of ideals of 'freedom', 'justice', 'humanity' and so on.[12] Yet unlike Levinas or Adorno, Laruelle will not look for an antidote to these tendencies in a new, critically inflected modality of philosophy (whether in an 'ethics of the Other' as 'first philosophy' or a 'negative dialectics'). Instead, Laruelle will look to an alternative mode of thought that cannot be conceived according to the customary parameters of the intensification, weakening, self-inhibition or questioning of philosophy itself. In Laruelle's view, all of these strategies merely *redeploy* philosophy in a variant form when what is needed is something other than philosophy as such. The logic of Laruelle's criticism is clear: if something *essential* to philosophy bears responsibility for the forms of totalitarianism and oppression critiqued by thinkers like Levinas and Adorno, then any critical response to such tendencies that is itself *philosophical* cannot avoid repeating what it aims to ameliorate. Strategies of weakening, decentering or attenuating philosophy (just as, on the other hand, programs of intensifying, transcendentalising or infinitising it) proceed by means of an operation – itself philosophical – upon the given material of philosophy. While such operations might alter philosophy in various important respects, by the same token they leave the object of the operation *essentially* intact.

Of course, the soundness of this logic depends upon a proper construal of philosophy's *essence*. It might seem that Laruelle is making use here of too narrow a conception of philosophy. He appears to presume that a fixed, identifiable essence of philosophy is already given, such that the thought of someone like Adorno or Levinas (or Derrida or Irigaray or . . .) only gives us 'more of the same'. Against this, proponents of these philosophers would no doubt point to the innovative concepts and methods introduced in their work. They are not doing 'just more' philosophy but a new and different kind of philosophy, a kind that precisely overcomes and ameliorates the failures, missteps and over-reachings of its predecessors.

Yet if we look at the history of modern philosophy at least since Kant, what major figure does *not* characterise himself as breaking with the preceding tradition in a more or less definitive way? Kant's critical turn against the deadlock of empiricism and rationalism, Hegel's simultaneous historicisation and absolutisation of reason against Kant, Nietzsche's rejection of truth as the event that would 'break History in two', Husserl's new foundation for philosophy through the bracketing of the natural attitude, Heidegger's existential break with the residual idealism of Husserlian phenomenology, Heidegger's later break with his own metaphysical presuppositions in *Being and Time*, Derrida's deconstruction of the metaphysics of presence still operative even in the late Heidegger, Deleuze's overcoming of the representational image of thought – all of these take the form of a critical rejection of previous tradition. Yet in each case, this occurs on the basis of conceptual innovations that generally admit at least selective identification with certain earlier aspects of that tradition. Indeed, this structure can be easily recognised prior to Kant going back to Descartes. How far back does it go? Through the debates of the medieval nominalists and realists? To the schools of Hellenism? To the Pre-Socratics? Is philosophy as such anything other than critique-of-and-identification-with-tradition?

Laruelle wants to take seriously the interplay between creative impulse and critical drive that courses through the dominant Western tradition of

philosophy. Rather than denying it, he takes this 'logic' of creative difference and self-overcoming as the very essence of philosophy. In this respect,
then, Laruelle is not putting forward a narrow conception of philosophy,
but one that is, if anything, so broad and open that any conceivable claim
to have critiqued or escaped the philosophical tradition would seem by that
very token to be necessarily re-inserted within the tradition itself. Western
philosophy is in this way understood as the untotalised history of its own
continual self-overcoming, at once conservative, critical and creative. Is
this open history not sufficient?

Nietzsche asks of any given idea, *who* (that is, what *type of will*)
thinks this?[13] Laruelle generalises this line of questioning. Who (and
with what desire) philosophises? And we should ask in turn: Who 'non-
philosophises'? Who may *really* critique philosophy as such? Laruelle's
own answer is: the 'ordinary human'. Anticipating later non-philosophical
emphasis on the 'subject' of non-philosophy who will be named 'Stranger',
Laruelle writes early on in *Philosophies of Difference*:

> If there is a power of the One, it is here: in this unilateralization of philosophy,
> its rejection to the abyss or to indifference which accompanies each person
> who comes into this World as into a strange land. The unilateralization or the
> duality, given their transcendental foundation in the One, cannot pass for an
> 'exit' beyond the World, beyond philosophy and its mixtures, but are rather
> what give us this indifferent and non-alienating access to the World as to phi-
> losophies.[14]

It is in light of this critique of philosophy's tendency to universalisation as
against the real human, that the following question will be posed regularly
to the models of Difference Laruelle examines: *What human reality is
excluded, denied or obstructed by these philosophies, or perhaps by philosophy
in general?* Constant if only periodically explicit reference to this question
will keep the ensuing analysis on track. Laruelle's own view is that the
complex problem of humanism and anti-humanism admits of a *theoretical*
answer, although *theory* will in this case be manifest not as a formal system
modelling some objective domain but instead as the immanent and immediate self-knowledge that characterises *gnosis*. The clearest break between
the philosophies of Difference and Laruelle's non-philosophy will thus
concern the status of the *human* with respect to philosophy. Are these two
terms *human* and *philosophy* co-penetrating and reciprocally determined
or are they definitively separate? If they can be held definitively separate,
from which side of the separation must the separation itself be thought?

Laruelle's *Philosophies of Difference* is an important moment in an
extended development that has taken non-philosophy through at least four
distinct phases (Philosophy II–V, see below). The relevance of *Philosophies*

of Difference today is in this regard largely due to its specific role within the broader project of non-philosophy. Especially with respect to the question of the human, it would certainly be a mistake to situate Laruelle's project merely in terms of the concerns and figures of French philosophy from nearly a half-century ago. Laruelle's thought is certainly rooted in that time, but its continued development over the past four decades also places Laruelle among the most current concerns of philosophy. Non-philosophy is not an artifact for intellectual historians, but an ongoing mode of thinking with significant contemporary relevance. Two points in particular are worth noting.

(1) One of the most immediate connections of Laruelle's work to present developments is in relation to the broad 'theological turn' or 'turn to religion' that has occurred in phenomenology and related fields over the last several decades. Associated with Levinas, Marion and Derrida's later work, but also figures such as Henry, Chrétien, and Anglophone commentators such as Bernasconi, de Vries and Caputo, this strand of continental philosophy has placed phenomenology and deconstruction in intimate relation with the traditional concerns of theology and the philosophy of religion: faith and reason, the transcendence and Otherness of God, political theology, the status of revelation, and so on. Some theologians have embraced this rapprochement of philosophy and theology, while others such as Milbank and the associated thinkers of Radical Orthodoxy have critiqued it as merely another variant of modern liberalism.[15] Philosophers too have approached these developments with varying degrees of appropriation, reconstruction and rejection. At first glance, Laruelle seems potentially appropriable by both sides of this internally diverse discussion to the extent that he draws on religious and theological materials yet asserts a thoroughly radical and heretical immanence. Nonetheless, Laruelle's own use of these materials runs counter to any theological appropriation *as well as* straightforward philosophical critique: there is no simple 'turn to religion' nor is there atheist rejection in Laruelle, but instead an application of non-philosophy within religious and especially theological materials. In the present intellectual context, non-philosophy thus promises a genuinely new path for advancing beyond increasingly sterile debates between secular and post-secular modes of philosophy of religion.

(2) More recently, the emergence of new forms of materialist and realist philosophies within continental circles demonstrates the continued relevance of the humanist/anti-humanist problematic well beyond any religious parameters and within the contemporary conjuncture (always political *inter alia*) of philosophy and science. Ray Brassier, one of the most accomplished interpreters of Laruelle, has levelled the criticism – especially against Laruelle's more recent work – that it remains con-

strained by an unnecessary reference to the human subject, even if that subject is radically reinterpreted as Stranger instead of functioning as the *subjectum* of worldly experience.[16] It is true that one of the most striking points of difference between Laruelle and mainstream continental thought is his insistence upon the term Man, in apparent opposition to the 'death of Man' proclaimed by post-structuralism more generally. Thinkers of the recent 'speculative turn' have taken up the critique of anthropocentrism anew on ostensibly 'realist' grounds.[17] Laruelle stands in an uneasy relation to this diverse movement: on the one hand, his project of non-philosophy has systematically worked through the rejection of 'correlationism' in philosophy in painstaking theoretical detail and rigour for some decades now, yet on the other hand, he continues today to use the term Man or Human (*Homme*) and makes use of theological materials in ways that can only appear conservative if not reactionary from the general point of view of the new realists. The ambiguity may be formulated as follows: on the one hand, non-philosophy is said by Laruelle to be a non-idealist form of science; on the other hand, this science itself is understood as a form of immanent, non-epistemological *gnosis*.

The contemporary scope of non-philosophy extends well beyond these areas, into ethics, aesthetics, even artificial intelligence research and the cross-pollination of philosophy and physics.[18] The above concerns, however, are probably those most immediately linked with the specific themes and problems addressed in *Philosophies of Difference*. In any case, the problem of how to 'situate' Laruelle with respect to his philosophical predecessors and contemporaries is a problem that draws in its train the entirety of non-philosophy. All of the stakes of non-philosophy are present in this question: how does non-philosophy stand with respect to philosophy and its history? Laruelle's response will consist in a *stance* within thought that is, however, not a *position*. As 'seen' from within this stance, all the problematics just surveyed take on a transformed sense, a generalised reality that is manifest as other than subject-to-philosophy.

PHILOSOPHIES OF DIFFERENCE *WITHIN LARUELLE'S OEUVRE*

The problem of how to 'situate' *Philosophies of Difference* is also local to Laruelle's own thought. Because of the breadth of Laruelle's work and its own internal differentiations, it is equally important to 'place' *Philosophies of Difference* with respect to the half-dozen or so books by Laruelle that preceded it as well as in relation to the main lines of the development of non-philosophy that have followed in its wake. *Philosophies of Difference* is located at a crucial juncture within Laruelle's own complex development.

Nearly four decades separate Laruelle's earliest work from his most recent, and during that period his output has been remarkably consistent, with a new book appearing on the average every two to three years. Laruelle himself has periodised his work into a sequence of phases that he now designates as Philosophy I through Philosophy V.

Within this schematisation, *Philosophies of Difference* is located squarely in the 'middle' of Philosophy II which, taken in its entirety, marks the initial conception and formulation of non-philosophy as such. More recently, Laruelle has spoken of these periods as successive 'waves', and this image is suggestive in several key respects. First of all, it suggests an underlying unity: the successive stages from Philosophy I through Philosophy V are more like differently inflected repetitions of a single, core insight than 'advances' toward a final position (indeed, the rejection of such 'natural' spatial metaphors in philosophy – 'position', 'neighbourhood', 'path', 'shift', etc. – will be one of the key elements of Laruelle's thought). At any rate, it would be precipitous and misleading to express the differences between these 'waves' as 'breaks' or 'discontinuities'.

What Laruelle now calls Philosophy I consists of his first (1971) book on Félix Ravaisson (something of an outlier in Laruelle's oeuvre) and then a quartet of books circling a common theme, namely how the philosophical problems of hermeneutics and writing, especially as raised by Heidegger and Derrida, become inflected and transformed politically in a materialist field of Nietzschean immanent forces. Even if Laruelle today brackets these early works as 'pre-non-philosophical' – that is, still philosophical – they address a variety of problems that remain in force for the later work and in fact provide a very important set of insights into the motivations underlying non-philosophy.[19]

The quartet of books *Textual Machines*, *The Decline of Writing*, *Nietzsche contra Heidegger*, and *Beyond the Power Principle* overlap considerably in their concerns and objectives.[20] To the extent that a 'development' may be registered from *Textual Machines* to *Beyond the Power Principle*, it is perhaps as a progressive distancing and finally a detachment from Nietzsche on the one hand and an increasing proximity to the late Heidegger on the other. The notion of a 'Nietzsche/Heidegger conflict' at the heart of contemporary thought will serve as one of the key structuring principles of *Philosophies of Difference*, and it is important to note that this conflict is something with which Laruelle had himself struggled already from a variety of theoretical perspectives in his four books preceding the emergence of non-philosophy. If the trajectory of these texts is, in broad strokes, away from an identification with Nietzsche and in the direction of a rapprochement with Heidegger, in *Philosophies of Difference* and, more generally, throughout non-philosophy, Laruelle will conceive his new form of non-philosophical thinking as no longer situated 'within' this problematic at all (whether to one side or the other) but rather outside of it entirely.

Philosophy II begins with *The Minority Principle*. With this text, Laruelle now in retrospect claims to have broken with the still philosophical approach that characterises the previous four books. The key innovation for Laruelle is a new conception of the One. Rather than treating the One as a limit or goal for thought or a term of absolute transcendence, with *The Minority Principle* Laruelle initiates an immanent mode of thinking that begins *from* the One and remains *in-One*. In Laruelle's view, this methodological inversion underlies a real critique of all forms of authoritarianism within thought and at the same time directly manifests in a new light the authoritarian essence of philosophy. The subtitle of Laruelle's subsequent book, *A Biography of Ordinary Man* – 'Of Authorities and Minorities' – both foregrounds this problematic and points to the 'dualist' solution that the non-philosophical One proffers.[21]

As Laruelle's new approach is extended into *A Biography of Ordinary Man* and then *Philosophies of Difference*, the outline of the new non-philosophical mode of thought becomes increasingly clear. In particular, Laruelle himself specifies *Philosophies of Difference* as a kind of application in the domain of the history of philosophy of the new conception of immanence organised in its immediate predecessor: *Philosophies of Difference* represents 'the effect, on philosophy and its history, of the theory developed in *Une biographie de l'homme ordinaire*'.[22] The definite distinction between philosophy and non-philosophy that marks the conclusion or result of *Philosophies of Difference* then becomes in turn the primary and initial focus of the book that immediately follows it, *Philosophy and Non-philosophy*.

Philosophies of Difference thus appears in the middle of a second quartet of books – coming after *The Minority Principle* and *A Biography of Ordinary Man*, and just before *Philosophy and Non-philosophy* – that together may be juxtaposed with the earlier quartet of Philosophy I. If the earlier books all share a common thematic of thinking hermeneutics and writing in broadly political terms under philosophical conditions of materialist immanence, the second group takes this same core problem and inflects it through a new method that marks a certain return of the theme of the One under conditions of contemporary philosophical Difference. This new method of thinking in-One or according-to-One vis-à-vis philosophy defines non-philosophy as such.

Within this group of Philosophy II, *Philosophies of Difference* stands as a kind of 'glance backward' toward the specific thinkers engaged in Philosophy I – especially Nietzsche, Heidegger and Derrida – now with Laruelle's understanding of their work transformed by the non-philosophical approach. For readers today new to Laruelle, this is part of what makes this text ideal for simultaneously encountering non-philosophy for the first time and understanding how this form of thought in fact grew out of a detailed engagement with the continental tradition. If contemporary continental philosophy continues to move within the broad terrain of dialectic and Difference marked out by Hegel, Marx, Nietzsche, Heidegger and various post-structuralist thinkers, *Philosophies of Difference* represents the most explicit point of encounter between this well-established tradition and non-philosophy.

After the second, non-philosophical quartet, two books from the early 1990s, *Inasmuch as One* and *Theory of Identities*, round out the phase of Philosophy II. *Theory of Identities* is especially interesting, as it fuses the non-philosophical mode of thought with contemporary scientific domains, particularly Mandelbrot's fractal mathematics and computer science. Against the background of the problem of artificial intelligence, *Theory of Identities* poses the problem of constructing an 'artificial philosophy'. It also introduces the theme of *cloning*, which non-philosophy disengages from its scientific origins in genetic engineering and develops as a thoroughly generic method for thought in Laruelle's subsequent writings.

Perhaps the main unanswered question for the works of Philosophy II (and among these, *Philosophies of Difference*) is the precise status of the philosophical *subject* as transformed within the theoretical stance of non-philosophy.[23] What Laruelle now calls Philosophy III consists of four books all of which engage the 'subject' of non-philosophy from various perspectives and elaborate the non-philosophical 'ethics' which that subject entails. In *Philosophies of Difference* Laruelle promises that 'a further work' will continue and expand the 'theory of philosophical decision' that consummates *Philosophies of Difference* and will aim at 'the transcendental foundation of an algorithm of decision'.[24] If this promise is kept – and no single work seems to meet this description exactly – it is in the establishment of a properly non-philosophical conception of the human subject as Stranger that such an 'algorithm' consists.

Of the works of Philosophy III, it is probably *Theory of Strangers* that comes closest to this earlier description. It takes the turn to a science of identity in *Theory of Identities* and applies it to the philosophical and psychoanalytical subject and the question of philosophically grounded 'human sciences'. The later *Ethics of the Stranger* continues this line of research especially with respect to Kantian and Levinasian ethics, as *Introduction to Non-Marxism* does with respect to Marx and particularly the neo-humanist Marxism of Michel Henry. Also within Philosophy III, the key work *Principles of Non-Philosophy* stands as the most comprehensive and systematic presentation of non-philosophy and its methods to date. It systematises the concepts of the non-philosophical subject as 'force (of) thought', the methods of conceptual 'dualysis' and 'cloning', and the non-philosophical reworking of intentionality conceived as a noetic-noematic correlation. All of these concepts are elaborated in a framework that generalises Husserlian phenomenological method according-to-One. For the reader new to Laruelle who hopes to catch up as quickly as possible to the astonishing non-philosophical output of the past decade (Philosophy IV and V), *Principles* is a natural complement and successor to *Philosophies of Difference*.

The appearance of a certain 'turn to religion' is manifest in the works from *Future Christ* to *Non-philosophical Mysticism for Contemporary Use* which constitute Laruelle's Philosophy IV. However, it would be precipitous to locate a definitive shift here. References to gnostic dualism (albeit stripped of all religious mythologising) are evident in Laruelle's writings from as early as Philosophy II. What is new in *Future Christ* and *Non-philosophical Mysticism* is an explicit engagement with Christian theological materials – especially Christian mystical theology – from Pseudo-Dionysus to Nicholas of Cusa and Meister Eckhart. One of Laruelle's long-standing concerns comes to the fore here, namely the importance of the intervention of a Jewish notion of transcendence and alterity into French philosophy, associated above all with the work of Emmanuel Levinas. On the one hand, Laruelle suggests that this insistence on absolute alterity and its relationship to ethics is among the most important elements of contemporary philosophy. But on the other hand, Laruelle's insistence on the radical immanence of thinking in-One tends to mark out theological transcendence as one of the most definite targets of non-philosophical 'critique'. In this respect, Laruelle's non-theological engagements present intriguing connections and contrasts with the work of other recent French thinkers besides Levinas such as Duméry, Henry, Marion and Chrétien. The analyses of Heidegger and Derrida in *Philosophies of Difference* provide important groundwork for this still-emerging discussion.

Finally, Laruelle's most recent period – Philosophy V – hearkens back in certain ways to the scientific concerns of *Theory of Identities*. The transitional book *Introduction to Generic Sciences* shows the influence of Laruelle's wife Anne-Françoise Schmid and her interdisciplinary work in epistemology and science studies.[25] This theoretically rich text serves as a methodological introduction to the massive *Non-Standard Philosophy* of 2010 and its closely connected supplementary text *Anti-Badiou*, which together mark a turn toward the particular science of physics, and in particular the mathematical models of quantum mechanics, as a new way to explode philosophical pretensions and, more importantly, to generate new forms of expression and new modes of exploration of the terrain opened up by non-philosophy's generalisation of philosophy. *General Theory of Victims* revisits the broadly ethical concerns of Philosophy III in this light.

The divisions into five phases are Laruelle's own. No doubt Laruelle stands in a privileged position to interpret and periodise his work. But at the same time, every historicisation and narrativisation – especially of oneself and one's own work – risks imposing an external order perhaps not fully present in the material itself. It would be wrong in any case to read the development from Philosophy I to Philosophy V as either a linear or a dialectical progression. The strength of Laruelle's thought, like that of any significant thinker, resides in the ultimate unity and integrity of its vision (whatever the diversity of its materials and effects). Non-philosophy does not constitute a whole, but the force of its insight is ultimately One. Laruelle's segmentation of his own intellectual trajectory into the periods of Philosophy I through Philosophy V should be taken as no more than an additional datum within this open field.

THE STRUCTURE OF PHILOSOPHIES OF DIFFERENCE

Before examining Laruelle's text in detail, it is useful to map out its overall structure and point to the plan of the present guide. Laruelle's book is organised in seven chapters, preceded by a brief set of 'Instructions for Use' that serves as Laruelle's own overview of his text. These 'Instructions' outline, in turn, the 'method', 'aims', 'problematic' and 'internal organisation' of the book as a whole. This self-reflexive pre-text is well worth studying in detail, as it foregrounds Laruelle's central concerns and provides a kind of interpretive template for reading the book as a whole. A few points are worth drawing attention to here as a way to get our most general bearings for what follows.

1. Laruelle characterises the overall 'articulation' of *Philosophies of Difference* in the following terms: 'to *reconstruct* the essence . . . of the most extensive of contemporary problematics from two correlative concepts, those of "Difference" and "Finitude"'.[26] In Laruelle's reconstruction of contemporary philosophy, the concept of 'Difference' will be primarily associated with Nietzsche and Deleuze and that of 'Finitude' with Heidegger and Derrida. However, this general Difference/Finitude problematic will not serve to divide the four main philosophers simply into two camps. Rather, the correlation of Difference and Finitude and its essential conflict will be located at the heart of each of the four thinkers themselves (although each time in a distinctive way).

2. Laruelle foregrounds a particular problem of the interlacing of object and method in his text: 'We will find constantly interlinked with one another the examination of the fundamental problems and gestures

of Difference and the exposition of the problematic that allows for this type of examination.'[27] In other words, there will be a specific instantiation in Laruelle's own text of the 'transcendental' problem of the methodological conditions of possibility (and reality) for a critique of philosophical Difference. Can Difference be understood without at the same time *using* Difference in order to do so? This question will lead in turn to Laruelle's insistence on the need for a form of thought that will have 'deliver[ed] itself from philosophy' and the justification of 'a thinking that claims, for precise reasons, to be "scientific": a science assuming in its proper mode the transcendental function that philosophy has captured for its own profit'.[28]

3. Laruelle poses as his ultimate 'thesis' the claim that 'in the One in the sense that we intend, we find the most immanent and most real radical unity of man and knowledge'.[29] It is this non-epistemological unity of the subject and object of knowledge that will qualify non-philosophical 'science' as 'a thinking of two principles', that is, a form of '*gnosis*'.[30] The two principles governing the problem of transcendental science for Laruelle will no longer be those of subject and object, but instead that of Philosophy or the World (the very site of contest between principles and anarchy, the One and the Multiple) and that of the One-in-One (the human as simply and ordinarily Real and thereby undetermined in essence by any contingent worldly situation). In this respect, Laruelle's argument in *Philosophies of Difference* should be understood to culminate in the vision-in-One and the peculiar form of dualism it entails.

After the 'Instructions for Use', Laruelle's text proper begins. The first chapter, 'Introduction', lays out the essential problems and methods that will be at stake throughout the book. It is worth summarising the main points here:

- It is possible to mark the displacement of the broad nineteenth-century problematic of historical Dialectic by that of Difference in twentieth-century philosophy after Nietzsche.
- A distinction between 'syntax' (philosophical ideality) and 'reality' (the remainder or Other of the ideal) is understood to define philosophy as such. It is the need to distinguish these two moments that will differentiate philosophical decision from non-philosophical science.
- There is a broadly 'historical' problematic in play: Difference is at once an 'unengendered' event and a historically conditioned effect. Moreover, this problematic is understood to manifest in its own restricted mode a more general concern with a constitutive philosophical difference between the empirical and the *a priori* and/or transcendental.
- Difference displaces Dialectic and accedes to the status of a principle

by (a) transcending its employment as a mere *means* or *instrument*, (b) exceeding its 'categorial' interpretation as merely one category among others, and (c) being elucidated syntactically for itself, independently of any correlation with identity or unity (this occurs especially in the work of Derrida and Deleuze).

- Difference *repeats* the Greco-Occidental problem of the unity-of-contraries and thereby *uses* the One implicitly in order to address this problem.

- There is a methodological and thematic problem of the relation between the plural 'philosophies of Difference' and the peculiar unity of 'the-Difference' which structures these. The latter structure only becomes fully visible from within the 'scientific' stance of non-philosophy.

- 'Philosophical decision' will come to be recognised as the ultimate invariant of philosophy.

- The *separation* of 'two principles' (philosophical Difference and non-philosophical vision-in-One) serves as the transcendental condition of 'real critique'. Such critique would not be a *negation* of Difference, but rather a generalisation of philosophy: '*Real* critique is a type of thinking that, without denying Difference, is content to deny what there is in it of restraint, limit or non-autonomy, its lack of the One and its hallucination with respect to the One which it believes itself to have the power to determine.'[31]

With these points of orientation in mind, the second and third chapters, 'Syntax of Difference' and 'Reality of Difference' introduce one of the fundamental organising principles of Laruelle's argument, the distinction and relation within philosophical Difference of a problem of 'syntax' and a problem of 'reality'. This distinction is reflected (albeit with certain *caveats*) in the difference between two of the three models of Difference, those of Nietzsche and Heidegger respectively. As we will see, it is this conflict – which we may designate here simply with the expression 'Nietzsche/Heidegger' – that functions as a kind of fulcrum for Laruelle's entire argument. As throughout the book, the method here elides the difference between general structure and particular instantiation. In this case, the 'general' distinction between syntax and reality is, at least in certain key aspects, not merely recognised *in* but rather identified *with* the 'specific' difference between Nietzsche and Heidegger. The analysis of Heidegger stretches primarily across chapters two and three, while Nietzsche is treated in passing.

The fourth chapter, 'Hegel and Heidegger', may be seen as a kind of appendix to chapter three, which focuses primarily on the interpretation of Heideggerean Difference in terms of the introduction of 'Finitude' into the general syntax of 'Difference'. One of the main purposes of this chapter is to demonstrate the specific 'epochal' character of Difference with respect to the earlier epoch of the Dialectic. Chapter five then analyses and critiques the philosophy of Derrida as a complex mixture of the two models of Nietzsche and Heidegger: deconstruction as 'Differance', the non-synthetic unity of Difference and Finitude.

Chapters six and seven, 'Critique of Difference' and 'Theory of Philosophical Decision' consolidate the previous critiques of Nietzsche-Deleuze, Heidegger and Derrida and sketch Laruelle's own proposal for a non-philosophical form of thought that would no longer remain caught up in the paradoxes, undecidabilities and aporias of Difference. Chapter six, which in the 'Instructions for Use' Laruelle himself designates as 'the most fundamental' of *Philosophies of Difference*, aims to generalise the previous discussions of Difference, Finitude and Differance and thereby unite the previous critical analyses into a comprehensive theory of Difference. Chapter seven then concludes by using this theory of Difference to undertake the more general task of a 'theory of philosophical decision' *as* a theory of philosophy. This final chapter clarifies how the non-philosophical critique of philosophy is conceived as distinct from philosophy's own self-critique. This distinction itself is made on the basis of the theoretical stance that has been employed implicitly throughout Laruelle's entire analysis and which now can be clearly designated: the non-philosophical vision-in-One.

The present introduction and guide develops broadly in step with Laruelle's own organisation of the material. However, instead of mirroring the analysis strictly chapter by chapter, we outline the critique of Difference in general terms first in order to lay out its basic elements, incorporating some of the results from Laruelle's chapter six into the introductory distinctions drawn in the book's early chapters: between Difference and the One, the metaphysical and the transcendental, and syntax and reality. If Laruelle's own organisation may appear to take the shape of an induction, treating the individual cases of Difference in order then to generalise to their common shape, it remains the case nonetheless that the general critique of Difference provides the essential interpretive framework for engaging each of the given models from the outset. Laruelle's at times complex analysis is structured everywhere by a single insight, a new way of considering philosophy (both itself and its constituent materials) in-One. It is the way traditional and perennial philosophical problems naturally characterised in terms of dichotomies (such as those of the One and the Many, objects and relations, form and content, genus and species and so forth) are taken up by Difference and transformed in a complex but structurally recognisable way that will serve as the initial 'object' of inquiry. But since

Difference subsists *as* this structural transformation, it will also necessarily transform the mode of inquiry into Difference itself. Only Difference will provide philosophical access to Difference. But this 'quality' or 'property' of Difference in turn will become the secondary – although from the stance of non-philosophy, 'first' – object of a new non-philosophical science, or *gnosis*.

After outlining the general critique of Difference, each of the three models of Difference – the 'Idealism' attributed to Nietzsche and Deleuze, Heideggerean 'Finitude' and Derridean 'Différance' – is then treated separately and in turn. In Laruelle's own text, the engagement with these three models is distributed somewhat unevenly across the separate chapters. As Laruelle puts it, 'It is a question of all of the authors in every chapter.'[32] While this may be true conceptually, it is less obvious thematically. By treating each model of Difference relatively independently, I hope to provide a provisional orientation that allows the argument as a whole to come into clearer focus. On the one hand, the three models may be conceived as concrete instances of Difference, variations on a common theme. But on the other hand, and more importantly, each model must be conceived to be oriented strategically with respect to the others. The three models taken together constitute a single, complex differential structure. For Laruelle, Difference is not a neutral form of thinking, but a violent contest among rivals: 'each type has its own singular manner of conceiving (itself as) the universal and reducing the others to a deficient modality of itself. There is *the* Difference of Heidegger, and that of Deleuze, and that of Derrida.'[33] The reason Laruelle treats 'all of the authors in every chapter' is that a key aspect of his analysis will consist in marking out this contest as itself *internal* to Difference, as in fact its very essence.

Finally, after the examination of the three models, the final chapter of the guide examines the non-philosophical theory of philosophical decision and its basis in the 'dualist' vision-in-One that serves as the conclusion and consummation of the argument of *Philosophies of Difference*. This key concept of vision-in-One becomes the foundation methodologically for all of Laruelle's later works of non-philosophy. The concluding analysis corresponds to chapter seven of *Philosophies of Difference*, 'Theory of Philosophical Decision'. The concepts developed there of the (non-)One and non-thetic transcendence are carefully reconstructed so as to understand how they undergird a conception of Difference that Difference itself remains unable to comprehend on its own terms. On the basis of these new non-philosophical concepts, the essence of Difference as *decision* then becomes visible and from there a theory of philosophy itself as decision emerges.

I have aimed throughout at highlighting what I believe are the most

important issues at stake in *Philosophies of Difference* and drawing out
the sometimes subterranean connections across its different chapters and
themes. There are many significant details and side issues that have been
passed over in silence. Some of these are touched upon in the notes for
each chapter, which function as a second layer of commentary serving
to indicate formally if not fill in certain gaps of the guide. *Philosophies of
Difference* is a book that bears more than merely cursory engagement. This
guide is meant to provide assistance in working through the main steps of
the non-philosophical critique of Difference; it cannot substitute for the
labour – difficult but necessary – of reading and thinking with care through
the dense foliations of Laruelle's provocative text.

NOTES

1. François Laruelle, *Philosophies of Difference*, p. xxii. Hereafter abbreviated *PD*.
2. *PD*, pp. 2–3.
3. This is the reason I chose to translate the subtitle as 'a critical introduction to non-philosophy'. Laruelle's text is not by any means an introductory 'reader's guide' to the philosophies of difference.
4. For those in need of broad and relatively thorough introductions to this material, I would recommend reading two books in conjunction: Lee Braver, *A Thing of This World*, for its clarity of insight, readability and conceptual rigour, and Reiner Schürmann, *Broken Hegemonies*, for its depth and historical contextualisation. Between these two texts, the matter and stakes of contemporary continental philosophy are made clear (with the unfortunate exception of contemporary Spinozism and, in particular, the philosophy of Deleuze).
5. See for instance Levinas's important early work *The Theory of Intuition in Husserl's Phenomenology* and especially its Heideggerean-inflected conclusion, pp. 153–8.
6. A clear and concise discussion of the emergence of post-stucturalism out of structuralism and their continuity is found in Tilottana Rajan, *Deconstruction and the Remainders of Phenomenology*, pp. 34–43.
7. Alexandre Kojève, *Introduction to the Reading of Hegel: Lectures on the Phenomenology of Spirit*.
8. See the selection of representative writings collected in David B. Allison, ed., *The New Nietzsche*.
9. See, in particular, Louis Althusser, *Philosophy and the Spontaneous Philosophy of the Scientists*.
10. Laruelle engages Badiou's philosophy directly in *Anti-Badiou* and earlier, under the pseudonym Tristan Aguilar, in 'Badiou et la non-philosophie: un parallèle', in Non-philosophie, Le Collectif, *La Non-philosophie des Contemporains*, pp. 37–46. Althusser plays little explicit role in these texts, but is the common source of a set of problematics (especially his understanding of the relations among philosophy, science and Marxism) for both thinkers. For

the relation between Laruelle and Althusser, see also Vincent Maclos, 'De la Science de l'Histoire à la Science en l'Un: Essai de transformation du concept althusserien de science par F. Laruelle' in Non-philosophie, Le Collectif, *La Non-philosophie des Contemporains*, pp. 7–34.

11. The twentieth-century debates in France between humanism and anti-humanism serve as the overarching conceptual framework for the fine intellectual history traced in Stefanos Geroulanos, *An Atheism that is Not Humanist Emerges in French Thought*.

12. On the commonalities and differences between Levinas and Adorno on this score, see Hent de Vries, *Minimal Theologies*.

13. See the discussion of 'Nietzsche's Method' in Deleuze, *Nietzsche and Philosophy*, pp. 78–9.

14. *PD*, p. 20.

15. See John Milbank, *Theology and Social Theory*, especially ch. 10.

16. Ray Brassier, *Nihil Unbound*, ch. 5, especially pp. 135–8.

17. For a good survey of the relevant figures, see the contributions to Levi Bryant et al., *The Speculative Turn: Continental Materialism and Realism*.

18. For connections with artificial intelligence, see François Laruelle, *Theory of Identities*, pp. 267–87. For Laruelle's theory of the conceptual 'fusion' of physics and philosophy, see *Non-Standard Philosophy*, especially ch. 6.

19. In a recent interview, Laruelle describes these early works as the first, 'negative' phase of his thought, upon which the second 'positive' phase of non-philosophy proper follows. 'Non-Philosophy, Weapon of Last Defence: An Interview with François Laruelle' in John Mullarkey and Anthony Paul Smith, eds, *Laruelle and Non-philosophy*, p. 239.

20. I translate Laruelle's French book titles into English in the text and chapter endnotes for ease of reading throughout. The titles are given in the French original with the English bracketed in the bibliography. Many English translations of Laruelle's later works are forthcoming at the time of writing.

21. Whether such a definite methodological break is really evident in that work and to what degree Philosophy II remains in continuity with the questions and arguments of Philosophy I are highly interesting questions that cannot be adequately dealt with here.

22. *PD*, p. xvii.

23. This problem is relatively obscured to the extent that Laruelle emphasises the scientific character of non-philosophy at this stage. See Anthony Paul Smith, 'Thinking from the One: Science and the Ancient Philosophical Figure of the One' in John Mullarkey and Anthony Paul Smith, eds, *Laruelle and Non-philosophy*, pp. 19–41.

24. *PD*, p. xxi.

25. See Jean-Marie Legay and Anne-Françoise Schmid, *Philosophie de l'interdisciplinarité*. Sections of Laruelle's *Introduction to Generic Sciences* have been translated by Taylor Adkins and published as 'The Generic as Predicate and Constant: Non-Philosophy and Materialism' in Levi Bryant et al., eds, *The Speculative Turn*.

26. *PD*, p. xiv.
27. *PD*, p. xvi.
28. *PD*, pp. xvi–xvii.
29. *PD*, p. xvii.
30. *PD*, pp. xvii–xviii.
31. *PD*, p. 21.
32. *PD*, p. xiv.
33. *PD*, p. 13.

2

The critique of Difference

Philosophies of Difference engages the philosophies of Nietzsche, Heidegger, Derrida and Deleuze in order to mark a distinction between philosophical thinking (which perhaps in the work of these thinkers is pushed in some sense to its limit) and a new, more general mode of thinking which will be called non-philosophy. Laruelle's text itself bridges the difference both methodologically and thematically between these two kinds of thought; it is *at once* philosophical *and* non-philosophical. Keeping in mind that non-philosophy is not meant to be a negation but rather a generalisation of philosophy, we should understand this 'at once' as in no way paradoxical. It represents instead a kind of overlay or 'superposition' of separate but unopposed theoretical frameworks. Thus, from one point of view, *Philosophies of Difference* may be understood philosophically as the critical exposition of a unique conceptual object: Difference. From another point of view, however, the same text appears as the exercise of a new mode of thinking: non-philosophy. This second viewpoint or 'stance' involves precisely the same exposition and critical arguments as the first, but these are conceived differently, in fact so differently that they no longer appear as expository or critical in the traditional philosophical senses of these terms.

There is in this way – apparently – a 'double' writing at stake in Laruelle's text that would require a corresponding 'double' reading. Nonetheless, such an effect of hermeneutic doubling and redoubling is in fact one of the primary philosophical symptoms that Laruelle aims to analyse and critique non-philosophically in the 'philosophers of Difference'. In a sense, Laruelle develops the notion of non-philosophy precisely to avoid the doubleness caught up in this general way of thinking about textuality, interpretation and so on. So it will be necessary from the outset to remain sensitive to an at least possible or hypothetical distinction between the most general image of thought usually available to us, which is everywhere characterised in terms of levels, divisions, sides, contraries, dualities and, in general, differences, and something that *prima facie* seems impossible or simply incoherent: a form of rigorous thinking that would not necessitate any differences or divisions whatsoever. This latter is what Laruelle will call the vision-in-One.

The argument of *Philosophies of Difference* serves as an introduction or passage into non-philosophy that begins from more familiar philosophical terrain. In following Laruelle's argument, we must proceed philosophi- cally only up to a certain point, a point at which another mode of thinking becomes possible, or rather becomes manifest to us as already realised but now no longer seconded or redoubled in this very moment of manifesta- tion. The entire plan of *Philosophies of Difference* is oriented finally not to the production of the reader's conviction with respect to one or another philosophical thesis but to a subtle shift of perspective in how the reader approaches and views philosophical discourse in general. Indeed, the very language of a 'shift of perspective' will itself turn out to be inadequate, since what is at stake for Laruelle is ultimately an indivisible theoretical 'stance' that cannot be captured by the visual metaphor of 'perspective' which implies an irreducible gap or distance between a viewer and what is viewed.

Nonetheless, in a preliminary fashion the core of the argument of *Philosophies of Difference* may be expressed in terms of three general theses:

T1. Contemporary philosophy in general, and in particular the philosophies of Nietzsche, Heidegger, Deleuze and Derrida, may be understood from the standpoint of a theoretical critique of their dominant structuring principle: Difference.

T2. The structuring of philosophy through Difference is not only limited to the contemporary epoch of philosophy stretching roughly from Nietzsche to Derrida, but in fact expresses an invariant core of Western philosophy as such: Difference as the essence of Greco-Occidental philosophy.

T3. There is a form of thought proceeding in a way other than according to Difference – and therefore (by T2) other than according to the essence of Western philosophy: Non-philosophy as thinking 'in-One' or 'according-to- One'.

These theses are interdependent, and at least on a first reading they develop logically according to the given order. T1 is a relatively restricted claim bearing on a limited set of philosophers who share various common problems, methods and points of reference. It opens onto the critical analysis of a definite (although highly abstract) concept, Difference. T2

29

then generalises this concept as extracted and clarified initially within the restricted domain of T1 by extending it to a much wider field, namely to the tradition of Western philosophy conceived in its extensive breadth but more importantly its essential intensive unity. Finally, T3 – ultimately the core thesis of the book and of Laruelle's non-philosophical project as a whole – posits that despite the generality of Difference expressed in T2, Difference (or philosophy) is not the sole form of thought available to us. There is a way of thinking that does not depend upon and proceed through Difference, but rather thinks 'in-One'. This latter form of thought is what Laruelle will call 'non-philosophy'.

There is a logically operative 'passage' from T1 to T2 and from T2 to T3. In the movement from T1 to T2 the intension of the concept of Difference does not change, but its conceptual extension is broadened. It is seen or recognised in places it was not originally obvious. The soundness of T2 thus clearly depends on the degree to which the given concept – Difference – as extracted from the restricted context of T1 exceeds or escapes, perhaps by virtue of abstraction, the limits of that context. Thus the essential relation or passage from T1 to T2 depends on a certain logic of *generalisation*. T3 then marks a limit to the generalisation of Difference and an apparent break with the conceptual structure of Difference as such. To make sense of T3 requires a new way to differentiate non-philosophy from Difference that does not itself depend on the structure of Difference. Thus the passage from T2 to T3 requires a specifically determined logic of *distinction*.

I introduce the term *distinction* here for purely heuristic reasons. It is not meant from the outset to designate a concept, but only to serve as an expository device to avoid unnecessary confusion. Clearly, if a thorough critique of the concept of Difference as mounted from a non-differential standpoint is what is at stake in Laruelle's analysis, then that analysis itself cannot employ any naive and uncritical operations depending on Difference except on pain of begging the question at issue. In particular, any invocation of a particular difference, any act of conceptual differentiation or, for instance, negation will depend in a more or less obvious way on the general structure of Difference. The problem here is that philosophy everywhere begins, proceeds and ends with and through differences and negations! *Prima facie* there is no viable alternative to Difference (if the purported generality of this concept is granted). For this reason, the term *distinction* (as distinct from 'difference') will here designate *any* opposition, contrast, difference, etc., that occurs in the course of exposition and argument at whatever level of naivety or sophistication, and which is understood to function without presupposing that its distinguished terms can be articulated through a more general structure or syntax. This allows us to pose from the very beginning the question whose full sense, as much as its answer, will only become clear at the close of the analysis: *How, if at all, does the very distinction between Difference and non-philosophy depend upon Difference?*

The formulation of T1 suggests a relatively familiar and straightforward logic. There is, on the one hand, a set of concrete instances or examples: four contemporary philosophies. There is then, on the other hand, an abstract 'structure' that is identified as common to all the members of the set. The basic form of reasoning would seem to be that of induction: from a set of specific instances, a general conclusion is drawn (*each* of these philosophies of Difference . . . thus *all* philosophies of Difference . . .). Alternately, this logic may appear as an instance of hypostatic abstraction: a recognisable property or relation is extracted from given material and turned into an independent term, a 'thing' (from these given philosophies, we abstract the new term: Difference).

At a first level of simply getting one's bearings such characterisations may be helpful, but in the long run they prove misleading. Laruelle's own strategy proceeds otherwise. On the one hand, he lays out specific critical readings of four influential philosophers: Nietzsche, Deleuze, Heidegger and Derrida. On the other hand, the primary impulse of his argument is not to critique these philosophies as such but to identify a structure they co–constitute, which is what Laruelle will designate as Difference with a capital D or *the* Difference (*la* Différence). This structure itself is understood intrinsically to undermine any clear divisions between abstract concepts (or structures) and concrete instantiations, as well as between the terms of other traditional philosophical dichotomies such as subject and object or thought and being. It is an infinitely supple mechanism, an elusive chiaroscuro. So the structure of Difference will itself challenge any simple and straightforward understanding of the means of its own abstraction from its concrete philosophical instances.

It is the global 'critique', then, of this ambiguous, self-deconstructing structure as a whole that is Laruelle's essential aim. Why place scare-quotes around 'critique' here? Because after having brought to light the concept of Difference on the basis of a series of contemporary philosophical examples, Laruelle will then retrospectively assign this concept as the very essence of the entire Western philosophical tradition, or what Laruelle calls the 'Greco-Occidental' (T2). Even if this explicit concept remains inseparable from a particular conjunction within the history of philosophy, namely the line stretching from Nietzsche through Heidegger to today, it is understood intrinsically to exceed this historical specificity and to extend itself across the entire tradition. Since the idea of 'critique' in both its general and its restricted Kantian senses are features of that tradition itself, Laruelle's 'critique' of Difference – if it is to avoid question-begging consequences and performative self-contradiction – finds itself in need of encompassing the very notion and practice of critique in the philosophical sense from a standpoint that would no longer be part of that tradition. For this reason, Laruelle's 'critique' will have to take a new, non-philosophical form that does not depend upon or reproduce Difference (T3).

Four key distinctions set forth in the first two chapters of *Philosophies of Difference* serve as guiding threads to help the reader stay on the path of Laruelle's argument throughout. If we adopt the convention that 'A/B' represents the distinction of A and B, we have four canonical or guiding distinctions as follows:

1. Difference/One
2. Metaphysical/Transcendental
3. Syntax/Reality
4. Models-of-Difference/The-Difference.

We examine each of these distinctions in a preliminary fashion in the following four sections. Taken together, they provide Laruelle's own most general framework for his critical analysis of Difference. The elaboration of these distinctions may at first seem unnecessarily complex and technical for merely introductory purposes. However, it should be kept in mind that the initially philosophical logic of these 'differences', in the context of Laruelle's argument, always invokes the very problematic at issue, that is, Difference as, finally, *the* invariant of philosophical thinking. In each case, the form of the distinction itself both separating and relating its two given terms should be understood as a particular instance of the more general structure of Difference that is at stake in the argument overall. This presents unique methodological difficulties for Laruelle's project and makes significant preparatory labours unavoidable. Because this point is so essential to grasping Laruelle's argumentation throughout *Philosophies of Difference*, it is worth clarifying here in some detail first, before examining the four distinctions themselves. We will call this the *(meta-)Difference problem*.[1]

Philosophy works through the making of distinctions and through reflection on its own practices. At times, philosophy finds itself in the position of reflecting on the *kinds of distinctions* it makes. It is then led to distinguish among various forms of distinction.[2] But there is a problem lurking here. If different kinds of distinction exist, and at stake in some particular context is how to distinguish between the various relevant kinds of distinction, then *either* (A) one of the forms of distinction at issue must be used to distinguish among the distinctions *or* (B) some relatively independent form of distinction must be imported to decide the question. (A) risks begging the question since part of what is at stake is used to decide the matter, while (B) precludes settling the issue for any presumed closed set of forms of distinction. What this argument schema suggests is that the problem of distinguishing forms of distinction can never be fully resolved philosophically. At the very least, the problem of classifying forms of distinction or difference involves a sort of 'strange loop' whereby the *objects* and *operations* of inquiry become ineluctably entangled.[3] Difference as the most general logic of differences seems inevitably to imply 'its own' (meta-)Difference. Is such a 'strange loop' essential to all thinking? According to what necessity?

Laruelle's mode of argumentation is especially difficult – but also especially powerful – because it functions at the level of philosophy's most fundamental operations and objects. In this respect, Laruelle appears to be pursuing a project of meta-philosophy, the philosophy of philosophy itself.[4] Yet one of the central claims that specifies his notion of non-philosophy is that instead of being a meta-philosophical project, non-philosophy should be conceived as a 'science of philosophy'. What this means in particular is that while philosophy does serve for Laruelle as a privileged 'object' of non-philosophy, non-philosophy itself does not employ the characteristic methods and operations – broadly speaking, the 'subject'-form – of philosophy with respect to that object. Even the most basic of philosophical operations become reconfigured for non-philosophy as themselves scientific 'objects' to be examined and recombined, not directly employed. In this way, Laruelle claims to have found a way to avoid a certain vicious-circularity and question-begging form of reasoning that he asserts is endemic to philosophy as such. The first-order, scientific and experimental knowledge of philosophy here replaces the self-inclusive, higher-order reflection of philosophy as meta-philosophy which is always structured ultimately by what we are calling here (meta-)Difference.

In place of philosophy's self-repetition whereby the *difference* between the method or 'subject' of inquiry and its objects determines at one and the same time their intrinsic *relation*, Laruelle thus substitutes what he frequently describes as the unary 'stance' or 'posture' of science according to which the problem of representation appears in a completely different light. In the context of the consolidation of the general 'Critique of Difference' that occupies chapter six, Laruelle writes:

> What is able to pass for paradox in the eyes of philosophy . . . is understood as perfectly simple once we have recognized here the posture of science with respect to the real or to its object: science does not constitute its object, but knows itself straightaway and non-thetically to be identical (to) this real even as its reflection. *Science is a representation that is non-thetic (of) the real, altogether distinct from what philosophy imagines as Representation.*[5]

Non-philosophical science for Laruelle is conceived here not as a method of empirical observation, hypothesis-formation and testing, but is understood rather as an irreducible 'stance' taken with respect to the real. It is the difference between this 'stance' and that of philosophy that distinguishes, for Laruelle, the non-philosophical 'science of philosophy' from any 'philosophy of philosophy' or (question-begging) meta-philosophy. Laruelle's distinctive concept of the 'posture' or 'stance' of science thus poses a unique methodological problem which is, in a certain sense, the central concern of *Philosophies of Difference* as a whole: *How can one conceptually articulate and elaborate both an 'object' and a 'method' that are intrinsically simple, immediate and 'non-thetic' rather than Differential and (meta-) Differential?* The four distinctions that follow outline Laruelle's own framework for both broaching and sustaining this question throughout his critical analysis of Difference.

DIFFERENCE AND THE ONE

To put matters as succinctly and straightforwardly as possible: philosophy and non-philosophy are both modes of thought, yet while philosophy thinks according to Difference, or by-Difference, non-philosophy thinks according to the One, or in-One. This distinction would be a simple matter, were it not for the fact that the differences of Identity and Difference, the One and the Multiple, Unity and Multiplicity, Monads and Dyads and similar constructions are already found everywhere throughout philosophy, to the point of *constituting* a basic framework for philosophical thinking. Even if we set the problem of the Multiple or the Many to one side, apparently leaving 'only' the One, it suffices merely to list a few names from the history of philosophy – Parmenides, Plotinus, Damascius, Kant, Badiou, for instance – to make it clear that there is more than just one One in philosophy.[6] As Aristotle might have put it, in philosophy *the One is said in Many ways.*

The One (and) Difference: between these two terms (if 'between' and 'two' do not already beg the question) hangs the entire argument, critical analysis and positive proposal of *Philosophies of Difference.* It is *their* difference, or rather their distinction, that is finally at stake in the text. However, this distinction is at stake not only *finally* but also *initially* and *formally.* Laruelle's argument takes the self-presupposing structure of a problematic relation of unity and difference between 'One' and 'Difference' – a circularity which resonates immediately with Hegelian dialectics and Heideggerean hermeneutics – as something *simply given*, indeed as something needing to be fully unfolded so as to be adequately understood. But this entire way of proceeding still remains relatively on the side of

Difference, according to Laruelle's way of thinking. What must be discovered or invented is a new kind of distinction between this complex, self-inclusive structure Difference/One on the one hand and the simple (non-structural) science of the One-without-Difference on the other.[7] Such a distinction is necessary for Laruelle because *if* the philosophical logic of the relation or unity of contraries always works by presupposing itself *and* that logic is itself universal for philosophy, *then* only a mode of critique that is not itself philosophical will be capable of critiquing this logic as such without begging the question.

This can be clarified in terms of the problem of (meta-)Difference indicated above. Let us express this somewhat formally. Given any two terms, A and B, representing differentiated concepts, objects, philosophers, etc., the *difference itself* between A and B will be represented as A/B. Now the structure of (meta-)Difference may be expressed as follows: the difference itself between the two terms, in other words the entire complex term A/B, is to be distinguished in its own way from one of the two terms it already includes, and identified with the other. So, for instance, for the variable B in the expression A/B, we substitute the entire expression A/B, that is, the difference itself of A and B is *distinguished* from its own term, A. Using parentheses to avoid ambiguity, the expression that results appears like this: A/(A/B). But the difference A/B is not only to be distinguished from A; it is at the same time to be *identified* with its other term, B. In the derived expression A/(A/B), the term 'B' thus remains relatively 'unanalysed'. It must be replaced with its equivalent, 'A/B'. So, from A/(A/B) we extend or unfold to A/(A/(A/B)). But clearly we now find ourselves in the same situation, only 'one level up' (or 'down', if one prefers). The process may be repeated indefinitely, generating the infinite or limit expression A/B = A/(A/(A/...)...B) = B.[8]

An alternate formulation of the same point, or rather the same basic problem, may be made in terms of the logic of *relations* rather than differences. Say we represent some given relation between A and B with a hyphen: A-B. We may then pose the analogous (meta-)relational problem: how do things stand when one of the terms thus related is in fact the relation itself? Formally, we assign the entire relation A-B to the term B. As above, we then substitute for B and, using parentheses for clarity, we have the expression A-(A-B). Once again, this process is interminable and we have the syntactical 'bad infinite' of A-B = A-(A-(A- ...)...B) = B. In both cases (difference and relation), what comes to light is the problematic structure of semi-self-inclusion, or one-sided redoubling: *a difference or a relation that is itself one of its own terms.*

Indeed, things can and do get even more complicated. One of the characteristic structures that Laruelle will engage and analyse as a crucial motif

of contemporary philosophy is that of the *chiasmus*, or crossed enfold-
ing. This structure, perhaps best known from the influential later work
of Merleau-Ponty, involves two terms or poles that mutually posit and
subsume one another in a complex mix of imbalanced alternation and symmetrical difference, like the sensation of two hands belonging to one and
the same person touching and being touched by one another.[9] In terms of
the formalism just introduced, notice that in the examples above one of the
two terms in each case remains fixed. But what if this term is also iterated?
What if it too is determined as its own 'interpretation' of the difference at
stake? As before, then, $B = A/B$. But now, by stipulation, $A = A/B$ as well.
Yet crucially, A is posited as not equal to B. Thus we have a 'conflict of
interpretations' over the difference itself between the two terms. But each
of the two terms *just is* this difference, and thus *is* this conflict itself.[10] From
the side or standpoint of B, we have, as before: $A/B = A/(A/(A/. . .) . . .$
$B) = B$. But now, from the side or standpoint of A, we have the symmetrical, but distinct structure: $A = (A . . . (. . ./B)/B)/B = A/B$. Combining
the two, we thus have: $B = A/(A/(A/. . .) . . . (. . ./B)/B)/B = A$, while
nonetheless B is posited as not equal to A since the difference A/B is precisely what is at issue. Such is the paradoxical abstract formula of chiasmic
(meta-)Difference.

So the (meta-)Difference problem may appear as a relatively one-
sided or, on the contrary, as a two-sided and hence doubly differential
essence of Difference. But either way, for Laruelle, such self-inclusive
differentiation and relation expresses Difference as such. In this manner,
Difference = (meta-)Difference. The formalism above is introduced in a
heuristic way simply to express the abstract structure of a certain paradox
or positive intensification (depending on one's point of view) that appears
in various ways in the philosophies of Difference as engaged by Laruelle.[11]
This structure, what we are calling here the (meta-)Difference problem,
is not simply a consequence or a latent possibility for Difference. Rather,
in the context of Laruelle's analysis, it *is* Difference – in person, as it
were. Difference is 'its own' transposition into a register that, by this very
transposition, at once takes 'itself' – that is, Difference – as an object and
yet nevertheless transcends its own objectification. Difference is something like a knife-edge that cuts itself, or a line split length-wise by a line
split length-wise by a line . . .[12] The fact that this structure is expressed
equivalently as (meta-)Difference or as (meta-)relation is important. A
good deal of Laruelle's argument works to substantiate the claim that every
philosophical difference (even, and especially, the peculiarly 'heterogeneous', 'absolute' or 'pure' differences of Difference) always in fact implies
a corresponding relation – in effect, that philosophy cannot tolerate a *real*
non-relation (namely, the real-without-syntax of the One).

To see how this logic applies more concretely, consider the generality of formulations arising in philosophy that take the shape 'X of X': for example, 'truth of truth', 'signification of signification' or 'principle of principles'. Such formulations are subject to diverse variations. For instance, the first and second appearances of X may be numerically varied: 'truth of truth', 'truth of truths', 'truths of truth', 'truths of truths'. Each of these variations produces specific inflections of sense and distinct philosophical effects. For Laruelle, formulations of this kind illustrate philosophical Difference in a particularly sharp fashion. We can analyse this according to the following two invariant tendencies that inevitably appear in such cases: (1) a tendency toward essentialisation; (2) a tendency toward relative destabilisation and indeterminacy.

If we take the example 'the truth of truth', for instance, tendency (1) appears in so far as 'the truth of truth' seems to signify a 'higher' truth, a truth that in applying to truth itself would extract from the concept of truth precisely that essence that makes it truly truthful. The basic logic here would be that of a doubling that consolidates, or a folding that purifies and potentialises. 'Truth of truth': *even more* true than truth. Tendency (2) on the other hand registers in this case as a sort of dark shadow concomitant to the former. From a slightly different point of view, the essentialisation of truth would also, even primarily, manifest its being called profoundly into question. We might grasp intuitively or empirically what 'truth' means, for instance, but when we are asked to identify the 'truth of truth' we feel ourselves called up short. It seems that *this* truth is relatively obscure and requires a deeper and more difficult mode of consideration that throws into relief the status of the very term 'truth'. Asking into the 'truth of truth' in this sense tends to *unground* truth from its own representation (truth or 'truth'?), to turn the folding of truth back onto itself into a duplicity of truth and untruth. 'Truth of truth': is this *still* truth?

Above all, in Laruelle's analysis the concept of Difference will always be subject to the syntax 'Difference of Difference' (which itself differentiates variably into its analogues: 'Difference of differences', 'differences of Difference' and so on). The distinctions that frame Laruelle's readings of the three models of Difference may then be schematised in a provisional way according to this logic of identical doubling and essential excess. On Laruelle's reading, Nietzschean and Deleuzean Idealist Difference will treat this effect of re-inscription primarily as an infinitisation and potentialisation of Difference.[13] This process maximises tendency (1). Heideggerean Finitude on the contrary will draw out a relative neutralisation of the former tendency which will tend to reduce the doubling structure to a more or less empty tautological identification of object and operation: 'language speaks', 'the nothing nihilates', etc. This will, in contrast to Nietzsche, tend to maximise (2), but in such a way that the 'essence' thus identified withdraws into the tautology of its own identity. The maximisation of essence thus entails Finitisation as withdrawal. Derrida, as we will see, represents a complex mixture for Laruelle of the Nietzschean and Heideggerean models. Perhaps the best way to characterise Derrida in the present terms is as a second-order reproduction of both tendencies as mutually interfering chiasmically with one another, (meta-)Difference of Nietzsche and Heidegger.

Other than these various forms of the 'Difference of Difference', however, is *the One*. What is at stake though is not an *opposition* of the One to Difference. As we will see when we reach the final third of Laruelle's book – the formulation of a theory of philosophical decision and the non-philosophical vision-in-One – the One is not, in itself or from its 'point of view', in any way distinguished or distinguishable from Difference. Thus whatever difference there is between Difference and the One is wholly on the side of Difference. Laruelle attempts to clarify the issue by making a terminological distinction between two kinds of 'two-ness': *duel* and *dual*. These correspond to alternate spellings in French that have been carried over to the English translation. The meaning of 'two-sided fight' in the English 'duel' is also carried by the French 'duel'. As we will see in the concluding chapter, Laruelle specifies the non-philosophical form of thought as a new kind of 'dualism' that is genuinely 'dual' and not 'duel', one in which the two terms remain simply separate rather than antagonistically opposed.

Laruelle identifies the 'duel' as the 'Greco-Occidental invariant' that structures Western philosophy from Heraclitus and Parmenides to Derrida and Deleuze, namely 'the combination . . . of an immanence and a transcendence, of an ideality and a supposed real'.[14] Laruelle emphasises that the essential character of every such 'coupling or . . . arrangement of two terms' is that it introduces a necessary moment that is 'continuous, reciprocal or symmetrical' and that this always holds 'despite all efforts to introduce asymmetry and unilaterality into their relation'.[15] In opposition to this philosophical 'duel' (but keep in mind that it is the character of this opposition itself that is at stake) Laruelle proposes a 'mode of thinking that is not *duel* but *dual* or dualist'.[16] This new form of thought is 'irreversible and ensues from the One'.[17] In a key formulation that is repeated in almost identical terms in many places throughout Laruelle's work, Laruelle specifies: 'Duality here is no longer as philosophy understands it: two heterogeneous terms finally equal or reciprocal in their exclusion or else in their unitary hierarchy. It is the unilateralisation and contingency of a "second" term by the One which however *does not posit* this second term and, consequently, is not determined in turn by it.'[18] This formulation indicates one of the key concepts of non-philosophy, that of 'unilateral duality', which in a sense encapsulates the whole of non-philosophy. To understand it fully is to know the non-philosophical One 'in person'. It is ultimately in order to show how this form of distinction enables a non-differential critique of Difference that Laruelle advances the readings of Nietzsche, Heidegger, Deleuze and Derrida that constitute *Philosophies of Difference*.

The stakes of the difference between the 'duel' of philosophical duality and the genuine 'dual' or 'dualism' of non-philosophy are set forth by Laruelle as embracing the Western philosophical tradition in its entirety: 'What duality, thus grounded transcendentally in a thought of the One, allows us to tear out at the roots is the oldest model of Occidental thought, that of which Difference is none other than the purest mode, the model of Unity-in-tension or the One-Multiple.'[19] This should be kept clearly in mind as the argument focuses more particularly on Nietzsche, Deleuze, Heidegger and Derrida. These 'philosophies of Difference' are understood to instantiate in 'none other than the purest mode' an invariant structure that determines all of Western philosophy – an operative, self-enabling distinction between the ideal and the real. To this philosophical Difference is *dual*istically (and not *duel*istically) 'opposed' the non-philosophical One.

FROM METAPHYSICAL TO TRANSCENDENTAL DIFFERENCE

Besides the overarching distinction of Difference and the One, Laruelle makes several schematic distinctions that are conceived as internal to Difference itself and which taken together serve as Laruelle's basic analytical framework. The first of these is an operative distinction that Laruelle identifies as being at work in each of the philosophies of Difference he examines and that underwrites the 'bootstrapping' effect of Difference being taken up into itself that we indicated above as the logic of (meta-)Difference. This distinction is that of the 'metaphysical' and the 'transcendental'. The terminological distinction between the metaphysical and the transcendental is here drawn first of all from Kant. Kant's transcendental analysis identifies structural conditions for the possibility of experience that do not imply metaphysical beings that would exceed experience.[20] In general, a broadly Kantian problematic is present throughout *Philosophies of Difference*. Difference in Laruelle's sense takes the difference between the metaphysical and the transcendental in Kant and generalises it by extracting the idea of an abstract 'passage' to the transcendental that may then be recognised in later thinkers who in other important respects may be said to have gone 'beyond' Kant. Laruelle himself thus takes over Kant's notion of the transcendental and transforms it while nonetheless showing its continued relevance for the philosophies of Difference. Among other things, then, the analysis of *Philosophies of Difference* aims to demonstrate the insistence of a certain Kantian problematic in all of the models of Difference, even and especially where they attempt to break with or surpass Kant.

This may occur by asserting a radical immanence as against the residual transcendence in Kant (Nietzsche), or by deepening this transcendence – particularly the withdrawal of the noumenal in-itself – as against the relative immanence of Kantian subjectivism (Heidegger). At any rate, attempting to surpass Kant is nothing new. As the standard history of modern philosophy after Kant emphasises, the innovations and transformations of Kantian philosophy in the nineteenth century – especially in the major German thinkers Maimon, Fichte, Schelling, Hegel and Schopenhauer, not to mention less obvious Anglophone figures like Coleridge and Peirce – largely define the space in which contemporary philosophy still moves. And as many have argued, Kant may be seen as the last common point of reference for what has become today the largely separate branches of philosophy as divided into analytic and continental traditions.[21]

It should be borne in mind that the notion of the transcendental in Kant is *first and foremost* opposed to metaphysical transcendence. The transcendental conditions of possible experience are precisely *not* transcendent entities that would exert some sort of causal efficacy with respect to the world. They are conditions that are immanent to experience itself, the conditions that the very essence of experience imposes on itself, if it may be put that way. It is this relatively immanent notion of the transcendental that will allow a thinker like Deleuze (or perhaps less radically, Husserl) to take over this terminology in the service of a philosophical immanence.[22] When Laruelle will ultimately critique the philosophical notion of the transcendental and oppose his own non-philosophical conception of the transcendental One, which is equally the Real, this will involve a separate notion of immanence. The movement from the metaphysical to the transcendental in Difference is for Laruelle precisely the highest immanence *of which philosophy remains capable*. As Laruelle will argue, however, this philosophical immanence remains always mixed ultimately with a surreptitious element of transcendence.

Laruelle writes, 'The mechanism of Difference as principle comprises two phases that form its process or its becoming and that are characteristics of philosophical decision in general.'[23] At the first level or phase Laruelle locates 'the meta-physical articulation of Difference'.[24] The hyphen here ('meta-physics' rather than simply 'metaphysics') is used to emphasise that this first level is already constituted by a differential structure. Indeed, Laruelle characterises this level in terms of the distinction between the empirical and the *a priori*. The 'meta-physical articulation of Difference' is the philosophical passage itself from the empirical or ontic to the *a priori*, the difference that first opens philosophy as such. Laruelle is careful to distinguish this very general conception of the *a priori* from that of Kant or Husserl. This, according to Laruelle, is not an 'ahistorical and rational' *a priori* but rather 'a plastic concept of the *a priori*, not only as "possible", but as historical "possibility" or possibility in becoming'.[25] In other words, the first stage of Difference constitutes an *a priori* possibilisation or potentialisation of empirical beings, their very 'power-to-be'.[26] This *a priori* is thus not merely some formal schema that might be filled in by one or another content, but is rather an effective although non-empirical feature of empirical reality itself, its very power to transcend, repeat and differentiate itself in its own processes of becoming.[27] While the *a priori* in this sense may be interpreted differently according to different philosophies, its basic structure is invariant; without some such minimal transcendence or intensification of the empirical, philosophy would simply collapse into an empty positivism. As Laruelle points out, the identification of such an *a priori* feature in any particular philosophy marks from the beginning a certain choice for the characterisation of the Being of beings *by* that philosophy.

The (meta-)Difference problem is already partly in play at this first level, since the difference between the empirical and the *a priori* is itself implicitly governed by the *a priori*. Despite, however, the already complex and self-reflexive structure of Difference at the meta-physical level, such a distinction between the empirical and the *a priori* remains too coarse and restrictive from the perspective of fully-fledged Difference:

> this *a priori* is always abstract because it is still too close to what it intends to leave behind: the sensible, beings, representation, reified metaphysical differences between Being and beings, etc., and their very multiplicity which is itself introduced here back into the *a priori*. It is threatened with falling back into what it proposes to leave behind, precisely because its principle remains transcendence, and transcendence, characteristically of meta-physics, is always insufficient and fragile, and risks becoming again empirical, foundering upon the facticity of the 'given'.[28]

In other words, once philosophy introduces the difference between the empirical and the *a priori* as the very opening of thought onto the possibility of philosophy, it must subsequently ensure that the level of the *a priori* does not merely reflect or redouble the empirical. It must possess its own self-determining consistency, coherence and relative autonomy.

Therefore, a second level must be founded and recognised: the 'transcendental stage of Difference'.[29] This stage marks for Laruelle the full 'coming into itself' of philosophical Difference. Here, every trace of relation to the empirical is left behind and Difference is conceived and affirmed in and for itself. On Laruelle's account, the seemingly arbitrary nature of the cut or division that would separate the empirical from the meta-physical must find its sufficient reason in itself and attain an immanent determination. The determinations of the metaphysical *a priori* which were 'born', as it were, through a generalisation or abstraction from ordinary actuality must be flattened onto the same level as empirical beings, so as to open up the pure *difference* between the empirical and the *a priori* as a new and relatively autonomous structure. Or, alternately, the *a priori* itself may be conceived as split from within into two differential poles, one intrinsically correlated with the determinately empirical or with actual beings and one oriented toward a pure indetermination or absolute transcendence with respect to the actual. In either case, the difference of the empirical and the *a priori* is redoubled or intensified through itself in a new way in order to manifest an immanent 'difference of differences' or (meta-)Difference.

It is at this stage according to Laruelle that the One is necessarily invoked by philosophy (either explicitly or implicitly) in its function of Unity or transcendental synthesis. The turn from the meta-physical to the transcendental marks in effect a decision for the second pole of the empirical/metaphysical difference. The metaphysical must not only be distinguished and differentiated from the empirical; the very operation of distinction or differentiation itself must relatively *side with* the non-empirical, metaphysical pole in its unifying function. Laruelle refers in this regard particularly to Heidegger's 'immense and overworn effort . . . to assign to Being *rather* than to beings, to Being itself *rather* than to Being-present, to the essence and truth of Being *rather* than to metaphysical Being and to man . . . the birthplace of contraries'.[30] Heidegger attempts to resist the 'forgetting of Being', that is, the reduction of Being to the status of a mere being, by thinking Being itself on the basis of a 'clearing' that would be both unconcealing and concealing, the indivision of truth and untruth. For Laruelle, such a strategy is nothing other than a reduplication and repetition of the first distinction between the empirical and metaphysical (or, as this structure appears in Heidegger's case, between ontic beings and ontological Being) but inserted now into the heart of the metaphysical itself: 'this mechanism is none other than the re-inscription of division, in particular the division of the meta-physical, *in* or rather *as* the Immanence of the One or the Absolute'.[31] Rather than serving as a secondary and derivative effect of Difference, the paradoxical, 'boot-strapping' character of (meta-)Difference is here set as the prior and initial *essence* of Difference.[32]

If the metaphysical level of Difference is constituted through the distinction of the *a priori* from the empirical but *on the basis of the empirical*,

for Laruelle the transcendental level of Difference takes this initial philosophical level as given and inverts its 'basis' in the sense of its relatively
concrete ground. At the transcendental level, Being (or its analogues: Will
to Power, virtuality, Body-without-Organs, differance, etc.) is not primarily determined through its relation (however broadly defined) *to* beings or
the actual, but rather through 'itself' as the relatively autonomous distinction of itself *from* beings and actuality. To be sure, the very syntax of 'itself'
as designating a self-relation is first and foremost drawn from the logic of
identity and exclusion that governs the empirical sphere of beings. So the
'determination through itself' of the transcendental will have to involve an
important critical element with respect to this 'itself' and to the received
logic of identity and difference in general.

This is the reason that the passage from the metaphysical to the
transcendental is in a sense the core of Difference. It involves a kind of
half-turn that 'inverts' the oppositional and dyadic logic governing the
metaphysical as such, even where this is relatively 'softened' or nuanced
(as in Heidegger's ontological difference).[33] Since the logic of meta-physics
envelops the classical binary structure that underlies any straightforward
notion of a logic of 'inversion', to 'invert' metaphysics into the transcendental is precisely to inaugurate a new logic that overcomes or overturns
the standard metaphysical conceptions of overcoming and overturning.[34]
This new logic is then incarnated in various ways in the multiple forms
of philosophical Difference. Laruelle aims to show in *Philosophies of
Difference* that this metaphysical/transcendental schema may be applied to
Nietzsche, Heidegger, Deleuze and Derrida (albeit in a distinctive manner
in each case). At the most general level, what matters here is the conception
of a passage from one stage of philosophical thought to another that has an
identifiable formal structure and yet manifests itself quite differently in
different concrete philosophies.

What, in short, is the status of the passage from the metaphysical to the
transcendental? It is for Laruelle the quasi-logical mechanism whereby an
original distinction, a first-level difference, is reduplicated and intensified
by including itself, that is, its very act or essence of difference, in and as
one of the terms it originally distinguished. This produces an effect of the
apparent absolutisation and auto-determination of Difference. The passage
to the transcendental in Laruelle's sense is a philosophical gambit through
which a more or less arbitrary division between the form and content
of thought (meta-physics) seems capable of grounding itself through its
own repetition or redoubling. Where and how does this take place? In
and through Difference itself. Difference is not thereby substantialised,
because it is 'itself' in this way only through its unlimited operation of
differing, dividing, etc. But without being substantialised or reified at an

43

initial level, it becomes quasi-reified in a strange new manner through its second-order iteration as difference 'itself', as 'its own' difference-in-itself.

FROM THE SYNTAX TO THE REALITY OF DIFFERENCE

For Laruelle, a second distinction internal to Difference cuts across the metaphysical/transcendental distinction. At his most general level of analysis, Laruelle understands Difference to consist of the disjunction and synthesis of a pair of philosophical problems, which he designates as those of 'syntax' and 'reality'. These are formulated as follows:

1. 'What is the syntax called "Difference" such that it may be distinguished, for example, from "Dialectic"? This is the problem of Difference as *form of order* or *articulation* of the real.'[35]
2. 'What is the specific experience of the real – the *experiences* – animating this syntax and rendering it concrete? What type of real does it articulate that specifies it in turn each time? Does it concern Being, Substance, Spirit, Power, etc.? the Other – which Other?'[36]

The first question, that of syntax, concerns in a broad sense the essential structure of Difference as we have sketched it above. At a relatively formal or abstract level, what is it that the philosophies of Difference share? How are they logically articulated in distinction from classical representation or dialectical *Aufhebung*? The second question, that of reality, poses the problem of the specific *relation* between this abstract structure and the particular interests of some given philosophy at issue. Given the common structure of Difference, we ask in any particular case: *which terms and/or relations* are conceived as essentially structured by Difference?

It is standard practice in formal logic, cognitive science and other fields to distinguish syntax from semantics. Syntax refers to the purely formal operations that regulate and transform strings of symbols or formulas. Semantics involves the assignments and interpretations of the various elements of the syntax such that statements in the syntax take on determinate senses and truth-values. In general, the specification of a semantics for some given syntax involves a mapping of formulas into truth-values in such a way that the combinatorics of the formal system are preserved. In this way, the distinction and relation between syntax and semantics are closely related to those of theories and models (see below). Laruelle eschews this standard language of syntax and semantics and writes instead of syntax and reality. Why? The difference between syntax and reality is for Laruelle in effect what the logical syntax/semantics distinction becomes when philosophical Difference is itself raised from the 'metaphysical' to the 'transcendental' level, that is, when it fully realises itself *as* Difference. It is then no longer a logical distinction, nor even a metaphysical or ontological distinction (like that between Being and beings), but rather a distinction that arises only in this specific form *for* the philosophies of Difference themselves. Reality, for Laruelle as for the philosophers of Difference, is not the object of a syntactical representation. It is precisely the problematic core of what escapes, exceeds or withdraws essentially from every such syntax or representational objectivity.

The two problems of syntax and reality are nonetheless interdependent for Laruelle. The way they relate to one another concerns precisely the nature and status of Difference. In this way Difference is set forth as essentially self-involved, auto-referential and auto-performative: 'Difference is a syntax, a manner of articulating philosophical language. It is also a thesis about reality, a certain experience – itself multiple – of the real. As the functional unity of a syntax and an experience, it is a principle, a syntax that is real and not merely formal, transcendental and not merely logical.'[37] There is no abstract correlation between syntax and reality in Laruelle's sense, but instead their strictly functional or performative unity such as some philosophy in any given case *instantiates* uniquely.

To clarify, at the 'metaphysical' level of the syntax/reality distinction we encounter one or another version of the distinction between Being and beings. Being – however understood – provides the ontological structure, the syntax, articulating and organising ontic beings, the reality. But this is only a first level. The syntax/reality distinction only becomes fully meaningful for Difference once it is raised from the metaphysical to the transcendental. This process begins with an act of abstraction away from the terms of the ontological/ontic difference, taking only the most abstract 'form' of this difference itself into view while prescinding from any questions of which term structures which in the relation, or which of the two is more formal or more real. There is no longer a given ontological/ontic difference, but only the pure Difference itself *of* this difference. This Difference itself then bifurcates in turn into two complementary oppositions – those of syntax and reality – that together form a chiasmus, each side of which is internally problematised by the chiasmus in its own way.

On the one hand, there is the problematic form of *syntax* as a structure defined solely against what remains 'exterior' to that structure, a real cut. What reality exceeds and escapes all philosophical determination? This opposition of syntax to the real *from the side of syntax* tends to produce from its side an abyss of undecidability, since Difference is the philosophical structure par excellence that includes its exteriority *as* exteriority or real difference. Is the opposed cut here internal or external to Difference? Rather than interiorising the different or Other as in Hegelian dialectics, Difference reproduces Otherness and exteriority indefinitely. In this sense, once Difference is articulated as a relatively determinate 'structure' – even as a simple term at this highly abstract level – the problem of its Other or its remainder inevitably appears as at once inside and outside Difference itself, as *barely* or *nearly* expressible syntactically.

On the other hand, there is the problematic form of *reality* as the 'same' distinction yet conceived from the side of the real cut itself. How is reality opposed to philosophical syntax *from the side of the Real?* This problem tends to produce a complementary abyss, one not of the undecidability of interiority and exteriority but of sheer exteriority and inexpressibility as such, as in the well-known aporias of negative theology. Here there is not a problem of the philosophical expression of philosophy's own limits, but of a more or less total dissolution of all philosophical expression whatsoever. It is one thing after all to speak of philosophy's need to be silent. It is something else entirely (or *almost* entirely) actually to cease speaking or to abandon philosophy altogether.

For Laruelle, the specific way any given philosophy links the problem of syntax with the problem of reality determines the internal structure of that philosophy itself: 'A concrete philosophical decision is each time the totality, the unity of the co-belonging and co-penetration of a syntax and an experience of what it calls the "real".'[38] The key point here is that in the philosophies of Difference, this general relation (roughly, that of philosophical *form* and *content*) becomes internally troubled and chiasmically reproduced in an especially complex fashion.

Against this complication and redoubling of syntax and reality through Difference, Laruelle asserts the simplicity of *science* as a mode of thought that does not require a 'scission' of syntax and reality at all. In an important passage that presages the key difference Laruelle will continue to elaborate in later works of non-philosophy between philosophical and scientific modes of thought, the distinction and relation between syntax and reality are identified in fact with the very essence of philosophy itself: 'Just as the scientific thinking of the One excludes its dismemberment into a syntactical side and a real side, so philosophy, which is a functional rather than theoretical activity, demands it and, like every practice stripped of genuine scientificity, founds itself upon the practical moment of scission.'[39] In other words, philosophy *needs* the two-sided problem of syntax and reality in order to be what it is. It produces and reproduces itself as this problem, whereas science does not ask into the structure of *the* Real but rather of *this* Real. Science does not aim at *determining itself with respect to* the Real, but *allows itself to be determined by* the Real.

Because of the peculiar self-scaling structure of Difference, its inclusion of itself in its own field of operations and its very definition of itself in terms of this self-inclusion, the relation of syntax and reality for the philosophies of Difference can never be confused with any simple mapping of the general onto the specific. It is not a question of ideal structures or types that would correspond to empirical particularities. The whole point of Difference as a philosophical strategy is to preserve thinking from its dependence on such simplistic and binary models. Because of this, the 'reality' at stake ultimately in the syntax/reality distinction can only be that of the absolute residue or remainder of Difference. It is not a matter of empirical reality, to be sure. But neither is it a matter of any thing-in-itself that would be correlated directly in a more or less Kantian manner with objects of experience. It will be a question of what – if anything – escapes and remains irreducible to the structure, that is, the syntax, of Difference altogether. Is there a Real beyond Difference? Difference is already, according to its own syntax, a generalised non-identity that would at every point both require and produce an irreducible or unrecuperable Other. The question of reality in Laruelle's sense of the syntax/reality distinction is that of an Other to this Other, which is itself already not *in* but precisely *of* Difference. What would be radically Other *than* (rather than Other *to*) Difference itself, if Difference is already the mode of philosophy that would be maximally 'affected' by the Other? This is for Laruelle the problem of syntax and reality in the context of Difference.

DIFFERENCE IN AND AS ITS MODELS

Finally, having set up the general framework for posing the problem of Difference in terms of the passage from the metaphysical to the transcendental on the one hand and the correlated problems of philosophical syntax and reality on the other, Laruelle proceeds to examine three distinct models of Difference which are conceived at once as generic types and as individual philosophical projects identified by proper names: Idealism = Nietzsche-Deleuze; Finitude = Heidegger; Differance = Derrida. The functioning of the metaphysical/transcendental distinction and the syntax/reality distinction then concern these concrete philosophical models in specifically determined ways.

First of all, the passage from the metaphysical to the transcendental is realised in a unique way in each of the three models, according to Laruelle's analysis.[40] These are summarised in a schematic way in the following table:

Difference:	Metaphysical	→ Transcendental
Models of Difference:		
Nietzsche:	differential forces	→ becoming-active of forces
Heidegger:	ontological difference	→ One-as-withdrawal, 'destinal' Being
Derrida:	differance	→ the Yes-to-Difference

In Nietzsche, a metaphysics that conceives of Being in terms of differential forces acting on and through present beings (Will to Power) is lifted to the transcendental level of a principle of affirmative selection among the whole circle of Being (Eternal Return), such that, as Deleuze emphasises, only the active and affirmative forces return: 'There is no other power but affirmation, no other quality, no other element: the whole of negation is converted in its substance, transmuted in its quality, *nothing remains of its own power or autonomy.*'[41] In Heidegger, ontological difference, that is, the incommensurable difference of Being and beings (manifest primarily through its having been forgotten or occluded across the history of Western metaphysics), is raised to the status of a tautological 'essence of Being', a withdrawn–withdrawing One that 'gives' ontological difference as such. This marks the terminal 'epoch' of Western metaphysics *but also* the unknowable possibility of philosophy's 'other beginning' – the possibility outlined in the later Heidegger. In Derrida, finally, the irreducible textual slippage of *differance* will be lifted to the status of an impossible and yet necessary object of Nietzschean affirmation. Laruelle conceives this lifting in a complex fashion in terms of a transcendental deduction of differance from Nietzschean Difference on the one hand and a kind of transcendental inscription of Derridean deconstruction onto a Deleuzean 'body-without-writing' on the other. The way the metaphysical/transcendental distinction is understood to appear in each model largely determines Laruelle's overall reading in each case.

Secondly, then, a redoubling and complication of the general problematic occurs similarly with respect to the syntax/reality distinction in so far as this is concretised in the relations among the three models. Laruelle in fact identifies the 'general' problem of the relation and difference of syntax and reality with the 'specific' difference that binds and separates Nietzsche and Heidegger. This Nietzsche/Heidegger difference overdetermines the works of Laruelle's Philosophy I and figures prominently in *Philosophies of Difference*. Laruelle describes a 'war' between two fundamental images of philosophy, represented by the key figures Nietzsche and Heidegger.[42] On the one hand this is conceived as a war between two conflicting models of Difference – the Idealist model of Nietzsche (and Deleuze) as opposed to the model of Finitude proposed by Heidegger. Yet on the other hand this conflict is understood as a war internal to Difference, a war that *is* Difference itself and is in this way internal to each of Nietzsche and Heidegger's philosophies considered independently. This opposition – described at times in terms of Difference and Finitude, at times in terms of syntax and reality – is more than just one element of Laruelle's overall critique of philosophy as Difference; rather, it is the very crux of the matter.

In a sense, the entire argument of *Philosophies of Difference* is intended to show that contemporary philosophy is caught in a dual (or rather, in Laruelle's terms, *duel*) orbit around the philosophies of Nietzsche and Heidegger, a tension the most general expression of which is the disjunction of syntax and reality at the heart of every philosophical decision. Laruelle's reading of Derrida situates Derridean deconstruction within this same problematic. This conflict thus remains a sustained theme throughout the entire text. It serves as both one of the overall argument's basic structuring principles as well as a determinate test-case for ultimately evaluating that argument. In Laruelle's final chapter, it will be 'the resolution we may bring to the conflict dominating contemporary philosophy: the conflict between Nietzsche and Heidegger, between absolute and finite Difference', that will mark the criterion of success or of value for the new form of thought – non-philosophy as the theory of philosophical decision – that Laruelle proposes.[43]

How should we read Laruelle's readings of Nietzsche, Deleuze, Heidegger and Derrida in terms of the metaphysical/transcendental and syntax/reality schemata? First off, it is important to be clear about what these interpretations are *not*. They are not 'critical readings' that would attempt to judge the internal consistency or philosophical acumen of the thinkers at issue. In the 'Instructions for Use', Laruelle paints a marvellously satirical picture of just such philosophical pretentions.[44] In contrast to such 'balanced' judgements which always involve a mixed yes-and-no, a mutually qualified affirmation and negation, Laruelle will insist on presuming at the outset the maximal internal coherence and philosophical completeness of each of the philosophies at issue: 'we will postulate immediately that all these authors are not only systematic but – taken in their totality – coherent up to the point of their sometimes unbridled manner of making Difference play'.[45] The muted qualification here ('up to the point . . . of making Difference play') is not intended as an external criticism or reservation but rather as an affirmation of what these thinkers themselves affirm. Their philosophies are understood as *more* than coherent, in excess of themselves, not incorporating but exploded by the Other – to the extent that this is what on their own terms they wish for. Laruelle's readings are 'generous' in this specific sense. They are not destructive (or deconstructive) readings.

The following chapters will follow Laruelle in presuming that the thinkers at issue basically succeed in their respective aims. Rather than undercutting their positions, the readings of the key figures of Difference are here meant primarily to bring Difference itself to light. The generosity of Laruelle's readings of Nietzsche, Deleuze, Heidegger and Derrida is ultimately in the service of a global critique of Difference: 'We will posit their internal rigor in order better to reject them globally.'[46] The philosophies of Nietzsche, Heidegger, Deleuze and Derrida thus do not represent individual tokens or species of some broader type or genus called Difference. The irreducible conflicts that both separate and conjoin these different philosophies *are* Difference itself. As Laruelle puts it, 'the types of Difference are *reciprocally* heterogenous, but . . . this *reciprocity*, that of their heterogeneity, is their unitary essence of mixture'.[47] The formal notion of (meta-)Difference sketched above provides an initial basis for understanding how the relations between the three types are to be conceived.

The language of 'models' is a natural one to describe the relation that Nietzsche-Deleuzean Idealism, Heideggerean Finitude and Derridean Difference each share with respect to Laruelle's conception of Difference in general.[48] It is important to characterise this relation correctly, because on the one hand it is understood to be immanent to Difference itself and is thus at stake in Laruelle's general critique of Difference, while on the other hand it is meant to preserve what is irreducible and incommensurable to any abstract generality in each of the three modes of philosophy taken individually.[49] In other words, here as elsewhere Laruelle has set himself a seemingly impossible task: the relation between Difference as such on the one hand and Nietzsche-Deleuzean Difference, Heideggerean Difference and Derridean Difference on the other must at once respect the formal structure of the relation of genus to species while simultaneously rejecting its general logic. The possibility of fully resolving this problem must wait for the 'theory of philosophical decision' that consummates Laruelle's overall argument, but a brief discussion of what it means to consider Nietzsche, Heidegger and Derrida not as *kinds* but rather as *models* of Difference will help to guide us toward that end.

The notion of 'model' is drawn here from the domain of mathematical foundations. An important branch of contemporary mathematics, *model theory*, has developed over the past half-century to become one of the key areas of research into the ultimate grounds of mathematics and its fields of application. Model theory is, in a very broad sense, the immanent mathematical ontology of mathematics. It studies the relations between formal axiomatic systems and their 'realisations' in various mathematical domains. More precisely, it establishes the conditions under which systems of objects and relations may be said to 'satisfy' a determined set of axioms. For example, the well-known Zermelo-Fraenkel axioms of set theory stipulate that certain relations, constructions and constraints hold with respect to an undefined binary relation, usually notated with the Greek letter *epsilon* and conventionally read 'belongs to'. These axioms are often naively thought to express *what* sets in fact are, or at least *which* sets may be said to exist. But in fact the axioms of set theory merely posit an abstract structure of complex relations; they do not specify *what* it is they relate. For this reason, formalist-leaning mathematicians have no ready answer to the apparently straightforward question 'What is a set?' Instead, their response can only be 'Well, anything whatsoever, I suppose, so long as it and its fellows enjoy relations that satisfy the axioms of ZF (or whatever other axiom system is in play).' In other words, while perfectly rigorous theorems may be generated deductively from an axiomatic system, precisely *what* those theorems refer to remains underdetermined. Indeed the *what* to which the axioms apply is determined only up to and precisely no farther than the system of deductive consequences generated by the axioms themselves.

Laruelle takes up the language of axioms and theorems as basic elements of his work subsequent to *Philosophies of Difference* precisely because of its rigorous delimitation of the problem of determinability and 'application'. Model theory examines the limits and degrees of freedom of general domains that instantiate given systems of relations.[50] In this way, to designate Nietzsche-Deleuzean, Heideggerean and Derridean philosophies as 'models' of Difference allows for the specification of a certain mode of abstract theoretical inquiry (into 'philosophy' and into 'Difference') without presupposing some pre-given logic of objectivity or ideality.[51] Laruelle adopts the generic axiomatic-model relation as a way to investigate the problem of *instantiation* in general, without presuming a metaphysics of objects and relations in which instantiation would already be explained. In general, Laruelle is wary of any formalisations of his theoretical approach, since the philosophical distinction of form and content compromises the 'unary' mode of non–philosophy. Yet thinking Difference and the philosophies of Difference *on analogy with mathematical formalisation* in terms of axiom-systems and models preserves the relation of philosophy *as* Difference on the one hand and the philosoph*ies* of Nietzsche, Deleuze, Heidegger and Derrida on the other from being conceived (wrongly) in terms of genus and species, type and token, or thesis and example. To think of these philosophies as models is to understand them as autonomous in their own right. The generic structure of Difference may be identified *in* them, but that does not imply that some external principle looms *over* them. Models are neither examples of generalities nor participants in ideal forms. They are autonomous realities that remain theoretically underdetermined except in so far as they satisfy certain structural requirements.

Finally, this brief detour through model theory helps us to understand quite clearly the often misinterpreted term 'non-philosophy' that in the wake of *Philosophies of Difference* will come to define Laruelle's project as a whole. Laruelle frequently makes clear that the 'non-' of non-philosophy expresses nothing negative but is rather a positive generalisation of philosophical modes of thought. To explain this, Laruelle often states that the 'non-' of 'non-philosophy' may be conceived as analogous to the 'non-' of 'non-Euclidean geometry'. Precisely what this means may be shown in terms of axioms and models.

Euclidean geometry is by far the best-known historical example of an axiomatic system. Its basic structure is widely familiar; it is for instance the only axiomatic system taught widely in general education curricula. Less well-known, and much less generally understood, are the non-Euclidean geometries that were first fully formulated in the nineteenth century. What exactly is the relation of non-Euclidean to Euclidean geometries? Euclid's axioms essentially license certain formal inferences (or diagrammatic constructions) when certain conditions are given. These may be intuitively grasped as aspects of ordinary space. For instance, given two non-identical points, there exists (or may be constructed) exactly one line passing through them both. Of course in the physical world, there is nothing corresponding exactly to an extensionless point or to a line with zero thickness. These are conceived formally, not physically. The deductive consequences of Euclid's axioms are thus in principle distinct from any 'matter of fact' about real space. Part of Euclid's genius was to have discovered that a large range of results in geometry may in this fashion be derived (that is, proven) on the basis of a highly restricted set of such axioms.[52]

Of these, one in particular sticks out as more complicated than the others, the so-called 'parallel postulate'.[53] Much work in the centuries after Euclid was spent in vain trying to find a way to derive this axiom from the others, precisely in order to make it unnecessary as an axiom (the fewer axioms, the more elegant the system). It was not until the nineteenth century that mathematicians thought to examine the consequences of simply removing the 'parallel postulate' altogether. There are then *fewer* theorems (which Euclid himself called 'propositions') that can be proven or deduced from the axioms. The axiom-system is 'weakened'. Yet model theory helps us to effect a shift in perspective that sees this decrease in the number of provable theorems as in fact an increase or enlargement of the field of applicability of the system. Without the parallel postulate in force, a large number of new models for the remaining axioms become available. An axiom serves as a *constraint* on the class of models that might satisfy it; it *excludes* precisely those models that do not. When an axiom is subtracted from an axiomatic system, therefore, the class of possible models for that system generally becomes larger. Fewer axioms means fewer restrictions and therefore more models.

The 'non-Euclidean' geometers Lobachevsky and Riemann independently examined the deductive consequences that ensue when Euclid's parallel postulate is replaced by an alternate axiom. From the standpoint of model theory we may understand this roughly as their exploration of an adjacent model-space with respect to Euclid's. In such exploration, Lobachevsky and Riemann do not in any way negate Euclid's results. They simply work within an enlarged space of possible geometrical models within which the class of Euclidean models becomes recognisable as just one proper subspace.

The analogy translates to the case of non-philosophy and philosophy as follows: if philosophy is conceived as the analogue of Euclidean geometry, it is clear that an analogous 'subtraction' of one or more of philosophy's 'axioms' (roughly, its enabling presuppositions) will in no way negate or disqualify philosophy as such. Instead, it will open up a wider range of possible models for the 'reduced' or 'simplified' system. All the philosophical models will be included in this larger class, but so will additional models that the now subtracted axiom(s) would have excluded. In this sense, non-philosophy is understood *to extend* philosophy, that is, it opens a more general domain of which philosophy represents only one restricted sub-domain. By calling the mode of thinking that proceeds in-One or according-to-One *non-philosophy*, Laruelle intends simply to designate that a *less restricted* form of thinking than that of philosophy (one involving fewer presuppositions) is thereby *more general*. In this way, non-philosophy engages a 'space' of thinking that includes (the models of) philosophy while also including other models that philosophy axiomatically excludes.

Charting Laruelle's analysis of three distinct philosophical models of Difference occupies our next several chapters. This analysis consists of three layers throughout: a narrativisation, a structural synthesis and a critical reduction. At a relatively superficial but not insignificant level, the analysis is organised as a historical trajectory of Difference. We treat Nietzsche, Heidegger and Derrida in turn. Nietzsche is read as initiating the philosophies of Difference, and Deleuze – the anachronism in the narrative – is thought alongside this relative 'innocence' of Difference as a return and non-identical repetition. Heidegger is then read primarily in terms of his reading of Nietzsche and the role of his study of Nietzsche in precipitating Heidegger's own distinctive 'Turn'. Finally, Derrida is interpreted on the basis of both Nietzsche and Heidegger, his two most important predecessors. This narrative, historical layer is necessary at an expository level simply to clarify Laruelle's readings, but it is certainly not Laruelle's primary concern. His analysis is not a genealogy. Nonetheless, Laruelle does often presuppose the historical connections linking Nietzsche to Heidegger and both to Derrida. It is important to lay out the basic framework of these connections in order to make sense of the analysis as a whole. In this regard, we will also consider important background relations to Kant and Hegel in these thinkers along the way.

A second layer, more structural, is more in tune with Laruelle's own explicit methodology. This layer – synchronic as opposed to the diachronic ordering of the former – treats the proper names Nietzsche-Deleuze, Heidegger and Derrida as indices of certain variants of Difference. Even more strongly, the *philosophies* themselves of these thinkers become thinkable as concrete instantiations of generic types. At this level, Idealism, Finitude and Differance become manifest as variants of Difference as well as the latter's co-constituents. Here, there is no narrativised continuity, but there is nonetheless the structural unity of a system/(meta-)system. Idealism, Finitude and Differance are not independent species of the genus Difference. The mirrorings and oppositions that distinguish and link one to another are themselves constitutive of Difference. With respect to this more 'systematic' conception, the opposition of Nietzschean Idealism and Heideggerean Finitude will be primary. The twist offered by Derridean Differance will be less an essential element of Difference than a forceful intervention into its problematic that partially exposes its irreducible 'exterior'. In this way, Derrida will represent a kind of 'halfway-step' in the 'direction' of non-philosophy, but only in the sense that the first step away from anywhere is already halfway to everywhere.

These first two layers correspond broadly to the distinction and relation of 'genesis' and 'structure' that is itself one of the key problematics of twentieth-century continental thought.[54] The third layer – which must await its full thematisation until the concluding chapter – represents Laruelle's specific critical overhaul of this entire problematic. This layer neither narrativises Difference nor schematises it in its (an-)architectonic structure. Instead, it registers at every point its unavowed exclusion of the One and thinks immediately *from* this excluded term (without thereby internalising the operation of being-excluded). Even if this layer remains relatively subterranean throughout the next three chapters, it should be recognised as pervasive by way of its essential independence and separation.

NOTES

1. This notation is meant to express the merely partial and always re-interiorised transcendence of the 'meta-' with respect to Difference. It also resonates with Laruelle's own more or less consistent use of parentheses, as in *(non-)One* and *force (of) thought*, where the parenthesised term is in each case relatively suppressed with respect to its philosophical *operation* while its relational *objectivity* remains intact. The term thus becomes a relation-that-does-not-relate for the thinking that makes use of it. This is Laruelle's particular way of writing and thinking *sous rature* (under erasure).

2. Paradigmatically, the Scotist distinctions among formal, rational and real distinctions. Also, Bergson's distinctions between differences in degree

and difference in kind. See the discussion in Gilles Deleuze, *Bergsonism*, pp. 21–9.

3. This term and the logic it describes are taken from Douglas Hofstadter, *I am a Strange Loop*, in which the proof-strategies in Gödel's incompleteness theorems are treated as intriguing analogies for the self-referential structures of consciousness.

4. The highly formal character of Laruelle's non-philosophical approach may be helpfully contrasted with Timothy Williamson's approach to the questions of epistemology and meta-philosophy through modal logic and the logical analysis of counterfactuals. For a relatively accessible introduction to Williamson's methods, see *The Philosophy of Philosophy*, particularly ch. 5, 'Knowledge of Metaphysical Modality'.

5. *PD*, pp. 159–60.

6. For surveys of the role of henology in Western philosophy, see Henry Duméry, *The Problem of God*, ch. 3, and Reiner Schürmann, *Broken Hegemonies*, chs. 5–7.

7. Laruelle will mark this distinction with the parenthetical syntax: science (of) the One.

8. A rigorous formal treatment of this self-inclusive logical structure is given in the analysis of the 're-entry of the form' in G. Spencer Brown, *Laws of Form*, pp. 56–68. This logic serves as the basis for Niklas Luhmann's sociological theory in *Social Systems*.

9. 'A veritable touching of the touch, when my right hand touches my left hand while it is palpating the things, where the "touching subject" passes over to the rank of the touched, descends into the things, such that the touch is formed in the midst of the world and as it were in the things'. Maurice Merleau-Ponty, *The Visible and the Invisible*, pp. 133–4.

10. There are certain congruences between this formal presentation and Peirce's mathematical understanding of the real continuum as prior to and in excess of all distinct individuals. See Charles S. Peirce, *Reasoning and the Logic of Things*, pp. 158–64. However, whereas Peirce essentially defines individuation as ruptured continuity (via 'secondness'), Difference prioritises discontinuity or difference *from the outset*. Difference is, in this sense, the Peircean continuum conceptually 'everted' (turned inside-out).

11. For a more rigorous formal treatment of the paradoxes involved in such self-modelling logical structures, see Graham Priest, *Beyond the Limits of Thought*, chs. 8–11, especially the 'inclosure schema' discussed on pp. 134–6 and 156–7.

12. In Laruelle's analysis of Derrida, for instance, this notion takes the name of the 'en-terminable', that is, 'the syntax of the *unlimited term*', *PD*, p. 137.

13. The logic here is akin to that of Schelling's notion of potencies that Deleuze develops through his esoteric reading of the calculus. See Gilles Deleuze, *Difference and Repetition*, pp. 176–82, 190–1.

14. *PD*, p. 15.

15. *PD*, p. 15.

16. *PD*, p. 17.

17. *PD*, p. 15.
18. *PD*, p. 15.
19. *PD*, p. 15.
20. A very clear discussion of precisely how this distinction underwrites Kant's position of *transcendental idealism* in the First Critique is given in Sebastian Gardner, *Kant and the* Critique of Pure Reason, ch. 5.
21. In this respect Lee Braver's framework in *A Thing of This World* for examining the 'anti-realist' strain of continental philosophy since Kant marks an important attempt to bring analytic and continental traditions into productive connection.
22. Among the recent work investigating connections between Kant and Deleuze, see Christian Kerslake, *Immanence and the Vertigo of Philosophy*, Beth Lord, *Kant and Spinozism*, especially ch. 6, Alberto Toscano, *The Theatre of Production*, and Edward Willat, *Kant, Deleuze, and Architectonics*. For an insightful and highly relevant discussion of the relation of Kant and Husserl, see the analysis by Laruelle's mentor Paul Ricoeur in *Husserl: An Analysis of His Phenomenology*, ch. 7.
23. *PD*, p. 27.
24. *PD*, p. 28.
25. *PD*, p. 28.
26. *PD*, p. 28.
27. Laruelle's understanding of the *a priori* and its distinction from the transcendental is quite close to the phenomenological theory worked out in detail in Mikel Dufrenne, *The Notion of the* A Priori, especially Dufrenne's distinction between formal and material *a priori*, chs. 2–3.
28. *PD*, p. 29.
29. *PD*, p. 29.
30. *PD*, p. 30.
31. *PD*, p. 30.
32. In general, the operative-objective logic of the 'boot-strapping' effect at work in Difference has been examined and formalised rigorously in a linguistic/pragmatic (and not metaphysical/ontological) register in Robert Brandom, *Between Saying and Doing*, chs. 1–2.
33. This metaphor of the 'half-turn' in the sense of 'half of an inversion' becomes relatively formalised in Laruelle's work *Non-Standard Philosophy* from the period Philosophy V as the 'quarter-turn' represented by the imaginary value *i*, the square root of -1, as interpreted in the complex number plane. See *Non-Standard Philosophy*, pp. 141–3, 263–8.
34. See, for an example of this, Gianni Vattimo's reading of Heideggerean *Verwindung* (partial overcoming) in *The End of Modernity*, pp. 164–80.
35. *PD*, p. 5.
36. *PD*, p. 5.
37. *PD*, p. 2.
38. *PD*, p. 5.
39. *PD*, p. 6.

40. *PD*, p. 31.
41. Gilles Deleuze, *Nietzsche and Philosophy*, 176.
42. See, in particular, *PD*, pp. 43–4 and 208.
43. *PD*, p. 208.
44. *PD*, p. xv.
45. *PD*, p. xv.
46. *PD*, p. xv.
47. *PD*, p. 15.
48. While Laruelle does not describe Idealist Difference, Finitude and Differance with consistent terminology (he generally uses the term 'types' but also suggests that 'even this word is now perhaps too much' at *PD*, p. 11), his own use of the term 'model' (for instance at *PD*, pp. 13, 15, 16, 25, 141 and 210) would seem to recommend its employment in conceiving the Nietzsche-Deleuzean, Heideggerean and Derridean instances of Difference, especially in light of later more consistent usage of the language of 'axiomatics'.
49. See *PD*, p. 17.
50. Badiou, for instance, has utilised Paul Cohen's work, which provides techniques for 'forcing' diverse models of the ZF axioms, as a basis for formalising his philosophical conception of the 'truth-event'. See *Being and Event*, pp. 410–30. See also Alain Badiou, *The Concept of Model* for a broad introduction to model theory and its philosophical import.
51. The particular way Laruelle understands axiomatics is clarified more fully in the context of the discussion of 'dualysis' in *Principles of Non-philosophy*, ch. 5.
52. In fact, Euclid himself formulated these in a slightly different way, distinguishing among definitions, postulates and common notions, of which his five postulates correspond most closely to formal axioms in the sense of contemporary mathematics. These differences are essentially irrelevant for the point at issue here. An analysis and critique of Laruelle's appropriation of axiomatic method is found in Michael J. Olson, 'Transcendental Arguments, Axiomatic Truth, and the Difficulty of Overcoming Idealism' in John Mullarkey and Anthony Paul Smith, eds, *Laruelle and Non-philosophy*, pp. 169–90.
53. Euclid, *Elements*, postulate 5: 'That, if a straight line falling on two straight lines make the interior angles on the same side less than two right angles, the two straight lines, if produced indefinitely, meet on that side on which are the angles less than the two right angles.'
54. See, canonically, Jean Hyppolite, *Genesis and Structure of Hegel's Phenomenology of Spirit*.

3

The Nietzsche–Deleuzean model of Difference: Idealism

And do you know what 'the world' is to me? Shall I show it to you in my mirror? . . . *This world is the will to power – and nothing besides!* And you your-selves are also this will to power – and nothing besides!

Nietzsche, in a fragment from *The Will to Power*

DIFFERENCE AS IDEALISM: THE REVERSIBILITY OF CONTRARIES

In the history of modern philosophy, after the systems of Kant and Hegel – systems respectively of the immanent critique and the apotheosis of Reason – the non-rationalist image of philosophy as anti-system or immanently creative Difference is born with Nietzsche. As the first of the three models of Difference analysed by Laruelle, Nietzschean Difference may be considered in an important sense as the base or standard model for the analysis overall.[1] Nietzschean Difference represents, from this point of view, the more general philosophical platform upon which the other, more specialised models of Difference will be constructed. Historically, it is with Nietzsche that Western philosophy, at least since Plato, most decisively confronts a conception of the Real that does not oppose truth to art or mere appearance. This overturning or evacuation of the concept of truth rebounds in turn upon the essence and practice of philosophy. It makes of the utterances of philosophers themselves an immanent play of forces and perspectives, an un-refereed contest of real drives to be interpreted symptomatically and deployed strategically for creative ends. The inner coherence of Nietzsche's perspectivism, his critical method of genealogy, his aphoristic style and above all his coordination of the key metaphysical concepts of Will to Power and Eternal Return of the Same together realise, after Kant and Hegel, a new kind of disruptive, anti-architectonic modality for philosophy, one that is intrinsically differential, creative and open. Such a philosophical modality is what Laruelle calls, in its broadest sense, Difference. Nietzsche writes self-consciously only for the 'philosophers of the future', thereby marking a certain closure of the epoch of Western philosophy since Plato that is not, however, a recapitulation or synthesis of what has come before.[2] In this respect, Nietzschean Difference inaugurates a philosophical break with Hegel and Hegelianism that would no longer represent a mere regression or failure to grasp the comprehensiveness of Hegel's project. In Nietzsche, Difference first emerges as a philosophical rival and epochal alternative to Hegelian Dialectic.

In one sense, then, in the context of Laruelle's analysis the Nietzschean model of Difference *just is* Difference. It is with regard to this Nietzschean 'standard model' that the modifications introduced into Difference by Heideggerean Finitude and, in turn, Derridean Differance will become comprehensible as variants on the Nietzschean theme. The Heideggerean and Derridean variants themselves then come to provide alternatives to the original Nietzschean model within contemporary post-Husserlian philosophy, and Deleuze on Laruelle's reading may be understood as reasserting the model of Nietzschean Difference in that later philosophical context. In *this* sense, then, as contrasted with the later Heideggerean and Derridean models, Nietzsche-Deleuzean Difference will appear as one fraternal and rival form of Difference among others. The Nietzsche-Deleuzean model is in this way both One and Different within the axiomatic of Difference.

It may seem surprising, initially, that it is in chapter four of *Philosophies of Difference*, which is concerned with the relation between Hegel and Heidegger, that we find the most extended discussion of Nietzsche in the book as a whole. Because of its importance, we will break up this long paragraph into two sections and elaborate it accordingly. Laruelle writes:

What is a *differential* 'relation of forces' for Nietzsche? It is the *a priori* structure of experience, the *a priori* or ideal constituent of the Will to Power that would be from its side its transcendental essence, its supreme principle of unification. Now such a relation is truly a 'difference', but this difference is integrally relative and ideal as a relation, each of the differends exhausts itself in its relativity to the other. Real beings are only a moment of the ideal field of presence, a field of presence that is never really present. It is not the Will to Power itself that would be able to escape this idealization and this reversibility without remainder of opposites. As the essence or possibility of relations of force, it is the transcendental and therefore real = indivisible factor, which communicates its reality to the otherwise divisible relations. But this is a 'mere-bit-of-reality' that it communicates to them: the One of the Will to Power is immediately closed upon the Idea and effectuated in the relations.[3]

Much of what is going on in this excerpt involves Laruelle's specification of the passage from the metaphysical to the transcendental as manifest
in Nietzsche's thought in particular among the philosophies of Difference.
This key issue is addressed more fully below. What is most important
first of all is to understand Laruelle's central claim about Nietzschean
Difference, namely that it is a kind of *idealism*. Laruelle reads Nietzsche as
reducing the reality of individual beings to that of an ideal, differentially
articulated 'field of presence'. In other words, 'idealism' is understood
here broadly as the prioritisation of relations over against the terms they
relate. The concepts of identity and self-subsistence that are concomitant
to the notion of the object or thing are evacuated in favour of relational
predicates that thereby take on the character of events or processes rather
than properties.

What Laruelle calls the reversibility of contraries in Nietzsche is not
the more or less trivial insight that the sense of terms can only be defined
through their opposites, as 'heavy' implies 'light' or 'true' implies 'false'.
Rather, Laruelle wishes to bring into view how Nietzsche's metaphysics
of Will to Power entails that existence itself occurs as decisive, relational
force. The relations in play are actual, not 'ideal' in the representational
sense. The reversibility of contraries is thus an *ontological* and not a *logical*
thesis. Rather than maintaining as a consequence of Nietzsche's thought
that since 'affirmation' implies 'negation', therefore 'it's all the same in the
end' (nihilism), the notion of reversibility at stake here throws any such
purportedly universal and objective judgement into relief as *only* a local
expression of Will to Power (reactive in this case) and 'nothing besides'.
Reversibility is not balance and harmony but precisely the opposites of
these, their *unsurpassable* opposites.

This Nietzschean tendency becomes fully explicit perhaps in Deleuze's
theory of the sense-event as developed in *The Logic of Sense*.[4] There, for
instance, the property of 'redness' is reinterpreted by Deleuze not as a
static predicate but as an active 'becoming-red'. The empirical difference
between 'X eats Y' and 'Y eats X' is relatively suppressed in favour of a
purely differential event of 'eating/being-eaten'. In general, the verbal
infinitive form ('to run'; 'to eat'; 'to be cut') takes precedence over the
nominative ('Joe'; 'the neighbour's cat'; 'an orange') since the former
series is precisely what coordinates a real communication of events prior
to their representation in the individuated, set-like matrix composed by
the latter. Deleuze effectively makes the logic of Leibnizian compossibility
(the combinatorial connections between events) and the metaphysics of
Nietzschean Difference (the affirmation of Becoming over Being) intersect
in this regard.[5] From there we may recognise the import of Deleuze's singular inflection of Stoic ethics ('not to be unworthy of what happens to us')

as a form of Nietzschean affirmation and *Amor Fati*.[6] For Deleuze, we must affirm and appropriate the events that befall us – not their representable contents, but their very form *as* active events-of-becoming. The Deleuzean critiques of objective identity and substantial unity with their corresponding rejection of the paradigms of Self, World and God appear then as the philosophical valorisation of chance and non-identical repetition.[7] Being is interpreted as pure Event.

For Laruelle, all of this is held in common by Deleuze and Nietzsche and is idealist in spirit in so far as it rejects the ultimate reality of anything *other than* this Event and its immanent production of differences. Laruelle continues:

> There is an immediation of the Idea and the One, of ideal and real immanence. It must be called precisely 'difference' (cf. the reinterpretation of Nietzsche by Deleuze, and Deleuze's entire oeuvre), but it remains at once *either* strictly unthinkable and merely postulated *and/or* immediately thinkable as simple Idea or purely ideal and divisible structure. This difference is simply itself infinitely, unlimitedly at stake; it is *integrally reversible*. The final triumph of the Will to Power over reactive forces and gregariousness is programmed straightaway as possible without remainder; gregarious inauthenticity and evil are only the appearances and phenomena of a supposed mimesis having no reality other than that of their objectivization-without-being, reality-without-the-real.[8]

In Laruelle's view, the passage from the metaphysical to the transcendental in the Nietzsche-Deleuzean model is effected as a simple and immediate identification of ideality and reality. These are conceived as immanent to one another, or rather their unity – the Nietzsche-Deleuzean One – *is* immanence itself: Being = Immanence. This immediacy, however, still becomes manifest philosophically as a *passage* or *becoming*: Being = Immanence = Creative Becoming. Nietzschean philosophy thus involves the movement from an interpretation of Being in terms of the differential relations of force between beings to an emergent yet fully immanent principle of selection as active force and affirmation. These phases participate in one and the same event of becoming, but this event is internally doubled and intensified through itself in creative affirmation. This twofold continuous becoming is precisely how Nietzschean thought is able to surpass the logical deadlock of relativism and nihilism. In the terms of Nietzsche's own concepts as crossed with Laruelle's schematisation of Difference, this movement may be conceived as the passage from the metaphysics of the Will to Power to the transcendental structure of the Eternal Return of the Same.[9]

Such are the basic points of orientation. Besides this relatively extended passage, much of Laruelle's analysis of Nietzsche remains implicit in *Philosophies of Difference*. The Nietzsche-Deleuzean model is frequently alluded to without being thematised in its own right. This is in part because Laruelle effectively builds upon a foundation laid out in several of his earlier books that expressly foreground Nietzsche's thought. Without referring to his own earlier work explicitly, Laruelle nonetheless draws upon the detailed analyses and applications of Nietzsche throughout the books from the period he now calls Philosophy I. It would take us too far afield to try to examine all of these works in detail. Yet by drawing on a few selections from these sources on the one hand, and anticipating Heidegger's critique of Nietzsche on the other, we may bring to light the two main problematics that Laruelle identifies as crucial in Nietzsche. Together, these provide a clear indication of the stakes of Nietzsche-Deleuzean Difference for Laruelle.

First, there is the complex interplay of the concepts of Will to Power and Eternal Return as indicated above. These constitute Nietzsche's 'metaphysics' in a broad sense as the expression of immanent Difference. This notion of a Nietzschean system constituted by the interplay of Will to Power and Eternal Return of the Same is at the centre of Laruelle's earlier analyses in *Nietzsche contra Heidegger* and *Beyond the Power Principle*. Second, there is the specific effect this metaphysics has when it becomes the principle for understanding the history of Western philosophy. This will be at the root of Nietzsche's genealogical method, his aphoristic style, and in general the methodological and stylistic concerns that in Nietzsche become essential to how the philosophy of the future is to think. Style and method in Nietzsche become the essential means of his immanent critique and creative overcoming of philosophical tradition. Thus closely related to this apotheosis of style will be Nietzsche's diagnosis of and prognosis for European nihilism.

Both of these issues as read by Laruelle draw upon Deleuze's reading of Nietzsche in his *Nietzsche and Philosophy* and also Pierre Klossowski's *Nietzsche and the Vicious Circle*, two of the most important works from the French Nietzsche renaissance of the 1960s and '70s. We examine this constellation of concerns and background sources in the next two sections in an overlapping fashion before then looking at how Nietzsche may be understood on Laruelle's terms partially to anticipate and respond in advance to the Heideggerean critique of Finitude that will be so crucial to the overall analysis of Difference in *Philosophies of Difference*. Finally in the last section, we address the question of Laruelle's identification of Nietzsche and Deleuze as avatars of a common model of Idealist Difference.

METAPHYSICAL WILL TO POWER AND THE
TRANSCENDENTAL ETERNAL RETURN

How is Nietzschean Will to Power conceived within Laruelle's general framework of Difference? The very designation of Will in Nietzsche, especially as taken over from Schopenhauer and then affirmatively transformed, becomes split for Laruelle between the metaphysical and transcendental levels of Difference. On the one hand, Nietzsche takes the manifest phenomena of worldly and material struggle, especially the Darwinian struggles for reproductive life, as important empirical signs of how real forces interact and are defined through their mutual interactions. But this struggle of living beings is itself ultimately no more than a sign, one just as likely to mislead or inhibit as to empower thinking.[10] What is really at stake for Nietzsche is precisely how such differential phenomena may come to serve as signs in this way at all and thus to become material for creative appropriation. What can be made (*Macht*) of such struggles and signs?

The concept of Will to Power is that of a generalised semiotics that moves the struggle among forms of life to the status of a structural *a priori*. This then elicits in turn the essential philosophical expression of Will to Power as a perspectivalism. From the unstable and vertiginous (meta-)perspective of perspectivalism, signs are understood as not just one kind of being among others but as the very Being of beings. There is not merely a semiotic exteriority within the play of material forces, the forces themselves are from this perspective precisely interpretive *forces* and not objects. Objects are moved by forces, but forces themselves involve an essential, non-objective determination as *self*-determining. This serves to indicate the intrinsic affirmative element that will then come to define active as distinct from reactive forces.

Consider an analogy with Newtonian mechanical forces. A force for Newton is conceived as the product of a mass and an acceleration: $F = ma$. Acceleration itself involves a second order relation; it is measured in units of distance *per unit time per unit time*. In other words, it is the measure of *a constant rate of change*. It is physical movement (*kinēsis*) redoubled through itself, motion or change as self-determining as though incarnating a Will. Of course, this can be no more than an analogy – Nietzsche most certainly does not reduce the interplay of living forces to Newtonian mechanics, and Newton is no vitalist. But, like Leibniz and Hegel before him, Nietzsche's thought is deeply influenced by the Newtonian notion of force and especially its crucial critique of Cartesian mechanism. What matters in the analogy for us is the formal character of force as a *self-relating difference*.

The most essential difference for Nietzsche is that between active and reactive forces. Now, it is clear from the above that reactive forces –

precisely *as* forces – must themselves involve some minimal affirmative component. There can be no *purely* reactive force. The minimal self-determining activity necessary to be an expression of the Will to Power at all is sufficient to eliminate any possibility of an absolute reactivity or absolute withdrawal from relation. It is on this basis that Laruelle will link his characterisation of the essential reversibility of Nietzsche's thought to the Nietzschean rejection of real finitude, which we will examine later. The identity-of-contraries is for Nietzsche obviously not an immediate identity: health is not sickness. But what then is the difference between active and reactive forces?

For Nietzsche active forces involve a positive self-overcoming. Beings possessed by active forces become other than themselves by *identifying with* these forces. It is here that Will to Power is concretely determined as a *continuous passage* from a representational, 'objective' notion of forces to a dynamic, metaphysical *a priori* of active force as such. For Nietzsche, Being as Will to Power does not transcend beings or forces. Being is fully immanent to beings. Yet beings themselves transcend their actual, objective particularities and limits *as* Will to Power. Beings overcome themselves via the active forces that are realised in and through them. The Nietzschean meta-physical in Laruelle's sense is thus the Will to Power of beings themselves, their very activity as Difference.

There is still, however, what Laruelle designates as the specific passage from the metaphysical to the transcendental in Nietzsche. Will to Power becomes a transcendental determination, that is, a genuine form of Difference, only when the immanent contest of forces circulates in and as non-identical repetition. This is the moment at which immanence itself is infinitely potentialised or made sovereign as Difference: the Eternal Return of the Same. The Eternal Return itself takes the form of a sovereign decision, and yet it dissolves any self or substance that would attain to the position of sovereignty. It functions as a transcendental temptation for the Will as such with respect to the sphere of finite, objectivised beings governed immanently by Will to Power. Nietzsche asks each one of us directly:

> How, if some day or night a demon were to sneak after you into your loneliest loneliness and say to you, 'this life as you now live it and have lived it, you will have to live once more and innumerable times more; and there will be nothing new in it, but every pain and every joy and every thought and sigh and everything immeasurably small or great in your life must return to you – all in the same succession and sequence. . .'. Would you not throw yourself down and gnash your teeth and curse the demon who spoke thus? Or did you once experience a tremendous moment when you would have answered him, 'You are a god, and never have I heard anything more godly.' If this thought were to gain possession of you, it would change you, as you are, or perhaps crush you.[11]

This terror of and desire for Eternal Return may be identified as the 'suspension' of all absoluteness, in particular any absoluteness of individual beings as distinct from the relations or 'distances' they may instantiate. It represents the 'moment' when, according to Laruelle, at the 'interior' of Nietzsche's philosophical syntax we note 'the insertion of the real: the diversity of this "distance" (forces, perspectives, etc.)' *and*, Laruelle then continues in italics, '*This diversity is straightaway ideal or ob-jective, a diversity of objectivity; this is supposed as autonomous relative to a being or a thing in itself that is suspended in a preliminary manner.*'[12] In other words, at the level of transcendental Will to Power it becomes possible to say 'Difference' as what eternally and non-identically returns rather than merely 'differences' as determined with regard to particular beings. The seemingly autonomous identities of the latter are, as it were, overwritten by the pure self-differentiation of the former.

How then does the Eternal Return of the Same stand with respect to Will to Power in terms of Laruelle's metaphysical/transcendental schema? On the one hand, the Eternal Return of the Same is nothing other than the transcendental determination of Will to Power as Difference. In Laruelle's view, Nietzsche takes the metaphysical empirical/*a priori* difference (beings/Will to Power) up into the transcendental without empirical or ontic remainder. Any Kantian thing-in-itself is thus 'suspended in a pre-liminary manner'. However, it is not that Nietzsche is thereby understood simply to identify the two levels of the metaphysical and the transcendental; Laruelle clearly maintains that the distinction and relation between the two levels is constitutive of Difference as such, and thus certainly of Nietzschean Difference. Rather, for Nietzsche as read by Laruelle the *content* of the two levels is one and the same – thus, an identical Difference with two distinct philosophical functions, at once metaphysical and transcendental. For Laruelle, Nietzsche conceives the transcendental real of Eternal Return as 'the diversity of objectivity or the *a priori* itself, and not an ontic-real diversity independent of the ideality of the *a priori*'.[13] In other words, not only each and every particular and individuated being but *the entire 'sphere' of all such beings taken together* is relatively 'dissolved' into the Eternal Return. Yet, in all rigour, the Nietzschean formulation of the passage from the metaphysical to the transcendental must still remain grounded in the play of relatively 'empirical' and imme-diate forces. 'Difference' cannot be too easily severed from 'differences' without losing its immanent determination and thus instituting a new transcendence.

In this way, as Deleuze notes, the Eternal Return must be thought relative to the question of European nihilism in Nietzsche, which is not some secondary, merely 'historical' determination of his thought. Deleuze asks, 'What happens when the will to nothingness is related to the eternal return?' And answers, 'This is the only place where it breaks its alliance with reactive forces.'[14] This would be because the selective function of Eternal Return is deployed as an 'active' negation or destruction: 'Active negation or active destruction is the state of strong spirits which destroy the reactive in themselves, submitting it to the test of the eternal return and submitting themselves to this test even if it entails willing their own decline.'[15] Here the Eternal Return becomes practically or operationally determined. The moment of active negation thus identifies the specific Nietzschean passage from the metaphysical to the transcendental (in Laruelle's terms) as a decisive practice and marks one key point where Laruelle's reading of Nietzsche aligns directly with Deleuze's.[16] Both Laruelle and Deleuze read the Eternal Return of the Same as the sovereign yet non-arbitrary decision *for* the annihilation of all reactivity, subjection and stasis within the sphere of particular beings. This 'state of strong spirits' impels their very self-transformation into positive and infinite Difference, their casting-off of all reactive finitude. As Deleuze puts it, Eternal Return as 'active negation' is the 'only way in which reactive forces *become active*'.[17]

Of course, for Nietzsche, this practice or event is not only an individual matter but one which extends across the civilisational history of the West. The 'epochal' stakes of Nietzschean 'reversibility' and 'destruction' are given, for instance, in the well-known short section of Nietzsche's *Twilight of the Idols* entitled 'How the "True World" Finally Became a Fable: the History of an Error'. In this famous passage Nietzsche outlines a six-part history of Western metaphysics that culminates in his own rejection of the canonical difference structuring philosophy at least since Plato, the difference between truth and appearance. In form it is simply a list, a series of interpretations of 'the true world' as indexed to a series of philosophical models (given here in brackets):[18]

> 1. The true world – attainable for the sage, the pious, the virtuous man; he lives in it, *he is it*. [Platonism]
> 2. The true world – unattainable for now, but promised for the sage, the pious, the virtuous man ('for the sinner who repents'). [Christianity]
> 3. The true world – unattainable, indemonstrable, unpromisable; but the very thought of it – a consolation, an obligation, an imperative. [Kantianism]
> 4. The true world – unattainable? At any rate, unattained. And being unattained, also *unknown*. Consequently, not consoling, redeeming, or obligating: how could something unknown obligate us? [incipient positivism]
> 5. The 'true' world – an idea which is no longer good for anything, not even obligating – an idea which has become useless and superfluous – *consequently*, a refuted idea: let us abolish it! [Nietzsche I]
> 6. The true world – we have abolished. What world has remained? The appar-

ent one perhaps? But no! *With the true world we have also abolished the apparent one.* [Nietzsche II]

There is a sequence of 'worldviews' represented here, even a dialectical sequence, but what matters for Nietzsche is not the historical narrative which that sequence implies but the pulsional forces it immediately incarnates and for which it decides. Truth (or 'truth' – Nietzsche can distinguish use and mention only in terms of relative intensity) functions here as mere material; it is both an effect and an instrument. Truth is stone, chisel and sculpture. For Nietzsche the epochal interpretations of Being indicated in the historical sequence are events, not representations, of Being. These are not world-pictures but world-deployments. And now something new is being willed in Nietzsche's own thought as written by Nietzsche's own hand: the abolishing of not only the 'true world' but equally of its *opposite* – 'the apparent one'.

What does this double abolition signify? What are its conditions of possibility? We are witness here to a particularly Nietzschean crux, one of many. The difference between stages five and six in Nietzsche's 'History' corresponds to a shift or 'turn' in Nietzsche's own thinking that comes to define that very thinking, a certain decisional break between a Nietzsche I and a Nietzsche II that itself makes Nietzsche Nietzsche.[19] In the text just after stage six, we find Nietzsche's own reflective commentary on this event: 'Noon; moment of the briefest shadow; end of the longest error; high point of humanity; INCIPIT ZARATHUSTRA.' This would be a moment in Nietzsche's own text where what Laruelle calls the passage from the metaphysical to the transcendental level of Difference is directly manifest. It is not accidental that for Nietzsche it is the history of Western metaphysics that is here at stake. All of Nietzsche's most forceful thought occurs as a sustained (although perhaps not always coherent) *decision on and for the tradition of Western metaphysics*. Thought always thinks the Real, or tries to. But here Nietzsche inaugurates something different – an immanent 'active destruction' (in Deleuze's sense) of the very idea of the Real as defined through the true world/apparent world difference that has determined the Western tradition at least since Plato.

Nietzsche replaces the true/apparent difference in philosophy with Difference as immanent Will to Power under the transcendental selective pressure of Eternal Return. There is a rigorous *logic* at work here that undergirds the method of Nietzschean genealogy as a structurally coherent enterprise. In fact, the reactive forces dominating Western civilisation, according to Nietzsche, should be understood on analogy (but of course a *forceful* analogy) with certain conceptual and syntactical errors whose 'correction' would mark local intensifications of Will to Power. In a separate text, for instance, Nietzsche himself diagnoses the general logical fallacy –

based in uncritical rationalism – that would infer metaphysical reality from the purely syntactical need of human thought to proceed via conceptual dichotomies:

> This world is apparent: consequently there is a true world; – this world is conditional: consequently there is an unconditioned world; – this world is full of contradiction: consequently there is a world free of contradiction; – this world is a world of becoming: consequently there is a world of being: – all false conclusions (blind trust in reason: if *A* exists, then the opposite concept *B* must also exist).[20]

Importantly, Nietzsche explains this logical mistake genealogically in terms of *reactive desire*, that is, *reactive will*.

> It is suffering that inspires these conclusions: fundamentally they are *desires* that such a world should exist; in the same way, to imagine another, more valuable world is an expression of hatred for a world that makes one suffer: the *ressentiment* of metaphysicians against actuality is here creative.[21]

In this way, we witness according to Nietzsche 'experiences derived from nature or society universalized and projected to the sphere of "in-itself"', that is, 'reason is thus a source of revelation concerning [purported] being-in-itself'.[22] In opposition to this false idealism, Nietzsche proposes instead an analysis according to 'the real genesis of the concepts' which in fact 'derives from the practical sphere, the sphere of utility', in other words, the necessary material struggles of life.[23] But now the problem repeats itself: is life something *other than* such creative valuation in response to suffering? And where would philosophy and its combination of logic and rhetoric fit into this schema? Does Nietzsche simply have recourse to another 'true-world' metaphysics, albeit in opposition to Plato one that would valorise matter and the immanent forces of life as against all philosophical ide-alisations? Via what philosophical syntax are the reactive forces that have dominated the West through metaphysical *ressentiment* to be *made active*? If nothing is true (or apparent, for that matter), what then is Real? In short, if the passage from the metaphysical to the transcendental is instantiated for Laruelle as the decisive relation of Will to Power to Eternal Return of the Same in Nietzschean Difference, what becomes of the coordinated problems of syntax and of reality for the same model?

THE REDUCTION OF DIFFERENCE TO ITS SYNTAX: NIETZSCHE AND HEGEL

There is a dilemma between materialism and idealism internal to Nietzsche's thought. In the end, do the finitist, anti-idealist and biological-materialist elements win out over the idealist and infinitist character of his metaphysics, or the reverse? Because of its rootedness in the material and biological sphere of empirical life, Nietzsche's thought always risks (or perhaps necessarily manifests) a *vulgar materialist* tendency that would effectively reduce thought to a matter of physics and chemistry. In many passages, Nietzsche presents a non-mechanistic but still essentially physical vision of Eternal Return. For instance, in the epigraph to the present chapter taken from Nietzsche's notes for his great, unrealised work *The Will to Power*, Nietzsche poses the question 'do you know what "the world" is to me?' In the ellipsis marked in the epigraph, Nietzsche's text provides an exquisitely Nietzschean image of the cosmos, worth citing nearly in full:

> This world: a monster of energy, without beginning, without end, a firm, iron magnitude of force that does not grow bigger or smaller, that does not expend itself but only transforms itself; as a whole, of unalterable size, a household without expenses or losses, but likewise without increase or income; enclosed by 'nothingness' as by a boundary; not something blurry or wasted, not something endlessly extended, but set in a definite space as a definite force, and not a space that might be 'empty' here or there, but rather as force throughout, as a play of forces and waves of forces, at the same time one and many, increasing here and at the same time decreasing there; a sea of forces flowing and rushing together, eternally changing, eternally flooding back, with tremendous years of recurrence, with an ebb and a flood of its forms; out of the simplest forms striving toward the most complex . . . and then again returning home to the simple out of this abundance . . ., blessing itself as that which must return eternally, as a becoming that knows no satiety, no disgust, no weariness.[24]

This statement should by no means be taken as a definitive account. How could there be such an account for an immanent philosophy of unlimited Becoming? Rather, the forces measured in the image should be understood to set determinate coordinates for posing the Nietzschean problem of the Eternal Return with respect to *any possible* representation of the cosmic embodiment of Will to Power. While Nietzsche is usually careful to distinguish his own notion of Eternal Return from the ancient conception of an endless cycle of repeated events, he never fully clarifies how his own version would differ from this relatively 'closed' model, more Stoic than Epicurean in its emphasis on a finitely extended cosmos, although not at all Stoic in its rejection of a unified rationality guiding this finite Whole. Whatever the complexities, there is undoubtedly a cosmic and 'materialist' problematic woven into the very fabric of Nietzsche's thinking.

Yet this materialism is equally a vitalism. Even an idealism? The counter-tendency in Nietzsche, the impulse that inherently excludes any vulgar and simply reductive materialism, is precisely the self-transcending, creative and semiotic element of Life as Will to Power. This living, creative moment is what determines Will to Power *as active and creative will*, rather than merely physical force. How are these two poles ultimately to be thought together in Nietzsche?

As Laruelle reads him, Nietzsche effectively reduces Difference to its philosophical syntax, even if this syntax itself is anti-representational and thus apparently manifests a 'realist' incarnation of forces. Thus, the idealist pole in Nietzsche is understood to incorporate and disguise itself as a materialist and immanent realism. This is its own immediately metaphysical aspect, the simple 'content' of Nietzsche's view of Will to Power and Eternal Return to the extent that this 'content' equally entails a specific 'form' of expression in Nietzsche's own writing and, more generally, an engagement with the problem of philosophical expression or utterance as such. Thus, in terms of the discussion in our previous chapter of the difference between the syntax and the reality of Difference, the Nietzsche-Deleuzean model is understood by Laruelle to reject in advance any recourse to real Finitude in the introduction of the syntax/reality distinction (which will characterise in particular the Heideggerean model of Finite Difference). It is from this perspective that Laruelle will – surprisingly – identify Hegel and Nietzsche as equally philosophers of 'idealism' despite Nietzsche's break with Hegelian Dialectic and his inauguration of Difference as such. In short, 'Every idealist usage of Difference, from Hegel to Nietzsche, conceives the *division* or *distinction* internal to Difference as having no more "reality" than that of a relation . . .'.[25]

In this respect, Pierre Klossowski's *Nietzsche and the Vicious Circle* is an important background source for Laruelle's reading of Nietzsche. In general, Klossowski works within a framework common to much French philosophy of the 1960s and '70s that would oppose Nietzsche to Hegel as the philosopher of untamed, sovereign, untotalisable and unrecuperable Difference to the thinker of the dialectical, rational and productive 'labour of the Concept'. Like Bataille, Deleuze and – at least in certain key respects – Derrida, Klossowski views Nietzschean thought as a critical instrument *against* the generalised form of thought of which Hegel is the supreme representative, namely the victory and closure of modernity and its culmination in the rationally ordered State. For all these thinkers, Kojève's influential reading of Hegel through the lens of the Master-Slave dialectic and its focus on a historical and socio-political determination of human essence serves as the key touchstone.[26] In contrast to this philosophical 'humanism', Nietzsche is understood to represent a break with all merely human and historical determinations of thought.

In Klossowski, this touches in particular on questions of reciprocity and communication in Nietzsche. Whereas Hegel presumes reciprocity and recognition as the very essence of thought, Nietzsche's thought *begins* from the experience of an irreducibly incommunicable and non-relational exteriority. Importantly, Klossowski presents this contrast itself from the Nietzschean standpoint:

> In his analysis of the unhappy consciousness, Hegel distorts the 'initial Desire' (the will to power): the *autonomous consciousness* (of the Master) despairs of ever having its autonomy recognized by another autonomous being, since it is necessarily constituted by a *dependent consciousness* – that of the Slave . . . In Nietzsche, there is no such need for *reciprocity* (this is his 'ignorance' of this passage of the Dialectic). On the contrary, given his own *idiosyncrasy – the sovereignty of an incommunicable emotion* – the very idea of a '*consciousness for itself mediated by another consciousness*' remains foreign to Nietzsche.[27]

In other words, the recognition by the Other as an immanent condition of the Hegelian Will to Mastery is rejected by Nietzsche in favour of a thoroughly non-relational, sovereign self-overcoming and self-creation. Note, however, that in this passage, which is intended to contrast Nietzsche and Hegel, Klossowski characterises Hegel's view already in Nietzschean terms: the 'initial Desire' of the Master which drives the Master-Slave dialectic is glossed in advance as an expression of Nietzschean 'will to power'. This mere textual detail in fact exposes an important conceptual point: the *contrast itself* of Hegel and Nietzsche cannot here remain philosophically neutral. One must already have 'taken sides' in presenting this contrast *as such*. Why? Because what is at stake in the contrast itself is precisely the extent to which different philosophies (in this case, those of Hegel and Nietzsche respectively) *necessarily* share a common ground or terrain. Is there an intrinsic milieu of thought within which different 'views' or 'positions' may be compared, contrasted and critiqued? If so, then the communication and reciprocity of different philosophies is already guaranteed, at least within certain limits. If not, then the very posing of the question of differential contrast among philosophies and the presupposition of their underlying common ground take on strategic functions; they are no longer neutral. In the former case, Hegel has already won the contest, since his philosophy just is the victory of a/the philosophy of philosophies. In the latter case, Nietzsche already holds the prize: the 'specific difference' of his philosophy is the absolutisation of strategic differences, in particular of philosophical differences as strategic expressions of Will to Power.

Even if Hegel and Nietzsche represent a crucial divergence for contemporary philosophy, it is thus important in this regard to note that even if and when Nietzsche breaks with the Dialectic, his thought still remains bound to a separate conception of essentially the same problem, although transposed into a different register. Rather than a dialectic of desire for recognition binding and separating Master and Slave, Nietzsche organises his thought around a typology of forms of Will to Power. To the value-creating affirmation of the Noble, Nietzsche non-dialectically opposes the reactive valuation of the Slave. Within Nietzsche himself, a certain 'dialectic' nonetheless unavoidably emerges that would problematise any unilateral opposition of Noble to Slave, of active to reactive force, or of reversible to irreversible difference. This occurs at the very moment of philosophical *utterance*.

The 'chiasmic' or reversible structure of Difference has itself a relatively 'positive' and effective essence. As Laruelle states the point, Nietzschean Difference entails 'that reversibility as equilibrium of contraries is still, in its essence, a form of irreversibility and that irreversibility always prevails, but it prevails only in appearing to deny itself, *the reversibility of contraries being not a third term, but only the primacy, or irreversibility, of the positive side, of Being or of Presence over Nothingness*'.[28] In other words, the very fact of metaphysical or *a priori* reversibility becomes an *essential and irreversible* property of beings as such. All the tangled conceptuality here amounts to this: Nietzschean immanence does not solve but rather clearly exposes the problem of difference, relation and self-inclusion at the heart of philosophical expression.

There is from this perspective, then, a certain 'dialectic' internal to Nietzsche's thought that may reverse or invert that of Hegel, but which *thereby* cannot be said to break absolutely with the latter. This dialectic concerns precisely the proper relation between the 'active' and 'reactive' forces into which the Will to Power differentiates itself. Whereas Bataille for example tends toward a relatively 'extremist' reading of Nietzsche that would identify the essence of the Will to Power with destruction pure and simple (as in his key formulation 'SOVEREIGNTY = NOTHING'), Klossowski recognises a deeper problem: despite its essential impulse to disequilibrium, the Will to Power necessarily takes relatively ordered and self-sustaining forms precisely as platforms needed in order to realise itself as creative overcoming.[29] In particular, this poses a unique obstacle for any straightforward conception of Nietzsche's 'anti-humanism'. Nietzsche himself cannot simply reject the most reactive and herd-like aspects of humanity, such as gregarious communication and the levelling tendencies of mass society. He must will their conversion into means for producing the Overman. But this puts Nietzsche in an ambiguous position. As Klossowski writes, 'The very anthropomorphism he was fighting against, and which he criticized even in the most "objective" theories of science, was now reintroduced by Nietzsche himself – he became an accomplice, certainly not in order to safeguard human feeling, but rather to "overcome" it, as he said; in fact, to dehumanize thought.'[30]

In its most general form, this problem ineluctably presents itself as soon as the sense and content of Nietzschean thought is itself *expressed* or *elaborated* in whatever way (purely theoretically, aphoristically, stylistically, etc.). Any representation of Will to Power, or conceptualisation of thought as force, cannot rigorously be held separate from a specific *deployment* of the very objects such concepts represent. An unavoidable corollary of the *immanence* of Nietzsche's notion of universal Will to Power is thus that Nietzsche's own acts of philosophical expression undergo an intrinsic bifurcation into two irreducible sides. They are at once *representations of* (the expression of Will to Power) and (representations of) *the expression of* Will to Power. Style then (and not Spirit) must be identified as philosophy's intrinsically equivocal Substance.[31] The Eternal Return, and especially its relatively 'esoteric' character, in this way become functions of a 'stylistic turn' in Nietzsche's thought. Nietzsche must *write* and thereby transmit the experience of the Eternal Return to the 'philosophers of the future'.

In his earlier book from Philosophy I, *The Decline of Writing*, Laruelle notes of the Nietzschean aphorism that it 'must be read twice', although this would imply 'not two readings, but one unique and redoubled reading'.[32] The aphorism must be read 'a first time in terms of the signified, and also of the signifier, of the process of signification and stylistic values'. But it must also be read 'a second time in function of a-textual forces, of their specific syntax or their coherence which is intense and without concept'.[33] Laruelle himself takes this problem of materialist hermeneutics as the primary focus in his works from the late 1970s that he now groups together under the pre-non-philosophical heading of Philosophy I. In particular, this is the shared theme of the pair of books *Nietzsche contra Heidegger* and *Beyond the Power Principle*.

Nietzsche contra Heidegger is a study of Nietzsche in the context of politics, desire and materialism.[34] Materialism itself functions in this early work as a contested term: dialectical materialism is contrasted with a Deleuzean-inspired 'machinic materialism.' The problem of politics is thereby conceived in terms of a radical distinction between two political 'poles' which are conceived as '"contradictory" (yet without mediation)': on the one hand, a 'principal' revolutionary pole: 'Rebellion'; on the other hand, a 'secondary' fascisising [*fascisant*] pole: 'Mastery'.[35]

Already at this stage – which precedes the break between Philosophy I and Philosophy II that inaugurates 'non-philosophy' – Laruelle is concerned with the abstract problem of a conceptual 'difference' that would not simply presuppose two terms and a principle of distinction/relation between them. He characterises the relation between the two 'poles' of Mastery and Rebellion as that of a 'duplicity', a form of difference that Laruelle consistently contrasts here with 'duality'.[36] This form of difference as duplicity is meant to open up a new ontological option which itself would elide the difference between monism and dualism: duplicity 'liquidates [*liquide*] the opposition of monism (philosophy of the Master *or* of the Rebel) and dualism (mediatised contradiction of the Master *and* the Rebel)'.[37]

Strikingly, Laruelle addresses the reader directly in the second person in this context, blurring the subject/object difference in the analysis between Nietzsche and Laruelle/Nietzsche's reader. It is neither 'you, the reader' nor 'Nietzsche' in isolation that is in question but rather the differential relation itself of these two 'terms', their disjunctive synthesis: 'It is *you or Nietzsche* that is in question: as the political subject that you must become, split by the cause, Revolution or Fascism.'[38] The reader's own relation to Nietzsche thus becomes caught up as an essential component in the inquiry into a Nietzschean politics: 'From the beginning, a scene at once unique and redoubled, a scene of reading from your side, a scene of writing from Nietzsche's side, two scenes that make but one [*qui n'en font qu'une*].'[39]

Ultimately at stake in this relation between a writer and a reader whose scenic stagings 'make but one' is a theory of sense itself – including the problems of signification, subjectivity, interpretation and so on – that would itself be deployed through an immanently 'political' and 'machinic' materialism. On the one hand, Laruelle accepts a more or less standard distinction between evident sense, subjective phenomenality and hermeneutics on the one side and a flux of a-textual forces, pure affects and power on the other. But on the other hand, Laruelle refuses to allow this very distinction to become a simple dualism between a world of ideal sense and a world of real force. Instead, the representations of forces are inseparably forces of representation, and the chiasmic relation between these two levels takes precedence over the two levels themselves conceived independently. In short, 'Nietzschean practice would imply at once an intervention or wrenching of a-textual forces, of anti-signifying powers *within* the signifying scene, and a "primacy" [*primauté*] of the relation of terms over the terms themselves.'[40] Or again, 'Nietzsche-thought [la pensée-nietzsche] is a question of immanent syntax and of flowing matter [matière fluante] proper to that syntax.'[41] Difference is both a real basis and a syntactical method for philosophy.

Beyond the Power Principle appeared in 1978, one year after *Nietzsche contra Heidegger*. In this book, Laruelle continues the project of developing a 'political materialism', yet an important shift starts to become noticeable. Laruelle aims here simultaneously at outlining a 'general hermeneutics' and a 'minor hermeneutics'. The latter depends upon a certain qualification of the infinite chiasmus of power and syntax:

Only a really minor thinking [*une pensée réellement mineure*] is a really political thinking, that is to say also anti?political, only a minoritarian power-to-
think renders the political field co-extensive with its internal limits, those of
anti?power. As these limits are transcendental in their own way, without con-
sisting in a subject, minoritarian thinking is thus universal by force of poverty,
inescapable by force of being without light or locus, inalienable by force of
being stripped bare. There is no radical political evil[;] even the seventh circle
of Hell, fascism, the only one to still be inhabited, contains a rebel postula-
tion.[42]

In distinction from the irreducibility of immanent, chiasmic forces in
Nietzsche contra Heidegger, here the 'poverty' of an 'anti?power' that would
perhaps escape the interplay of reciprocal relations altogether is sounded.
Together, these two books register a unique reading of Nietzschean politics *as* hermeneutics.[43] At the same time, with the advantage of hindsight,
the contours of the problematic that will occupy non-philosophy are also
clearly evident. Perhaps most importantly, *Beyond the Power Principle*
moves somewhat away from Nietzsche in the direction of Heidegger in
rejecting the infinite, syntactical intensification of Difference as Power and
opening the space for an absolute 'beyond' with respect to Nietzschean
immanence that would in effect reduce Nietzschean Power to Hegelian
Idealism. In *Beyond the Power Principle*, Laruelle seems to 'side' relatively
with Heidegger in rejecting the chiasmus of force and representation with
respect to an absolutely impoverished Finitude that would cut the infinite,
idealist reversibility of sense and force in advance.

Here we should note a characteristic rhetorical or argumentative reversal in Laruelle that we will have occasion to see again in other contexts.
Laruelle's own readings of other thinkers tend first to bifurcate: an initial
interpretive level (usually a more conventional one) is distinguished from
a second level at which the first level is overturned or inverted. Then, in a
final step, Laruelle posits an ultimate level from the standpoint of which he
rejects (rather than sublates) the sense or principle that would discern the
previous two levels or readings as meaningfully distinct. In non-philosophy
this final step will take place only at the ultimate point where indifference
to philosophical Difference is effected through the vision-in-One. In
the present case of Nietzsche, we have A: the anti-Hegelian reading of
Nietzsche common to Bataille, Klossowski and Deleuze; B: the problematic relation of Hegel and Nietzsche as perhaps equally philosophers of
idealist immanence (although undecidably perched in this relation between
dialectics and non-dialectics); and then C: this very (meta-)Difference
between the difference and relation of Hegel and Nietzsche registered as
indifferent with respect to the definitive break of Heideggerean Finitude.
It is worth noting that the structure just outlined (A: initial interpretation,

B: inverted interpretation, C: cancellation of the difference A/B) bears a clear similarity but also an important contrast with Hegelian dialectic – which is precisely the philosophical question at issue! Once again, the importance of the structure of (meta-)Difference for Laruelle's argument is evident. Is there another 'side' to this infinite, vertiginous play of the syntax of Difference and (meta-)Difference? And what exactly is Heidegger's role here?

THE REJECTION OF FINITUDE: NIETZSCHE AND HEIDEGGER

For Laruelle, what from the Nietzschean standpoint appears as the identity of syntax and reality appears from the perspective of Heidegger as the denial of essential Finitude. This contrast is one important instance of what Laruelle will call in general 'unilateral difference': the very difference between the models of thought that Laruelle calls Difference and Finitude is itself 'visible' only from the standpoint of Finitude. It is a difference that exists for only 'one side' of that difference. From the Nietzschean perspective, there is no real opposition between finite and infinite. There is only an inclusion of the finite within the infinite. Any assertion of the rights of Finitude as against the infinity of Eternal Return will necessarily appear as a simple deployment of reactive forces, a failure to adequately traverse the passage from the metaphysical to the transcendental. It will appear as a mere assertion of the reality of objectivity and empirical positivity that remains as such unable to consider those aspects of experience in the light of Eternal Return and active negation.

The Nietzsche/Heidegger distinction is central to *Philosophies of Difference*, and it is important even within the purview of Laruelle's analysis of Nietzsche-Deleuze to anticipate the introduction of Finitude which will concern us in the context of Heideggerean Difference. In this respect Laruelle himself takes up a broadly Heideggerean standpoint throughout the book, at least in a provisional manner. He makes extensive use of the syntax/reality distinction, which he at the same time ascribes specifically to Heidegger *as against Nietzsche*. Just as in Laruelle's view the Nietzsche-Deleuze model of Difference reduces Difference to its ideal syntax, this model would mark by the same token – particularly from the standpoint of the philosophising subject – the rejection of reality as irreducible finitude. Whereas in Heideggerean philosophy all thought will remain irreducibly and essentially conditioned by mortality and epochal closure *as by a real, exterior limit*, in Nietzsche the Eternal Return makes all such finitude and limitation a mere effect *interior to the syntactical play of immanence*.

This question of finitude returns us to the problem of the reversibility and/or irreversibility of Difference. As we saw above, the relation between these two concepts *requires* the equivocation of 'and/or' while nonetheless remaining inadequately expressed by this syntax. The *content* of the two terms at issue infects the determinability of the relation itself – (meta-)Difference. The question of finitude may thus be restated as the question of the extent to which this problem necessarily remains internal to the terms taken in themselves. Is there any non-Differential remainder of Difference? This bears more generally on the problem of determination: not only the question as to what extent things are determined from within (from their essence) or, to the contrary, determined from without; more important, even in the case of essential or tautological determination, is such determination always intrinsically differential?

In a key fragment from Nietzsche's notes to *The Will to Power*, Nietzsche addresses this problem of tautological valuation with respect to morality and art. This passage is worth examining, as it demonstrates clearly how Nietzsche both poses and responds in his own mode to the problem of differential tautologies. He begins by treating this problem in terms of ethics:

> 'Morality for morality's sake' – an important step in its denaturalization: it itself appears as the ultimate value. In this phase it has permeated religion: e.g., in Judaism. And there is likewise a phase in which it separates itself again from religion and in which no God is 'moral' enough for it: it then prefers the impersonal ideal – This is the case at present.[44]

The differential tendency toward essentialisation is prominent here. Morality conceived as its own end, as the 'morality of morality', tends to purify morality and invest it with an 'impersonal' and 'denaturalised' ideality. In the same passage, Nietzsche then addresses the same critique with respect to aesthetics:

> 'Art for art's sake' – this is an equally dangerous principle: therewith one introduces a false antithesis into things – it culminates in a defamation of reality ('idealization' into the ugly). If one severs an ideal from reality one debases the real, one impoverishes it, one defames it. 'The beautiful for the sake of the beautiful', 'the true for the sake of the true', 'the good for the sake of the good' – these are three forms of evil eye for the real.[45]

As with morality, the folding back of art onto art produces an effect of ideal essence *as distinct from* real existence. Immanent determination as tautological withdrawal is understood as idealism, as rejection of reality. Why? Because for Nietzsche reality is *only* relational, differential, reversible. This in turn implies that transcendent and tautological values should in fact be traced to their practical utility:

> Art, knowledge, morality are *means*: instead of recognizing in them the aim of enhancing life, one has associated them with the antithesis of life, with 'God' – also as the revelation of a higher world which here and there looks down upon us through them.[46]

Finally, this civilisation-level category mistake (objective instruments of bio-engineering misconstrued as external moral authorities) is generalised and reinterpreted at the metaphysical level of individuated entities as such. For Nietzsche *any* individuated being requires its unique 'adversary' (at the limit, its environing world) with which it struggles in its own self-constitutive way. Tautology is only an idealist refusal of the reality of the 'essential war' of Difference:

> 'Beautiful and ugly', 'true and false', 'good and evil' – these distinctions and antagonisms betray certain conditions of existence and enhancement, not only of man but of any kind of firm and enduring complex which separates itself from its adversary. The war that is thus created is the essential element: as a means of separation that strengthens isolation.[47]

This is how Nietzsche finds his own distinctive idiom for rejecting the Kantian thing-in-itself through its genealogical 'active negation'. In the context of Laruelle's overall analysis of Difference, this aspect of Nietzsche's thought thus appears as, in a sense, anticipating and rejecting in advance Heidegger's critique of idealism via the finitude of the Real.

In a trio of Nietzschean references to Kant, the 'untimely' response of Nietzsche to Heidegger is sounded:

1. In one passage, Nietzsche expresses his critique of the strategic alignment of truth and untruth, belief and unbelief, in the service of defending a radically unthinkable transcendent term, a last refuge for the absolute: 'The problem of truth can slip away into hiding places of all kinds; and the greatest believers may finally avail themselves of the logic of the greatest unbelievers to create for themselves a right to affirm certain things as irrefutable – namely, as *beyond* the means of all refutation – (this artifice is today called "Kantian Criticism").'[48]

2. In another, he asserts the definitive rejection of the 'thing-in-itself' on the grounds of an immanent, pragmatist metaphysics of relational forces: 'The properties of a thing are effects on other "things": if one removes other "things", then a thing has no properties, i.e., there is no thing without other things, i.e., there is no "thing-in-itself".'[49]

3. In a third, he sketches a genealogical critique of the very notion of a 'thing-in-itself' as a mere by-product of human language and especially the herd-quality of communication: 'The "thing-in-itself" nonsensical. If I remove all the relationships, all the "properties", all the "activities" of a thing, the thing does not remain over; because thingness has only been

invented by us owing to the requirements of logic, thus with the aim of defining, communication (to bind together the multiplicity of relationships, properties, activities).'[50]

All of these passages point clearly to a Nietzschean rejection of Kant. Beyond this, they point to the possibility of a rejection in broadly Nietzschean spirit of the appropriation of the theme of Kantian finitude that we will examine subsequently in Heidegger. In this sense, the Heideggerean critique of Nietzsche appears from the Nietzschean 'point of view' as an element already fully grasped by Nietzsche himself, and the apparent 'exteriority' of this critique is foreclosed in advance. Will Heidegger be 'inside' or 'outside' Nietzsche? Again, we seem here to face an irreducible philosophical condition of *chiasmus* as *aporia*: (meta-)Difference.

THE CONFLATION OF NIETZSCHE AND DELEUZE

Laruelle identifies Nietzsche and Deleuze as equally representative of the Idealist model of Difference. What relation between the two thinkers is in play here? We should attend first to Nietzsche and Deleuze themselves. Deleuze writes in *Nietzsche and Philosophy*:

> The succession of philosophers is not an eternal sequence of sages, still less a historical sequence, but a broken succession, a succession of comets. Their discontinuity and repetition do not amount to the eternity of the sky which they cross, nor the historicity of the earth which they fly over. There is no eternal or historical philosophy. Eternity, like the historicity of philosophy amounts to this: philosophy always untimely, untimely at every epoch.[51]

We need here to understand the 'un-' of 'untimely'. Is this a negation, a transcendence, a difference? What Laruelle understands as Nietzsche's rejection of Finitude bears directly on the problem of the relation of negativity to the Real and to time. It is certainly not a question here of logical negation.[52] What is at stake is the status of an irreducible remainder with respect to any and all becomings or differentiations. Nietzsche and Deleuze hold out at least the possibility of an unlimited affirmation, a pure Repetition with respect to which every finite or restricted repetition would find its principle of selection. The pure intensity of the Eternal Return and the *Eventum Tantum* in Nietzsche and in Deleuze relativise *every* finite and determinate event, every relative becoming. Such becomings (or in Deleuze's collaborations with Guattari, deterritorialisations) are grounded in an absolute Becoming (or absolute deterritorialisation), a virtual-real eternity of untimeliness.

The previous discussion has focused almost entirely on Nietzsche.

In Laruelle's view, all of these Nietzschean elements or axioms are fully evident in Deleuze's thought as well. Laruelle makes the strong claim that the philosophies of Nietzsche and Deleuze may thus be identified with respect to the general perspective of the problem of Difference. For Laruelle, there is a single model of Difference common to Nietzsche and Deleuze, a Nietzsche-Deleuzean Idealism. This single model will itself be oriented vis-à-vis those of Heidegger and Derrida respectively. We should ask two questions of this: What motivates this identification of two philosophers? What specific consequences are entailed when Nietzsche and Deleuze are identified in this way?

As for motivation: the particular way Deleuze interprets and repeats Nietzsche helps to make explicit the metaphysical underpinnings of Nietzsche's thought. Undoubtedly, if Laruelle says significantly less about Deleuze than about Heidegger and Derrida in *Philosophies of Difference*, it is not due to any implicit judgement of his relative importance for understanding Difference. If anything, Laruelle is perhaps more 'Deleuzean' in his basic *philosophical* outlook than anything else. As he himself says, 'If [Deleuze's] oeuvre is not examined thematically but only marked out and designated, although quite regularly, this is also because it is constantly present and active here.'[53] Indeed, immediately following this reflection on the virtual textual presence of Deleuze, Laruelle indicates the key theoretical role Deleuze plays in the overall analysis of Difference: 'Deleuze has produced a systematic internal analysis of "Difference" and has made appear, by the very excess of the variations that he has operated upon it, its invariant nature.'[54]

In any event, the key role of Nietzsche in Deleuze's thought cannot be gainsaid. After the publication of his first book, the study of Hume, Deleuze withdrew for the better part of a decade without any significant philosophical output until the appearance of *Nietzsche and Philosophy* in 1962. In terms of his own philosophical trajectory, this work on Nietzsche seems to have played a key role in Deleuze's singularly self-creative project, as though Nietzsche were a crucial teacher and 'turning-point' for Deleuze. Nietzsche breaks Deleuze's own philosophical history in two, just as he claims to break History itself in two.

Besides the study *Nietzsche and Philosophy*, Nietzsche of course plays a central role in Deleuze's *Difference and Repetition*. In that work, Nietzsche is set within a genealogy of univocity which begins with Duns Scotus and passes through Spinoza, where ontology progressively sheds transcendence and realises immanence until it finds in Nietzsche the immanence of Difference. Then, as we already saw, in *The Logic of Sense* – itself a kind of systematic complement to *Difference and Repetition* – Nietzsche plays a crucial role in determining the chiasmus of the surface of sense-events and the depth of bodies, the very genesis of sense. There, Nietzsche provides a differential supplement with respect to Leibniz. To summarise: Leibniz advances the shift from the logic of identity to the logic of the event by substituting the distinction of compossibility and incompossibility for the distinction of identity and contradiction. Incompossible predicates do not directly negate one another but the positing of one precludes the positing of the other in one and the same subject. Thus the permutations of predicates that are compossible with one another define a class of possible worlds. Deleuze's primary criticism of Leibniz is that this proliferation of differences is ultimately restricted by the axiom that there may only be one actual world and therefore God must be introduced to function as the agent of a principle of selection: the rational = good choice of the 'best of all possible worlds'. Relative to Leibniz, Nietzsche subtracts the transcendent selective function of God and thereby allows the differences among possible worlds to 'communicate' immanently by way of a new, immanently selective principle, precisely Difference as Eternal Return.

So what purpose is served by focusing on Nietzsche's metaphysics but nonetheless equating Deleuze with this interpretation of Nietzsche? The key relation again is that of Nietzsche and Heidegger. Deleuze represents an advance in this debate to the extent that he comes after Heidegger and is able to coordinate Scotus, Spinoza, Nietzsche and Heidegger in a single genealogy of univocal Being. If Deleuze is essentially Nietzschean in spirit, the logic or syntax in which this spirit is expressed is nevertheless that of *Spinoza after Heidegger*. Deleuze unconditionally accepts Spinoza's philosophical method, which begins with 'absolute infinity' and remains there in immanence. For both Nietzsche and Deleuze, like Spinoza, thought is essentially *affective*. To think is, for both these men, to be grasped by events as material forces and to channel such forces into new configurations that are at once states of feeling ('power is joyful affirmation') and active affects ('concepts are creations'). Both thinkers thus uphold the equation: concept = affect. In this respect, the philosophy of Spinoza serves as a kind of common denominator of Deleuze and Nietzsche. If Nietzsche recognises Spinoza as a philosophical precursor and ally and yet rejects the trappings of his intellectualism, Deleuze senses the vital energy of a Nietzschean creative will beneath the logical rigour and uncompromising intellectual honesty of Spinoza's *Ethics*. On a Spinozist terrain the metaphysics of absolute immanence may express itself in unlimited forms, but whatever its mode of expression the affirmation of immanence will everywhere be philosophically One.

Here then are the consequences: Laruelle's biconditional 'equation' of Nietzsche and Deleuze has effective force in both directions.[55] On the one hand, Laruelle's reading in effect 'essentialises' Deleuze by reducing the pluriform Deleuzean model of philosophy to that of Nietzsche. All the innovations and conceptual creations of Deleuze's thought are conceived as more or less accidental variations or expressions of a fundamentally Nietzschean standpoint in thought. The important point is that this apparent 'reduction' of Deleuze to Nietzsche is made from within the more general non-philosophical critique of Difference. In the context of Laruelle's larger argument, it is not the status of Nietzsche's and Deleuze's philosophies in themselves that are at stake but the model of Idealist Difference whose axioms may be extracted, Laruelle claims, from their work.

On the other hand, perhaps less obviously, Laruelle 'resolves' Nietzsche into Deleuze by taking the latter's unequivocal stance with respect to the infinite and absolute character of Eternal Return. Deleuze is in this respect much more clearly a differential Idealist in the sense attributed by Laruelle to Nietzsche than is Nietzsche himself. Methodologically, Laruelle would seem to be justified in such a procedure only to the extent that his critical aim would be directed at neither Nietzsche nor Deleuze taken as a whole, but rather toward a motivated 'extraction' of a philosopheme that may exist only as a particular cross-hatch of the two thinkers juxtaposed in a certain way. Since Laruelle clearly delimits his project as that of an exposition of models of Difference rather than analyses of particular philosophies, it would appear that he is able to ward off any criticisms that would claim he is too 'reductive' of either thinker. Instead of adequacy to their respective textual corpuses, the relevant criterion becomes that of utility in clarifying a new philosophical 'object', that of an Idealist Difference.

Is it fair to conflate Nietzsche and Deleuze as avatars of a common model of Difference? Probably that is the wrong question. We should ask instead how this very approach to philosophy must be understood. However that question will not be able to be answered, according to Laruelle's own argument, until the formulation of the theory of philosophical decision that closes the book. To what extent is Deleuze's thought Nietzschean? The most important point is that by treating Laruelle's philosophical models as themselves generic, the 'identification' of Nietzsche and Deleuze does not in any way imply that there is a general Nietzschean form that would subsume Deleuze nor that there is a common generality within which both would be included. Laruelle's generic is not general.

In Deleuze and Guattari's late text *What is Philosophy?*, Laruelle's non-philosophy is briefly discussed in a note. In response, Laruelle composed a statement of non-philosophy in sharp contrast to Deleuze's philosophy in particular. In the present context, we can draw several key points from this essay (which post-dates *Philosophies of Difference* by approximately a decade). Even though the presentation of non-philosophy in Laruelle's

'Reply to Deleuze' incorporates some of the many new developments that stretch from *Philosophies of Difference* up to *Principles of Non-philosophy*, the critique of Deleuze that structures that essay throws light on both why Laruelle considers it legitimate to assimilate Deleuze and Nietzsche and on the critique of the Nietzschean-Deleuzean model itself.

Laruelle draws the conclusion there that Deleuze's philosophy marks a disparagement of actual beings, of 'empirical' reality:

> The consequences for 'empirical data' are disastrous: not only are they deprived of reality, they are also, above all, necessarily conceived as deficient or degraded, as the reification or 'actualization' of becoming. Their reality is an illusion, an appearance, a deficiency of their auto-position in and by the [Moebius] strip [as a chiasmic topology] . . . This is the most general presupposition of every absolute idealism, and perhaps of all philosophy, an idealism that is here equally an absolute realism ('real without being actual, ideal without being abstract'): 'experience' is generally construed from the outset as devoid of reality.[56]

Here, Laruelle cites Deleuze's well-known formula of the virtual from *Difference and Repetition*, 'real without being actual, ideal without being abstract'.[57] In this critique of Deleuze, Laruelle is roughly in line with the position outlined in Peter Hallward's *Out of this World*: the distinction between the virtual and the actual, due to the very excess of virtuality over actuality, leads to the denigration or even – at the limit – the negation of the actual as such.[58] For Laruelle, this chiasmus of the actual and the virtual may be indifferently characterised as an 'absolute idealism' or an 'absolute realism'. For Hallward, on the contrary, Deleuze's idealism and 'otherworldliness' is contrasted with the real as 'concrete' with its evident political exigencies.

The specific criticism levelled by Hallward and Laruelle that Deleuze in fact denigrates or rejects the actual necessarily depends on an independent conception of what the actual really amounts to. The point only has critical traction and thus only makes sense *as* an effective critique if the actual that Deleuze is said to reject philosophically may be identified with a 'real actual'. After all, Deleuze is not criticised for rejecting *his own concept* of the actual, but rather *the* actual, Hallward's 'this world'. Thus *on Deleuze's own terms* the actual cannot be conceived as denigrated or rejected unless the virtual/actual 'system' – in effect Deleuze's entire ontology as such – is conceived as immediately and straightforwardly inconsistent and self-contradictory. Both Hallward and Laruelle require a conception of the actual or Real *external to Deleuze* from the standpoint of which the criticism of *Deleuze's* actual would make sense.

On this latter point, the advantages of Laruelle's critique over and above Hallward's are clearly evident. Hallward relies on a more or less common-sense notion of actuality that cannot help but beg the question when confronted with the undeniable philosophical sophistication and subtlety of Deleuze's approach. Laruelle, on the other hand, conceives of his critique of Deleuze as an *effect* – it would even be appropriate here to say a *mere effect* – of his own independent conception of non-philosophy as a rigorous science (of) the One. *If* indeed a sound and complete critique of Deleuze's philosophy can be mounted, it is much more likely that it would be grounded in a sophisticated theoretical apparatus of its own than that it would rest on simple demonstrations of inadequacy or inconsistency in Deleuze's own account. One does not adequately critique any fully developed philosophical system of the scope and range of Deleuze's on the basis of common-sense and mere *ad hoc* argumentation.

With this brief sketch of Laruelle's later treatment of Deleuze in view, the core of Laruelle's reading of Nietzsche-Deleuzean 'Idealism' in *Philosophies of Difference* perhaps comes into clearer focus. On this reading, the syntax/reality distinction simply cannot be thought in a strong sense on Nietzschean or Deleuzean (or Spinozist) terrain. This is because the metaphysics of differential immanence on which both thinkers rely in order to mount their respective critiques of transcendent absolutes and reifications requires that no term in thought or being fully escape its essential reversibility with respect to its Other(s). For Laruelle, Nietzsche and Deleuze are not idealist in a simple and straightforward sense, but only in the relatively autonomous, transcendental sense of Difference. By no means is Laruelle claiming that Nietzsche and Deleuze endorse the thesis 'only ideas are real'. If anything, Nietzsche and Deleuze are both materialist rather than idealist at this 'metaphysical' level. Instead, Laruelle identifies the way the critical power of both their philosophies depends upon a transcendental decision for immanence that disallows not just the possibility of the real transcendence of finite, empirical objects, but of *any* real transcendence that would limit or qualify the creative-destructive power of Difference. Nietzschean and Deleuzean Difference is 'pure' Difference in the sense that it locates thought within a milieu of thoroughgoing differentiation and mixture and thereby entails the critical rejection of every pure or absolute distinction between thought and being just as among diverse entities themselves.[59]

For Laruelle, Nietzsche and Deleuze both remain faithful in their own ways to a metaphysics of *unlimited* Difference that identifies the Real as such with the events of its immanent articulation and differential production. This means that the distinction between syntax and reality as used by Laruelle to characterise Difference in general functions particularly in Nietzsche and Deleuze as no more than a formal distinction and never as a real one, that is, it falls for both thinkers relatively on the side of syntax rather than reality at the self-scaling level of (meta-)Difference. In short, Nietzsche-Deleuzean Difference ultimately situates the philosophical problem of reality *only within* the problem of philosophical syntax. The infinitisation through Difference of syntax as the very essence of the syntax/reality distinction effectively turns 'reality' into no more than the effect of a limit at the interior of syntax itself:

$$\text{Syntax}/(\text{syntax}/(\text{syntax}/\ldots)\ldots\text{reality}) = \text{Syntax} = \text{Idealist Difference}.$$

Nietzsche and Deleuze's philosophies are 'idealist' for Laruelle only and exactly in this differentially articulated sense.

NOTES

1. The notion of a 'standard model' comes in particular from contemporary mathematics (Zermelo-Fraenkel set theory on the one hand and the 'non-standard analysis' of Abraham Robinson on the other). For insight into Laruelle's appropriation of this vocabulary, see François Laruelle, *Non-standard Philosophy*, pp. 219–44.
2. Nietzsche's most detailed discussion of his orientation toward 'philosophers of the future' is in *Beyond Good and Evil*, the subtitle of which is 'Prelude to a Philosophy of the Future'. See especially section 212.
3. *PD*, p. 82.
4. Gilles Deleuze, *The Logic of Sense*, especially pp. 12–22, 28–35.
5. Compare the relation of Leibniz and Nietzsche in Gilles Deleuze, *Difference and Repetition*, pp. 44–58.
6. Gilles Deleuze, *The Logic of Sense*, p. 149.
7. See Joshua Ramey, *The Hermetic Deleuze*, especially ch. 3.
8. *PD*, pp. 82–3.
9. Laruelle does not hold Will to Power and Eternal Return separate from one another in Nietzsche, but sees them precisely as forming an integral system. As early as his 1977 text *Nietzsche contra Heidegger*, Laruelle expresses this 'algebraically' with the formula WP/ERS (VP/ERM in the French).
10. See the section entitled 'Anti-Darwin' from *Twilight of the Idols* in *The Portable Nietzsche*, pp. 522–3.
11. Friedrich Nietzsche, *The Gay Science*, section 341, in *The Portable Nietzsche*, pp. 101–2.
12. *PD*, p. 41.
13. *PD*, p. 83.
14. Gilles Deleuze, *Nietzsche and Philosophy*, p. 70.
15. Ibid.
16. In general, for a solid account of Deleuze's philosophical apprenticeship and friendship with Nietzsche, see Gregory Flaxman, *Gilles Deleuze and the Fabulation of Philosophy*, pp. 22–71.

17. Gilles Deleuze, *Nietzsche and Philosophy*, p. 70. There are clear links here to Deleuze's Spinozism and the formation of active affects in the *Ethics*.
18. *Twilight of the Idols* in *The Portable Nietzsche*, pp. 485–6. The bracketed segments in the citation condense Nietzsche's own parenthesised commentary at each 'stage'. In *A Thing of This World: A History of Continental Anti-Realism*, Lee Braver provides an analysis of this six-stage genealogy of Western philosophy as what he calls Nietzsche's 'Six-Step Physics'.
19. The attribution of a difference between 'Nietzsche I' and 'Nietzsche II' in the genealogy is meant to anticipate and mimic the distinction between 'Heidegger I' and 'Heidegger II'. In both cases, an internal 'passage' constitutes the philosophy 'in itself'. When Heidegger examines this text in the first of his four-volume study, *Nietzsche*, he emphasises the relation between each of the six stages of this 'history of Platonism' and the interpretation of human essence each supports. In Heidegger's view, stages five and six together mark the transformation of Western metaphysics evident in Nietzsche's own philosophy, and in particular stage six represents a key final step in Nietzsche's own trajectory. For Heidegger this step bears especially on Nietzsche's understanding of human being: 'At the end of Platonism stands a decision concerning the transformation of man', essentially Nietzsche's ultimatum as the choice between the 'last man' and the 'Overman'. Martin Heidegger, *Nietzsche*, vol. I, p. 208.
20. Friedrich Nietzsche, *Will to Power*, pp. 310–11.
21. Ibid.
22. Ibid.
23. Ibid.
24. Ibid., p. 550.
25. *PD*, p. 83.
26. Alexandre Kojève, *Introduction to the Reading of Hegel*, pp. 3–30.
27. Pierre Klossowski, *Nietzsche and the Vicious Circle*, p. 12.
28. *PD*, p. 67.
29. Pierre Klossowski, *Nietzsche and the Vicious Circle*, pp. 113–20.
30. Ibid., p. 113.
31. See Nietzsche's remarks on Sterne from *Mixed Opinions and Maxims*, aphorism 113, which Laruelle comments on in *The Decline of Writing*, pp. 143–4. This problem of style conforming to the matter to be thought is one of the key themes of Laruelle's study of Ravaisson *Phenomenon and Difference* which John Mullarkey has analysed in his discussion of Laruelle in *Post-Continental Philosophy*, pp. 147–56. Compare Derrida's discussion of Nietzsche's style(s) in *Spurs*.
32. François Laruelle, *Decline of Writing*, p. 127.
33. Ibid.
34. In this respect, *Nietzsche contra Heidegger* shares many of the same concerns as Badiou's *Theory of the Subject*.
35. François Laruelle, *Nietzsche contra Heidegger*, p. 9.
36. Ibid.

37. Ibid.
38. Ibid., p. 10, emphasis added.
39. Ibid.
40. Ibid.
41. Ibid., p. 12.
42. François Laruelle, *Beyond the Power Principle*, p. 142.
43. More recent commentators on Nietzsche, such as Alenka Zupančič, have taken an approach to Nietzsche that resonates strongly with Laruelle's early work. Indeed, Zupančič's formulations – particularly her conception of the non-representational relation between the Real and the Real's linguistic 'declaration' – may sound quite close to those that eventually come to define Laruelle's non-philosophy, as in the claim that beyond the deadlock of classical representation and postmodern 'sophism' lies 'precisely a *duality,* a duality that has nothing to do with the dichotomies between complementary oppositional terms (which are ultimately always two sides of the One): this duality is not (yet) multiplicity either' (Alenka Zupančič, *The Shortest Shadow*, p. 12). The apparent similarities with Laruelle are belied by the fact that Zupančič goes on to describe this duality as 'perhaps best articulated in the topology of the edge as the thing whose sole substantiality consists in its simultaneously separating and linking two surfaces' (ibid.). In this respect, Laruelle's view may also be compared, for instance, with Gregory Bruce Smith's Straussian-influenced reading of Nietzsche: 'Nietzsche had to say different things to different people – that is, to philosophic and nonphilosophic humanity – and different things to present and future man, and to say them all simultaneously. His distinctive mode of writing was adopted in response to these requirements.' Gregory Bruce Smith, *Nietzsche, Heidegger and the Transition to Postmodernity*, p. 162.
44. Friedrich Nietzsche, *Will to Power*, p. 168.
45. Ibid. Compare the Hegelian end-of-history understanding of 'art for art's sake' as neo-animalistic instinctual production in Alexandre Kojève, *Introduction to the Reading of Hegel*, pp. 158–62.
46. Friedrich Nietzsche, *Will to Power*, p. 168.
47. Ibid.
48. Ibid., p. 145. Reflecting on this aspect of the relation of Nietzsche and Kant, Nick Land writes, 'the Nietzschean problem with the *Ding an Sich* was not its supposed dogmatic materialism, but rather that it proposed "an ideal form of matter" as the transcendent (quarantined) site of integral truth, a "real world". There are no things-in-themselves because there are no things . . . The *Ding an Sich* is a concept tailored for a God (supreme being) desperately seeking to hide itself: a cultural glitch turned nasty, but on the run at last.' Land, *Fanged Noumena*, pp. 210–11.
49. Ibid., p. 302.
50. Ibid.
51. Gilles Deleuze, *Nietzsche and Philosophy*, p. 107.
52. The idea of determination as a simple negative limit that since Hegel has been

unfairly ascribed to Spinoza ('omni determinatio est negatio') is in play for neither Nietzsche nor Heidegger.

53. *PD*, p. xv.
54. Ibid.
55. The mathematical model of just such a 'quasi-inverse' or reciprocal 'local isomorphism' in category theory is that of the adjunction of functors (adjoints). See Saunders Mac Lane, *Categories for the Working Mathematician*, pp. 79–108.
56. François Laruelle, *The Non-philosophy Project*, p. 70.
57. Gilles Deleuze, *Difference and Repetition*, p. 208.
58. In this way, Laruelle also agrees in certain key ways with Badiou's criticism of Deleuze's philosophy as a cosmic One-All in Alain Badiou, *Deleuze: The Clamor of Being*. However, while Badiou will contrast a 'pure multiple' as drawn from Zermelo-Fraenkel set theory, Laruelle will think the One-in-One as a real transcendental, thus neither an All nor a synthetic function (Badiou's 'count as One'). See François Laruelle, *Anti-Badiou*.
59. To put the point in Pre-Socratic terms: Nietzsche and Deleuze combine a Heraclitean emphasis on eternal flux with Anaxagoras' notion of the unlimited mixture of the ingredients of the cosmos. They posit in this way *the infinite becoming of the mixture of Becoming and Mixture*.

4

The Heideggerean model of Difference:
Finitude

The essence of truth is un-truth . . . the *negative* belongs intrinsically to truth, by
no means as a sheer lack but as resistance, as that self-concealing which comes
into the clearing as such.

Heidegger, *Contributions to Philosophy*

DIFFERENCE AS FINITUDE: IRREVERSIBILITY AND ONTOLOGICAL DIFFERENCE

If for Laruelle Nietzsche establishes the standard model of philosophy as
Difference, Heidegger marks the full taking-stock of Difference in relation
to the Western tradition as such and draws out the consequences of its
immanent critique as the culmination of metaphysics. Whereas Laruelle
characterises the Nietzschean model of Difference as one of 'Idealism',
he designates the Heideggerean model as that of 'Finitude'. Laruelle's
reading of Heidegger follows the late Heidegger in treating the thought
of the ontological difference of Being and beings as still determined and
thus relatively constrained by the history of metaphysics. Thus for the
late Heidegger, as glossed by Laruelle, the key question for philosophy
becomes something more profound than ontological difference and the
Destruktion of onto-theology. Even deeper than the question of Being is the
question of the *essence* of Being and the decisive epochal possibility on its
basis of an 'other beginning' to the West.

The essence of Being is finite – this is *in nuce* what Laruelle understands as
the distinguishing mark of Heidegger's model of 'Finite Difference'. What
does this shift from 'Being' to 'the essence of Being' signify? Rather than
aiming to understand the structure of a certain difference – the unique,
non-logical form of the correlation of Being and beings (ontological

difference as occluded for the most part by the history of metaphysics) – the focus of inquiry turns instead toward what cannot be grasped in terms of *any possible* structure of correlation or difference. This is the problem of reality as understood from the very side or standpoint of the Real, independently of any syntax whatsoever.

Since the syntax of the Being/beings difference is conceived as the universal framework for any possible experience, intelligibility or manifestation at all, anything that would 'escape' this correlation remains necessarily outside the limits of experience, unintelligible in itself and thoroughly non-manifest. In other words, it possesses all the characteristics that Western philosophy ever since Parmenides and especially after Neo-Platonism has 'attributed' to the One as *epekeina tes ousias* ('beyond Being'). Heidegger himself, in his later work, feels compelled to move beyond the thematisation of Being and truth and toward the questioning of the essence of these as the non-synthetic *indivision* of Being and Nothing, manifestation and withdrawal.

In an attempt to break with the broadly Platonic tradition, however, Heidegger will offer a finite and realist interpretation of Indivision or the One. The One will not govern the Being/beings difference through an infinite transcendence beyond Being, but will instead at once enable and restrict this difference via the finite transcendence on the side of beings – not 'beyond' but 'beneath' Being/beings as the dark and finite Earth to the horizonal clearing of their World.[1] In both cases, what is at stake is an *absolute* transcendence, a One that cannot be 'framed' within the correlation of Being and beings. Yet while the Neo-Platonic One transcends beyond the Being/beings correlation in the direction of ideal Being (although *beyond* this), for Heidegger the direction of transcendence is rather on the 'side' of real beings as the ontic trace of the occluded depth of the Earth in the strife of Earth and World.[2] It is not simply that objective beings transcend Being in the sense of possessing their own relatively independent identity; this is precisely their role in the Being/beings difference and correlation itself. Rather, the very possibility of this objective particularity of beings is understood to depend upon a real, *non-objective transcendence* that separates, as it were, each particular being into two formally distinct 'sides': one side turned toward the twofold movement of concealment and unconcealment that characterises the Being of beings, and one side turned away from both these 'directions' of Being equally, indifferent both to concealment or withdrawal as to unconcealment or manifestation.[3] This second side – a generalisation and transformation of the Kantian noumenon well beyond the sphere of human subjectivity and the problems of epistemology – serves to relativise Being itself. The opening of ontological difference, Being *as* the difference of Being and beings, depends thus upon a prior finite Real whose symptom within Being (symptom rather than effect since any direct relation is precluded via transcendence) will be the qualities of objectivity and particularity in beings themselves.

In contrast to the reversibility of contraries that characterises Laruelle's reading of Nietzsche and Deleuze, a new, *irreversible* element is introduced into the general pattern of Difference with the turn to Heideggerean Finitude. Heidegger's critical *Destruktion* of metaphysics is thus situated for Laruelle with respect to the problem of idealist reversibility: 'Heidegger intends, against Hegel, against Nietzsche and all metaphysics, to reinstate irreversibility as such, *or the form of irreversibility that does not finally deny itself.'*[4] As against the continuity and reversibility of contraries in Nietzsche which effectively inflates the reality of Becoming to the ideal infinity of its philosophically structured syntax, Heidegger is understood to introduce the problem of the *real origin* of irreducibly finite, negative and inauthentic modes of experience such as failure, stupidity, suffering and, at the limit, death. What matters here are not these experiences themselves, but what is ultimately *real* in such experiences. To be sure, as a philosopher and a man Nietzsche was by no means unaware of suffering, mortality, stupidity or failure. But such phenomena are always, for Nietzsche the philosopher, differentially articulated. They are always, in themselves, perspectives on the contraries that dominate them and thus potentially sites for the becoming-active of forces.[5]

Laruelle's reading of Heidegger is perhaps the most complex as well as the most crucial of the three interpretive models of Difference. Laruelle's own position is in many respects 'closest' to Heidegger's among the three models, and Laruelle's distinctive reading of Heidegger finds or intro-duces several of the key elements of non-philosophy directly in Heidegger himself. As Laruelle himself makes explicit at one point, Heideggerean irreversibility marks 'the way, the first step, still uncertain and purely indicative, toward a radically irreversible transcendental condition' that would bear necessarily on 'the essence of the One as such'.[6] In other words, Heideggerean Finitude in important respects already leads in the direction of the key insight that underwrites non-philosophy. Nonetheless, Laruelle will insist that the 'difference' between Heidegger and non-philosophy remains incommensurable and in this sense Heideggerean Finitude rep-resents no less than Nietzschean Idealism a model of philosophical Difference that is as such no 'closer' to non-philosophy than the latter. At times, Laruelle presents Heidegger in such a way that Laruelle's own cri-tique of Difference is almost indistinguishable from Heidegger's critique of Western philosophy from Plato to Nietzsche. One of the significant drawbacks of Laruelle's own generous readings of other thinkers is that it can be difficult at times to distinguish Laruelle's own critical voice from his exposition. It will thus be a central task in this chapter to clarify precisely where and in what respects Laruelle 'differs' from Heidegger.

This is especially true to the extent that Laruelle emphasises the critical dimension of Heidegger's project. Rather than Heidegger 'in-himself', it is Heidegger's critical relations to the figures from the tradition with whom Laruelle is also particularly concerned (above all Kant, Hegel and Nietzsche) that it is necessary to decipher and unfold.[7] In addition, Heidegger's own critical relation to himself, manifest most clearly in his *Kehre* or 'Turn', serves a key role. By emphasising the critical and relational aspects of Heidegger's project, his philosophical and hermeneutical *Mitsein*, over and above Heidegger's own isolated 'views', Laruelle foregrounds the problem of Heidegger's continuity and break with the tradition that precedes him. To be sure, Heidegger himself already makes this problem quite explicit. Indeed, it is at the very centre of his thought and serves as one of the 'invariants' that cuts across its various phases. Throughout his work, Heidegger conceives his project in terms of its critical relation with respect to the Western tradition as a whole – this is the core of his critical *Abbau* of metaphysics and onto-theology. In this sense, Laruelle is only developing Heidegger on his own terms. He nonetheless introduces a slight but important shift in how the critical relation of Heidegger to the tradition is itself understood.

Laruelle's reading of Heidegger is spread out across several chapters of *Philosophies of Difference*. Much of the important structural characterisation of Difference as Finitude is set forth in chapter three, 'Reality of Difference', which in part serves to map the syntax/reality distinction onto the conflict within Difference between the two philosophical models Idealism (Nietzsche) and Finitude (Heidegger). Chapter four, 'Hegel and Heidegger', continues the elaboration of Heideggerean Finitude and situates it with respect to Hegelian Absolute Idealism. Finally, several key themes – especially with respect to Heidegger's 'tautological' syntax that emerges in tandem with the Turning – are sounded most clearly in chapter six, 'Critique of Difference.'

In what follows, we will look first at how Laruelle characterises Heidegger's relationship to Kant. This often overlooked element in Heidegger's work is placed front and centre in Laruelle's reading. On that reading, by radicalising Kantian finitude in thinking it not subjectively but ontologically, Heidegger charts out the basic orientation toward real Finitude that will aim his thought in opposition to every form of idealism. This line of analysis continues through Laruelle's critical juxtaposition of Heidegger and Hegel. The stakes of Heidegger's reading of Kant prove to be of interest for Laruelle's analysis of Difference especially in terms of how the Heideggerean model thereby becomes placed with respect to Hegel. This latter distinction will schematise the generic relation of (twentieth-century) Difference to (nineteenth-century) Dialectic, which will be important for understanding the generalisation of Difference across philosophy (T2). Finally, especially in relation to Nietzsche, there is the question of Heidegger's *Kehre* or Turning, the explicit self-narrativisation of Heidegger's later thought. Laruelle reads Heidegger's Turning against Heidegger himself in terms of a turning of Difference 'in and as the One'. The introduction of the One – even as a still-philosophical term – into the general fabric of Difference opens up a thematic that will serve as a particularly direct point of contrast between the philosophies of Difference and non-philosophy. Thus understanding the claim Laruelle makes about the role of the One in Heidegger's Turning will provide an initial means for grasping the difference between philosophy and non-philosophy. The Turning depends in a very particular way on Heidegger's delimitation of Nietzsche within the history of Western metaphysics. So in this sense, the question of Heidegger's relation to Nietzsche becomes the fundamental concern for understanding the Heideggerean model of Difference as Laruelle conceives it. Here, then, we return to some of themes of the previous chapter on Nietzsche and examine how they have been transformed in light of Heideggerean Finitude.

Despite the historical order of presentation here – Kant, Hegel, Nietzsche – Laruelle's analysis of Heidegger's relation to the tradition is not itself genealogical in structure. For Laruelle, Heidegger's relations to Kant, Hegel and Nietzsche do not constitute three separate stages of an argument, but rather three inflections of one and the same basic point. The point is to understand Heidegger's relation to the tradition in terms of a critical reduction of Western philosophy since Plato to a series of metaphysical idealisms of various sorts (the long epoch of onto-theology and the metaphysics of presence), of which Nietzsche marks a certain closure or consummation (more so than Hegel). For Laruelle, Heidegger's thought provides a model of Difference as Finitude that introduces the problematic of the irreversible One into the framework of Nietzschean Idealist Difference, yet in a way that ultimately remains incapable of treating the One as otherwise than through negative and transcendent determination.

HEIDEGGER AND KANT

Heidegger's early work arose in many ways as a resolute opposition to dominant Neo-Kantianism in early twentieth-century German philosophy. Yet Heidegger's thought up to and including *Being and Time* may itself be understood from a certain standpoint in terms of a critical reworking and generalisation of Kant's transcendental project. Whereas Kant takes secure scientific knowledge – above all, Newtonian mechanics – as a given with respect to experience and aims at providing the transcendental conditions of its possibility, Heidegger takes the question of Being – the fold of Being and beings – as primary and makes use of the condition of facticity – human Being-in-the-World – as a unique mode of access to Being, a transcendental method in a radically new sense for ontology.[8] A hermeneutics of Being as grounded in the existential analytic of human *Dasein*, that is, the interpretation of human Being-in-the-world as governed by the ecstatic temporality of 'care' (*Sorge*), then becomes possible.[9] Human facticity becomes a new kind of transcendental clearing for the understanding of Being.

Like Kant, too, the Heidegger of *Being and Time* looks to ground experience in transcendental structures linked specifically to human beings. Where Heidegger breaks with Kant is above all in his rejection of subjectivity and noumena on the one hand and his reinscription of the problem of Being at the heart of Kant's primarily epistemological concerns on the other. The transcendental structure in Heidegger is ultimately the temporal horizon of Being, to which philosophy has access only through that being whose own temporal character is that of thrownness, presence and ecstatic projection into individual and historical existence, or human *Dasein*.

Heidegger generalises Kant's transcendental project (and at the same time marks a partial return to Kant as against Husserlian idealism) by shifting the terrain from subjectivity to hermeneutical ontology. This ontological reading of Kant is expressed most clearly in *Kant and the Problem of Metaphysics* which appeared in 1929, two years after the publication of *Being and Time*. Much of Heidegger's argument in this work turns around an interpretation of *schematism* and the transcendental imagination in Kant's *Critique of Pure Reason*. But on the whole, Heidegger's reading of Kant is as interesting for its method as for its content. Essentially, Heidegger applies the insights of the generalised hermeneutics codified in *Being and Time* to the inner dynamics of Western philosophy as a concrete, ontico-ontological tradition. The traditional problems of philosophy thus become events of disclosure that take on meaning through their interpretive repetition:

> By a repetition of a fundamental problem we understand the disclosure of the primordial possibilities concealed in it. The development of these possibilities has the effect of transforming the problem and thus preserving it in its import as a problem. To preserve a problem means to free and to safeguard its intrinsic powers, which are the source of its essence and which make it possible as a problem.[10]

This broadly hermeneutical approach to the problems of philosophy allows Heidegger to equate the interpretation of the metaphysical tradition with the very act of 'laying the foundation' of metaphysics. In philosophy, according to Heidegger, one 'lays foundations' not by inventing new forms of thought *ex nihilo* but rather by reworking and uncovering the 'established ground' that has been settled as well as covered over by the tradition: 'What takes place in the Kantian laying of the foundation? Nothing less than this: The establishment of the intrinsic possibility of ontology is accomplished as the disclosure of transcendence, i.e., the subjectivity of the subject . . . The establishment of metaphysics is an interrogation of man, i.e., it is anthropology.'[11]

From Kant Heidegger inherits the notion of intrinsic finitude, a conception of the finite that would not be determined logically as a limitation or restriction of the infinite. However, while Kant presents such finitude primarily in terms of the possibility of knowledge with respect to experience, Heidegger wishes to generalise this aspect of Kant such that it embraces Being as the folding of the ontic and the ontological both through and as human *Dasein*. Indeed, the main argument of Heidegger's *Kantbuch* is that the purely 'epistemological' interpretation of Kant's *Critique of Pure Reason* misses the real import of that text: 'the true result of [the Kantian] endeavor lies in the disclosure of the bond which unites the problem of the possibility of metaphysics with that of the revelation of the finitude in man'.[12]

Human finitude here is not a mere property of one particular kind of entity, nor is it a simple restriction or conditioning of scientific knowledge. Rather, it is the very structure of openness to beings in the world and is in this sense a positive condition for the disclosure of such beings, that is, for Being. Human finitude *is* the form of the comprehension of Being:

> As a mode of Being, existence is in itself finite and, as such, is only possible on the basis of the comprehension of Being. There is and must be such as Being only where finitude has become existent. The comprehension of Being which dominates human existence, although man is unaware of its breadth, constancy, and indeterminateness, is thus manifest as the innermost ground of human finitude.[13]

Finitude is not a property of existents, but the ground of existence. Most precisely: 'More primordial than man is the finitude of the *Dasein* in him.'[14]

The introduction of an irreversible element into Difference marks, in Laruelle's view, Heidegger's reassertion of the full generality of the Kantian problematic of the 'thing-in-itself' as against its restricted, epistemologically oriented interpretation by Neo-Kantianism. It is noteworthy that the only full citation of Heidegger in *Philosophies of Difference* comes from *Kant and the Problem of Metaphysics*:

> What is the significance of the struggle initiated in German idealism against the 'thing in itself' except a growing forgetfulness of what Kant had won, namely, the knowledge that the intrinsic possibility and necessity of metaphysics, i.e., its essence, are, at bottom, sustained and maintained by the original development and searching study of the problem of finitude.[15]

In effect, Heidegger's book on Kant serves to reclaim the notion of Finitude that Kant marshals against metaphysical dogmatism and to show that such Finitude is not merely an intrinsic epistemological limit, but functions much more generally as a constitutive ontic-ontological ground. Thus it is not just a characteristic of human *Dasein* in particular but is the mark of *Dasein* itself *in* human activity and experience. In this way, Heidegger is able to employ his generalisation of Kantian Finitude as a critical instrument *against* all forms of idealism, 'saving Finitude from its psychological and empirical forms and raising it to the status of *a priori* or ontological structure'.[16] But this is still only the first step, which in Laruelle's more general framework corresponds to the passage from the empirical to the *a priori*, or metaphysical. It still remains to shift from this metaphysical usage of Finitude to a properly transcendental usage.

When Laruelle originally characterised the 'generalisation of the passage from the categorial [or metaphysical] to the transcendental' in chapter two of *Philosophies of Difference* he indicated the way that 'the categories thus "appropriated" to their essence detach themselves from one another in order no longer to possess anything other than the form of the Same or of superior tautology'.[17] Laruelle points out that under this transformation the categories of thought take on an immanent operativity: 'operation has become immanent to their essence: Nothingness nihilates, Essence essentializes, Language speaks, Desire desires, the World worlds, etc.'[18] These phrases allude no doubt to Heidegger's writings in particular, but they are meant to apply to all the models of Difference, even if Heidegger's thought is here paradigmatic. 'This becoming-immanent in the form of tautology is fundamental. The sur-mounting of any metaphysical category, its appropriation to its essence or ownness, its unary "turning", absolves it of its metaphysical relativity and frees it from its contrary.'[19] This movement is for Laruelle the general way the transcendental level of Difference constitutes itself in its relative indeterminacy and autonomy.

Our task now is to see how this general formulation of 'becoming-immanent in the form of tautology', which is itself drawn and generalised from Heidegger yet applies to all three models of Difference, is meant to apply back in turn *specifically* to Heideggerean Finitude. In other words, what qualification must be introduced into the passage in general from the categorial or metaphysical to the transcendental in order to identify the particular way this happens in Heidegger (where the turn toward a 'tautological syntax' is clear and easily demonstrated)? What takes place in Heidegger in this regard, on Laruelle's reading, is that the tautological syntax is thought on analogy with the Kantian thing-in-itself as an essential withdrawal, as withdrawal-in-itself as the essence of Being.

This is, for instance, in contrast with Nietzsche, for whom according to Laruelle the basic tautological structure is also in play after its own fashion. As we have seen, for Nietzsche the Same is first of all the differentiated Same of Eternal Return; its basic impulse is one of transcendental infinitisation and potentialisation. It is Difference as redoubling and non-identical repetition. When the Same appears in the form of tautological determination, Nietzsche tends to evaluate this as a reactive withdrawal from real becoming and a confusion of means and ends (as in 'art for art's sake' or 'morality for morality's sake'). For Heidegger, like Nietzsche in this regard, the 'sense' of tautology is conceived as basically inhibitory and negative. Yet for Heidegger this inhibition is not simply a function of reactive forms of willing (that is, reactive forms of being or historical life). Instead, tautological syntax expresses in the only way it can the *finite* reality and autonomy of worldly beings. For Heidegger, finitude as tautology represents the symptom of a lack or gap introduced into thought by the inevitably inauthentic association of Being with empirical or actual beings. This lack is manifest not as purely negative, but as the minimal positivity of a negative 'operation', the factical condition of *Dasein* as temporal and 'mixed' nihilation rather than as simple negativity or logical negation. Philosophy's proper relation to such tautologies is less to express them than to 'let them be', to dwell with the phenomena they can only partially indicate and to refrain from subjecting them to any determination or redoubling through ideality.

There are thus for Laruelle two distinct levels or strata of Finite Difference. The 'metaphysical' layer of Finitude in Heidegger distinguishes 'finitude as everyday self-forgetting' from Finitude 'as *factum a priori*'.[20] In other words, the first stratum of Heideggerean Finitude, for Laruelle, consists of a lifting of the empirically derived notions of forgetting, inauthenticity and finitude to the *a priori* characterisation of philosophy *as* metaphysics. Finitude here concerns therefore the very difference of Being and beings in so far as this difference determines Western philosophy 'not in its [own] metaphysical self-interpretation, but for the first time as reduced to its *a priori* essence as precisely "metaphysical"'.[21] This first level is thus understood as the dimension in which Heidegger delimits Western philosophy *as* metaphysics, or metaphysics *as such*.

With this framework thus established, according to Laruelle's schema, the second stratum constituted through the passage from the metaphysical to the transcendental consists of the self-inhibition of Heidegger's own philosophy as it enfolds *itself* within the metaphysical delimitation it has effected. Heidegger's delimitation of Western metaphysics 'seeks the "grounds for its possibility" in Finitude *as such*, here in so far as it has become if not a principle, at least a quasi-principle that would be itself finite and have the "form" of Turning'.[22] The distinction invoked here by Laruelle between a 'principle' and a 'quasi-principle' is crucial: the central problem posed is that of an enacted refusal or restraint that would give Finitude its real due rather than idealise it into just one more component of a more-embracing philosophical syntax. What the rigour of Heidegger's thought makes necessary is a 'tempered reduction . . . that would respect or disengage Finitude' and that would in fact 'be itself finite in its essence or its possibility'.[23] The tautological turn of Heidegger's late thought allows this rigorously finite Finitude to be 'let be' (*Gelassenheit*) and thus to become minimally manifest (as essential withdrawal) without thereby determining any correlative and reciprocal syntax.[24]

Laruelle takes the final outcome of this analysis to rest in a radicalisation of the determination of the essence of Being as Finite:

> Thus the thinking that engages itself in its highest task, the determination of essence, remains throughout in this dimension of Finitude that is the making use of Difference for this very task. The essence of Finitude is itself finite in the sense that it is finitude alone that is able to become essence, and is thus capable of subtracting essence (of Being, of Nothingness, of *Ereignis*, etc.) from the empire of Logic and the closure of the Concept.[25]

As Laruelle writes, 'There is thus Turning, but *it is finite*.'[26] It is Laruelle's insistence upon interpreting Heidegger's Turning on the basis of Finitude rather than the reverse that guarantees the passage from the metaphysical to the transcendental level of Finite Difference. It is only this that underwrites Heideggerean philosophy as relatively autonomous with respect to Nietzschean reversibility and thereby as capable of sustaining a model of Difference that would be 'complete' on its own terms rather than as merely one moment or aspect of Difference as Nietzsche understands it (namely as a Kantian-reactive moment).

What matters here is the precise conception of negativity and nothingness in Heidegger and its relation to the key notion of *withdrawal*. The problem is that if withdrawal is conceived as one pole of a duality, as in the couple withdrawal/presencing, then the Nietzschean reversible model of Idealism stages its resurgence. The problem for Heidegger is how withdrawal may be conceived in and for itself, that is, without essential reference to its Other. Laruelle states: 'The Withdrawal "turns" as such or comes into its appropriating essence not in the idealizing mode of a dialectical lifting or as the other of Forgetting forgotten, but in the mode, itself finite, of a Forgetting that "turns" rather than a Turning that suppresses Forgetting.'[27]

What distinction is Laruelle making here and what exactly is its import? The difference between 'a Forgetting that "turns"' and 'a Turning that suppresses Forgetting' is precisely the difference between a Finite, or irreversible characterisation of Differential negativity and an Idealist, or reversible one. What is at stake is the possibility of the negative pole or term of a relation to detach itself absolutely from the relation as such, to be absolutely rather than merely relatively negative. But what would an 'absolute negation' mean? It could only be the absolute as such, which is why Laruelle names it as the One. A 'Forgetting that "turns"' is an absolute Forgetting, or Forgetting-as-One which can only have an inauthentic and analogical relation to any empirical, historical or even logical and structural characterisation of forgetting or loss. The Forgetting with which Heidegger is concerned is the Western forgetting of essential Finitude, a forgetting so radical that it can only conceive it as a historical problem to be resolved through global technoscience and the en-framing of all things including Man.[28] Heidegger thus turns back to the Kantian problematic of the thing-in-itself at least in part in order to preserve thinking from its absolute subsumption into the historical Idea and its effective worldly realisation.

HEIDEGGER AND HEGEL

If the primary stakes for Laruelle are between Heidegger and Nietzsche, it is nonetheless with respect to Hegel and Hegelian Dialectic that the Nietzsche/Heidegger distinction itself appears most clearly. Chapter four of *Philosophies of Difference* marks something of a detour from the flow of the argument and the overall organisation of the text. After having distinguished the syntax of Difference (manifest most clearly in Nietzsche's reversible contraries) from the specific problem of the finite reality of Difference (as introduced by Heidegger), it is as though Laruelle chooses to take a step back and to reconsider in some detail the theme with which he briefly opened his introductory first chapter: the epochal shift in Western philosophy from nineteenth-century Dialectic to twentieth-century Difference.

From the standpoint of Laruelle's analysis of Difference, Hegel stands as a liminal figure. His break with the representational emphasis of Kant and his insistence on the immanence of the transgression of limits to the very thinking of limits makes him already an avatar of Difference. Yet the notion of the circle of Spirit as a completion that would not open out onto a future of radical Otherness (like that of Nietzsche's Overman or Heidegger's 'other beginning' for Western thought) places him rather on the side of the Dialectical *as against* Difference.

The last two sections of chapter four – 'Systematic Dissolution of the Resemblances of Hegel and Heidegger' and 'The Hegel-Heidegger Conflict and the Impossibility of a Decision' – may be summarised in the following theses, which are ordered successively as a rough argument:

A)   Despite superficial similarities, there is a real and genuine difference between the philosophies of Hegel and Heidegger.
B)   Nonetheless, there is no independent criterion by which we might adjudicate between the philosophies of Hegel and Heidegger.
C)   Thus, the difference between Hegel and Heidegger must itself be understood as an instance of chiasmic and self-implicating Difference.

The upshot of this argument is that Difference is a philosophical structure rich and robust enough not only to function *within* Heidegger's thought but equally to envelop and exceed Heidegger and thereby to order the relations *between* Heidegger and the tradition (and its figures) which he attempts to delimit. This broad conception of a liminal Heidegger whose thought is at once *within* and *beyond* the metaphysical tradition (as well as undecidably *between* these relations) is itself very much in line with Heidegger's own self-interpretation, especially in his late work.[29] Laruelle diverges from Heidegger, however, in claiming to be able to designate this liminal condition *precisely*. Difference is not merely an instrument of philosophy but is philosophy's very milieu, its most general locus of activity, sometimes despite its own intentions. Crucially, then, the very power and range of Difference, its universality and inescapability up to the point of its identity with philosophy as such will be marked by an inherent self-limitation. The lack of any exterior criterion according to which the difference between Heidegger and Hegel might be judged results in fact from the *strength* of Difference. This lack is actually a mark of Difference's power. But this means that any philosophy that makes use of Difference must already situate itself within Difference.

For Laruelle the problem of the relation of Hegel and Heidegger advances through a series of qualifications: first, certain commonalities between the two thinkers suggest themselves, but finally these commonalities must be rejected in favour of a deeper and more fundamental disjunction. Secondly, then, this very disjunction – a difference between them that does and should *matter* for thought – would seem to suggest both the possibility and the necessity of judging between them, but no such criterion can be found. In other words, in differentiating himself from Hegel, Heidegger succeeds only too well. The 'difference from system' that marks Heidegger's break with Hegel induces an incommensurability that makes the break itself meaningless. If Heidegger represents the 'general economy' that exceeds the 'restricted economy' of Hegelian reason, the problem of the (economic) relation of general to restricted economies remains entirely undetermined and indeterminable. Escape from the system can only be thoroughly ambiguous. In the conflict between Heidegger and Hegel (just as in the conflict between Heidegger and Nietzsche), Difference 'itself' wins.

The clearest commonality between Hegel and Heidegger is the shared reference to negativity – to negation, the Nothing, etc. – as an essential feature or operation of thought. In Laruelle's reading, this reference to an essential and functional negativity – at least at a first level of interpretation – distinguishes both Hegel and Heidegger equally from Nietzsche. The basic difference between Hegel and Heidegger is manifest most clearly in the way their respective standings with respect to the negative impart divergent conceptions of the relation of Being to History. For Hegel, history is the instrument of the identity of being and thought. For Heidegger, history is the relation of being and thought.

In chapter six, Laruelle returns to this relation between Hegel and Heidegger, using it to mark the ultimate failure of Heideggerean Finitude to achieve its aim of reducing Idealism through the introduction of an irreducible and irreversible finitude into the work of philosophy. It is not that Laruelle denies Heidegger's difference with respect to Hegel, only that this differentiation remains finally unable to meet its goal of genuinely reducing the transcendence of ideality. In Laruelle's words:

> If Finitude and what it introduces into Difference prohibit any confusion of the Heideggerean project with a mere repetition of Hegel, it is still however not this – here is the last reservation, yet a decisive one, as little Hegelian as possible, constraining us to abandon Heidegger himself – that is able to claim *really* to have liquidated Idealism and its avatars in Hegel and Nietzsche. The One, even as an absolute transcendence, is experienced here still as a mode of transcendence in general; its reality and its immanence are sacrificed to what remains *despite everything* of a transcendence of theological origin in the 'thing in itself' and Finitude.[30]

This passage is crucial because it clarifies both what Laruelle understands as the aim of Heidegger's overall project and at least in part why that project cannot fully succeed. For Laruelle, Heideggerean Finitude aims at the 'liquidation' of 'Idealism'. In other words, Heidegger's philosophy takes the reduction of Being to the Idea as its essential critical target. From this standpoint, the unity of Heidegger's critique of metaphysics as stretching from Plato to Hegel and Nietzsche becomes visible, as does the specific function of Heidegger's critique of truth as correctness and his attempt to recuperate a more original figure of truth as *aletheia*, or unconcealment. In each case, it is the 'idealist' destiny of the West that is at issue, the overarching tendency toward the determination of Being by Thought in the Western tradition. From this perspective, then, Heidegger's critique of *Ge-Stell* as the modern understanding of Being through technological 'enframing' also comes into clear focus as one inflection of this more general anti-idealism.

For Laruelle, the ultimate limitation of Heidegger's project is then evident at last in his dependence on the positing of a unique beginning to the history of Beyng. Even if history must be thought on the basis of Beyng and not the reverse, Beyng itself must be thought in terms of its 'first beginning' in the Platonic and Aristotelian reorientation of Pre-Socratic *physis*. The very difference in Heidegger's late thinking between a 'first beginning' and the 'other beginning' mitigates against the drive to immanence in his ontology. The openness of Being (even of Beyng) depends on an originary event. From the identification of this event, its naming, follows the disastrous political conservatism of Heidegger's philosophy, his duplicity of 'tradition' which is always at once the very essence of tradition *and* a particular tradition, at once historicity *and* this particular history of the West. Even if the cultural chauvinism is mitigated in some later works, Heidegger cannot for reasons intrinsic to his philosophical conception accept the possibility of a thought that would not be rooted in the Earth, native-born at its origin.

What then becomes of Heidegger's project? In Laruelle's view, Heidegger is correct in one sense to make the 'turn to the One' that guarantees a real Finitude within thought. But for Laruelle, Heidegger's use of the One remains a kind of half-measure, a *mere* use rather than a genuine inquiry into the One's essence. 'Heidegger re-activates against Hegel a generalised Kantianism, but he remains dependent upon the thematic of an extrinsic Finitude.'[31] In other words, the One invoked by Heidegger that makes of Beyng a unique clearing/withdrawal that cannot close into any circle or return, even an Eternal one, depends upon the irreducible finitude of beings. Being itself is made finite, but on the basis of the finitude of beings. What this means is that, according to Laruelle, Heidegger confuses the simplicity of the One with a conception of Finitude that is ultimately derived from or at least inextricably mixed up with that of empirical beings. In short, for Heidegger the One is thought finally in relation to the Difference of Being and beings.

Laruelle's ultimate evaluation of Heidegger with respect to Hegel is thus twofold and inherently ambiguous, like Difference itself. On one side, Heidegger risks with respect to the System of the Absolute Idea what Laruelle comes to name 'the philistine remedy of extrinsic Finitude'.[32] In chapter four Laruelle describes this as follows: 'From a certain point of view Heidegger cannot claim to have outflanked the closure of the Hegelian *Concept* except by giving the appearance, like all those who have searched for the "real" that Hegel misses, of a "stepping-back", of a pre-Hegelian regression: like Feuerbach, Kierkegaard and others.' Laruelle specifies: 'It would be a matter here [in Heidegger] of a Kantian regression.'[33] And it is true that Heidegger's recuperation of the Kantian 'thing-in-itself' in a more purely ontological register risks simply reinstating a naive, pre-Differential distinction of appearance and reality. Yet it would be too simple to leave things in this way. As Laruelle specifies further:

> on the one hand the Kantian apparatus is purified in Heidegger of its epistemological determinations and constantly generalised in view of the conquest of a horizon of Being that would be really universal and no longer simply rational = general = regional; this implies a radically non-rational concept of Difference. On the other hand, the real, in the name of which thinking tries once more to circumvent the high walls of the System, is in Heidegger no longer an empirical and given form of the real, a mode of the object (the sensible Object, the Thou, the I, Practice, etc.), but the real inasmuch as it 'holds itself' precisely in withdrawal, more exactly as it (is) withdrawal, the non-objectivizable par excellence or the transcendental form of the non-objectivizable.[34]

In other words, Heidegger's generalisation of Kant's 'thing-in-itself' from epistemological to ontological terrain allows this concept (a concept of the without-concept) to serve a function that is no longer restricted to the purposes of philosophical rationalism and at the same time preserves the 'real' from being equated with the merely empirical or 'philistine' exteriority. So from this latter perspective, then, 'Heidegger seems not to regress in relation to Hegel except insofar as he initiates . . . the only "hither side step" still possible, . . . absolute withdrawal, without term, and without term because the One – the real – is no longer a term in a relation' – although Laruelle is careful here to 'withhold a last reservation'.[35] This 'last reservation' is important because without it Heidegger would have already accomplished with his introduction of Finitude what Laruelle aims at with the instauration of non-philosophy.

It is noteworthy that these more general points are made here in the particular context of the relation between Heidegger and Hegel since, as we have seen, this relation for Laruelle encapsulates at once the problem of the relation of syntax and reality *within* Difference (in so far as Hegelian Absolute Spirit may be assimilated to the Nietzschean model of Idealist Difference as distinguished from Heideggerean Finitude) *and* the historical and epochal shift within philosophy from Dialectic *to* Difference (in so far as Difference's break with Dialectic marks for Laruelle one of Difference's leading historical causes). By finessing the distinction in this way between the conflicts internal to Difference on the one hand and the differences separating Difference as such externally from other 'epochal' philosophical concepts, Laruelle opens the way for his more general argument and critique which will treat Difference as a specific figure through which Western philosophy as such may be conceived and critiqued from a non-philosophical standpoint.

NIETZSCHE AND HEIDEGGER'S 'TURN' TO THE ONE

In the abundant literature on Heidegger's thought, one of the continuing points of controversy remains the status of his *Kehre* or 'Turning'. The late Heidegger steers away from the project of fundamental ontology by way of the analysis of human *Dasein* that characterises *Being and Time* and toward a more primordial structure of the 'appropriating-event' (*Ereignis*) or the 'there is/it gives' (*Es gibt*). These latter are understood to stand in some sense prior to the opening of the difference between Being and beings or to be this very opening itself. It is largely an unresolved question to what extent the post-*Kehre* Heidegger breaks with the earlier work and to what extent it depends upon it. Laruelle's own intriguing suggestion is that the later Heidegger may be understood in terms of a particular requisitioning and usage of the One.

Since William Richardson's study *Heidegger: Through Phenomenology to Thought* it has become conventional to distinguish 'Heidegger I' from 'Heidegger II'.[36] The hinge that both connects and distinguishes these two figures is the Turn itself.[37] Heidegger gathers the various themes that constitute his 'turn' above all in his *Contributions to Philosophy (Of the Event)*. In this collection of notes and discussions of varying lengths whose overall system of organisation is unclear, Heidegger aims at renewing his philosophical project on a new basis. On the one hand, he shifts the 'question of the meaning of Being' that provided the central principle of organisation for *Being and Time* toward a new questioning of the history of Being in terms its own intrinsic 'appropriating event', or *Ereignis*. At the same time, this shift entails a new conception of the relation between Being and human *Dasein*: Heidegger signifies this new conception by writing the question governing his inquiry as that of 'beyng' [the Old German *Seyn*] rather than of 'being' [*Sein*].

An equally important source for understanding the 'turn' is Heidegger's essay 'On the Essence of Truth', which clarifies and extends many of the formulations found in *Contributions*.[38] Reading 'On the Essence of Truth' alongside section 44 of *Being and Time* precludes any simple disjunction between an 'early' and 'late' Heidegger with respect to this question as well as any easy narrativisation of the 'development' from the former to the latter. Heidegger II is neither a philosophical extension of Heidegger I nor a critical self-revision. A new *kind* of difference separates these two stages, which is what Heidegger II aims to explain. Heidegger himself makes this point in *Contributions* in terms of the rejection of any 'historiological' approach to the *Kehre*:

> There is no gradual 'development' here. Even less is there that relation of the later to the earlier according to which the later would already lie enclosed in the earlier. Since everything in the thinking of beyng is directed toward the unique, to fall down is, as it were, the norm here! This rules out the historiological procedure: to renounce the earlier as 'false' or to prove that the later was 'already meant' in the earlier. The 'changes' are so essential that their scale can be determined only if in each case the *one* question is pervasively asked out of its own site of questioning.[39]

For Heidegger, this entails an irreducible performative dimension to the task of thinking beyng. Because 'every historiological support is withdrawn from this question', the 'way' of thinking becomes instantiated in finite and singular human expressions, 'not as "personal development" but as the human exertion (in a completely non-biographical sense) to bring beyng itself to its truth in beings'.[40] This necessity for singular human exertion ensures what 'has to happen ever more decisively, namely, the fact that the thinking of beyng must not become a "doctrine" or "system".'[41]

Importantly, Heidegger invokes Nietzsche at this point: 'This occurs for the first time as Nietzsche's thinking; and what confronts us there as "psychology", as *self-dissection* and dissolution and "*ecce homo*", along with everything contemporary to that desolate time, has its genuine truth as the history of thinking.'[42] Nonetheless, Heidegger reasserts his charge here against Nietzsche that the latter remains after all 'in the sphere of *metaphysical* questioning'.[43]

For Heidegger, Nietzsche's essential philosophical aim is both creative and redemptive. As against the pervasive nihilism that he diagnoses at the heart of modernity and indeed as the consummation of the post-Socratic and Christian traditions of philosophy, Nietzsche calls for a 'revaluation of all values', an essentially creative act. On his own account, he himself *is* this act, or is at least its precursor, its incipience. Nietzsche's final, uncompleted work – provisionally entitled *The Will to Power* – was intended to gather the insights of Nietzsche's last lucid years in which degenerative disease and encroaching madness provided the stimulus to explode his thought in an absolute surpassing of limits. This final project was to have been a plan for the future, for Europe's future in particular and more broadly for a future that would take humankind through its decisive passage into the Overman.

Yet Nietzsche's creative orientation to the future is everywhere determined by his relationship to the history of the West and the present it has brought forth. Nietzsche's creative project would succeed on its own terms only to the extent that it would be capable of 'redeeming' this past by instrumentalising and overcoming its essentially slavish and reactive spirit. In *Thus Spoke Zarathustra* Nietzsche describes 'the bridge to the highest hope' as the possibility *'that man be redeemed from revenge'*.[44] 'Revenge' and (elsewhere) 'the spirit of revenge' is in fact the ultimate target of Nietzsche's critical genealogy of the West. This is Nietzsche's most vital project. Yet the spirit of revenge also marks the moment of greatest negativity in Nietzsche, or rather the threat of an unendurable negativity entering into the very substance of philosophy (even Nietzsche's own) in the form of the 'ugliest man' and his shame.[45]

When Heidegger glosses these passages concerning revenge in the second of his four-volume study of Nietzsche, he emphasises their strictly *metaphysical* bearing. These are not analyses of human moral failings or mere psychological or biological quirks but rather interpretations of the meaning of thought itself and thereby of the relation of beings to Being. Taking a highly general point of view, Heidegger places Nietzsche here in continuity with both the tradition of German idealism after Kant – especially Schelling, but also Fichte and Hegel – as well as the great critic of this tradition, Schopenhauer. What do all the antagonists in this philosophical *Kampf* share? The interpretation in one way or another of Being as Will. This interpretation, which appears for Heidegger 'in modern metaphysics . . . for the first time expressly and explicitly', provides the common framework for Schelling, Hegel, Schopenhauer and Nietzsche.[46] This framework serves as both the positive condition for the creative upsurge of Nietzsche's thought and ultimately, for Heidegger, the constraint or limit that will in turn entrap Nietzsche within the long epoch of Western metaphysics that opens essentially with Plato.

In what sense is the spirit of revenge a *metaphysical* spirit? For Heidegger, the key passages are the following, both taken from the section of *Zarathustra* entitled 'On Redemption':

[1] *'The spirit of revenge*: my friends, up to now that was man's best reflection; and wherever there was suffering, there also had to be punishment.'

[2] 'This, yes, this alone is revenge itself: the will's ill will toward time and its "It was."'[47]

Both statements, to be sure, are not directly those of Nietzsche but rather of Nietzsche's literary creation Zarathustra. Furthermore, this authorial slippage is not irrelevant here since part of what is at stake is the very possibility of a 'subject' or, perhaps better, a 'name' that would become capable of supporting the affirmation of life that would escape the 'spirit of revenge'. If the gregariously expressive and communicative functions of language have been constituted not just accidentally but essentially via 'the will's ill will toward time', then the problem of the diagnosis of the spirit of revenge will necessarily imply a correlative problem of the expression and formulation – precisely the performance – of the diagnosis. Statement [1] determines revenge, or rather its spirit, with respect to thought: the 'best reflection' of human beings has been the reciprocity of suffering and punishment, the latter as properly equivalent consequence of the former. Statement [2] reveals the properly metaphysical dimension of this conception of thought as revenge. The ultimate object of such thought is time itself.

Recognition of the spirit of revenge against time as the essence of modern (and not only modern) thought grounds at once a diagnosis of actual nihilism and the prognosis for a possible schema of redemption:

First, Heidegger's account of the Nietzschean *diagnosis*: 'Time and its "It was" is the obstacle that the will cannot budge. Time, as passing away, is repulsive; the will suffers on account of it. Suffering in this way, the will itself becomes chronically ill over such passing away; the illness then wills its own passing, and in so doing wills that everything in the world be worthy of passing away.'[48]

Next, Heidegger's interpretation of Nietzsche's *prognosis*: 'For Nietzsche redemption from revenge is redemption from the repulsive, from defiance and degradation in the will, but by no means the dissolution of all willing. Redemption releases the ill will from its "no" and frees it for a "yes." What does the "yes" affirm? Precisely what the ill will of a vengeful spirit renounced: time, transiency.'[49]

These passages outline Heidegger's method for granting the radicality of Nietzsche's philosophy and yet ultimately including Nietzsche within the metaphysical tradition with which he otherwise in many key respects breaks. How exactly are the 'no' and 'yes' opposed here? Their common object is time. Yet the respective acts of negation and affirmation modify this object. They are not simply judgements, but *decisions*. For Heidegger, this traces the genealogy of the doctrine of the eternal recurrence of the same: 'Redemption from revenge is transition from ill will toward time to the will that represents being in the eternal recurrence of the same. Here the will becomes the advocate of the circle.'[50]

In this way, the passage from diagnosis to prognosis in Heidegger's reading of Nietzsche offers a canonical instance of what Laruelle calls

Difference. On the one hand, the 'negativity' of the spirit of revenge is brought under critique from the perspective of a possible redemption. On the other hand, the 'positivity' of redemption consists in the valorisation of what revenge would disparage, namely time itself. But how is this valorisation to be effected? By giving Becoming the one-sided but also two-levelled characterisation of eternal recurrence of the same. It is one-sided – 'same' – because Becoming is All; it is without-Other. But this All is itself divided in and through itself; it is at once 'eternal' and 'recurring'. In this way the act or operation of valorisation depends upon a bifurcation within one of the two opposed terms. Given the opposition of Being and Becoming, it becomes necessary to bifurcate Becoming itself: on the one hand, Becoming must be valorised as against the (vengeful) negation of Becoming in favour of Being; on the other hand, Becoming must take on the very role of Being in a new, transcendental sense: the valorisation of Becoming is inseparable from its reinterpretation *as* thoroughly immanent and differential Being. In other words, in order to overcome the opposition of Being and Becoming, Becoming itself must internalise a new, more complex differentiation involving a characteristic doubling or reduplication of itself, a dual opposition within Becoming both to its misinterpretation by the metaphysical spirit of revenge on the one hand and to 'itself' on the other. This is not a dialectical relation, but precisely Nietzsche's philosophical Will to Difference.

The encounter with Nietzschean Difference becomes the basis for Heidegger's Turn. In the course of the Turn, Heidegger tends to rework the difference between the ontic and the ontological that structures *Being and Time* in terms of a more primordial opening or difference that would 'give' Being itself (together with all its internal structural differentiations, such as ontological difference). This is expressed as a shift from the thematisation of being to that of truth and its 'appropriating Event' (*Ereignis*), as the fundamental 'rift' of World and Earth opened by cultural artifacts, and perhaps most intriguingly as the 'fourfold' (*Geviert*) of mortals, gods, earth and sky.[51] All of these indications are understood to mark a shift to a thematic of truth as *aletheia* that places the duality of concealment and unconcealment at the centre of the question of the *essence* of Being.

For Laruelle, the 'Turn' in Heidegger corresponds in his own particular philosophical trajectory to the 'passage from the metaphysical to the transcendental' that we examined in chapter two. If the early Heidegger certainly poses the problem of ontological difference on the basis of the *heterogeneity* of Being and beings and the forgetting of this heterogeneity across the tradition of Western philosophy, the characterisation of Being in terms of the ek-static care-structure of *Dasein* nonetheless suggests a relatively fixed, 'structural' interpretation of the conditions for the interplay of Being and beings. Despite Heidegger's careful provisions to the contrary, the existential analytic of *Dasein* in *Being and Time* ends up taking on the character of a more or less Kantian set of transcendental conditions for experience. Even if the Kantian problematic is generalised such that transcendental synthesis becomes ontological *existentialia* and subjective experience becomes ontic (*existentiell*) reality, the form of this difference itself remains ultimately one of conditions to conditioned, even if these are relatively flattened onto a reversible plane of existence as *Dasein*. Factical existence remains here a condition *with respect to* its inevitable lostness in inauthenticity and ideality. Thus while the early Heidegger is able to critique the reduction of Being to the status of *a* being – the fundamental error of onto-theology – he remains unable to 'overturn' the form of thought that would remain structured by this problematic itself.

How does Heidegger's 'turn' stand with respect to his earlier reworking of the Kantian problematic of the thing-in-itself? Rather than a definite break with the Kantian framework, the Turn may be understood as a deepening of the problematic beyond even the residual 'structuralism' of ontological difference. If the problem of the thing-in-itself remains too closely bound, in the early Heidegger, to a universal and ahistorical onto-logical model and is determined primarily in relation to human *Dasein*, in the later Heidegger (profoundly impacted by Nietzsche), the difference of concealment and unconcealment determined not in but as history, not in the ontic/ontological difference but as Beyng, takes the rejection of idealism outside of any correlation to factical human being and puts the difference of authenticity and inauthenticity at the heart of Being as such (even if this is itself still coordinated in some sense with Man's *essence*).[52]

The scope and ambition of Heidegger's late work are immense. After Nietzschean Difference, Heidegger sees that philosophy stands in a new relation to its past and its future. The 'other beginning' of thought Heidegger then proposes, or rather gestures toward without being able – for intrinsic reasons – to characterise exactly, is meant simultaneously to close the history of Western metaphysics and to open a way of thinking that would be sufficiently different from metaphysics that it would inaugurate a new epoch entirely, one in which the fundamental categories of history, human being, reason and so on would have to be radically reconceived. Laruelle's own project of non-philosophy bears at least superficial similarities to the late Heidegger in this respect and it therefore becomes important to clarify how these two projects relate to one another.

What Laruelle is at pains to illuminate in Heidegger is the pertinence of a distinction between (A) the structural role of the Real as irreducible to conceptualisation and idealisation yet still as an immanent determination of thought and (B) the One Real as absolute withdrawal. Both Heidegger and Laruelle emphasise the inherent instability of this distinction. For both thinkers, it is a radically *undecidable difference* from the standpoint of philosophy. At the end of the day, how are we to distinguish the intra-idealist, merely structural 'real' from the genuinely counter-idealist 'Finite Real'? After all, the assertion of an absolutely irreducible withdrawal is still just that, an assertion, and thus part of a philosophical syntax. How can the difference between syntax and reality avoid everywhere falling back into the internal differentiations of syntax?

If we designate philosophical ideality as what falls between parentheses, how can we avoid the equation: (syntax)/reality = (syntax/reality)? One possible answer is simply stipulative: if we cannot articulate or conceptualise what is essentially One and non-conceptual without producing a performative contradiction, that does not preclude us from recognising this aporia as such and 'naming' in a straightforward, first-order manner what escapes all names. In this way Finitude would be not a concept but something like a proper name of the Other. A second possibility is to generalise the problem so that it does not function as merely one problem that arises for thought but is instead the very milieu of thinking, thought's own arising as such. In this way, 'there is no point or zone that would be neither authentic nor inauthentic, but all are both one and the other'.[53] Here, Finitude would be a generalised *pathos*, or non-conceptual philosophical mood.

There is no clear way to hold separate these two possibilities. What is at stake is thus the undecidability of a shift in point of view that is not registered by any distinguishable mark and in principle never could be so distinguished. It is clear on the one hand that:

> In Finitude, the real is not a supplement or surpassing programmed by the syntax itself, even if it manifests itself symptomatically by such a supplementarity at the interior of syntactical effects. There is a hierarchy that is non-invertible once and for all, *irreversible*, between the real and the syntax, an ultimate submission of Difference to the experience of the Other.[54]

But it is equally clear on the other hand that this irreversibility itself receives no mark of determination from its 'experience of the Other' anywhere other than 'at the interior of syntactical effects'.

Laruelle's critical stance with respect to Heidegger then amounts to showing how the framework of Heidegger's own characterisation of Finitude precludes him from conceiving of such Finitude as *positive*. Even if Heidegger on Laruelle's reading is able to conceive the priority of the Finite One to Being, Heidegger's own thought of this priority is itself situated on the side of Being. This entails that the characterisation of the One as tautological withdrawal can only be negative, critical and limiting. 'Thus the essence of irreversibility, instead of being thought in itself, as effect of essence, remains finally still a mode of negativity that cannot, by definition, become radically positive or of which the positivity would remain permeated by facticity.'[55]

In other words, while Heidegger is able to properly thematise the relativisation of Being by the One, he only conceives this prioritisation from the side of what is relativised, namely the folding of Being and beings. Therefore, in Heidegger the One retains its traditional philosophical character of transcendence, negativity, unknowability and Otherness. This accounts for Heidegger's pathos of belatedness and the ultimately depressive character of his thought. Laruelle's point of view will be very close to Heidegger's, with the sole element of 'reversal' being that of taking the 'side' of the One here rather than of Being. This will allow Laruelle to think the One as fully positive, immanent and knowable (in the sense of *gnōsis* rather than *epistēmē*) while nonetheless maintaining the philosophical determinations of the One as Other, transcendent, etc. (but only from within the restricted and relativised standpoint of philosophy). For Laruelle, these determinations may be necessary to philosophy, but they are not essential to the One itself or to a thinking that stands in-One.

The Nietzsche/Heidegger conflict becomes in its own way the repetition within Difference of the original tension between Plato and Aristotle that has served as one of the great refrains of the Western tradition.[56] If Nietzsche may be cast as the Plato of Difference, the founder of a model for thought the criticisms and variations of which will subsequently appear as endless footnotes, then Heidegger becomes Difference's Aristotle, the great critic of the founder, the reflective 'empiricist' to the founder's intuitive 'idealist'. Ultimately, however, all such analogies and the distinctions they might mark remain secondary to what is fundamentally at issue here, namely the most basic distinction structuring philosophy as such: Thought/Real.

For Laruelle, this difference itself has always been marked in Western thought by the idea of transcendent *theos* in one form or another. If Nietzschean immanence aims to reject such a distinction between thought and the real entirely in face of the death of God, Heidegger looks to revive this distinction in a new way against the lingering metaphysics he sees as still at work in Nietzsche. In this respect, Laruelle will place Heidegger and Derrida together in relative opposition to Nietzschean immanence. What Derrida will make fully explicit, according to Laruelle, is what is already constitutive of Heidegger's Turning, namely a ceaseless reference of thought to the real conceived as a quasi-theological Other. Laruelle writes in this regard: 'Difference is devoted to thinking the real as Difference or, better, as the *différance* or *differancing* of Difference, as Other in general.'[57] But Laruelle then poses a series of loaded questions that indicate precisely the point at which non-philosophy will separate itself from this way of proceeding: 'Is this the ultimate experience that we have of the real? Or indeed is this an experience that is still historico-metaphysical (namely religious) and contingent? And is this perhaps, as measured against the One in its essence, a philosophical hallucination of the real?'[58]

For Laruelle, Heidegger is not just one philosopher among many, but is rather *the* contemporary philosopher who most clearly poses the problem of ideality and reality governing the Western tradition as a whole. In this respect, Laruelle does not aim at deflating the claims Heidegger makes with respect to his own philosophical project. If anything, Laruelle is willing to grant Heidegger the somewhat grandiose role of prophet of the destiny of the West that Heidegger at times suggests of himself. What Laruelle denies – and it is far from clear that he is unlike Heidegger in this – is that Heidegger manages to unveil a clear and viable alternative to the tradition he critiques. In short, according to Laruelle, 'Heidegger has no means for exiting from the confusion of the real and the ideal', that is, from the confused and collusive 'region of [philosophical] mixtures, the only region in all likelihood where thinking necessitates violence'.[59]

NOTES

1. 'The opposition of world and earth is strife.' Martin Heidegger, 'The Origin of the Work of Art' in *Basic Writings*, p. 174.
2. 'The earth appears openly cleared as itself only when it is perceived and preserved as that which is essentially undisclosable, that which shrinks from every disclosure and constantly keeps itself closed up.' Ibid., p. 172.
3. For a full analysis of this aspect of Laruelle's reading of Heidegger, see Ray Brassier, 'Laruelle and the Reality of Abstraction' in John Mullarkey and Anthony Paul Smith, eds, *Laruelle and Non-philosophy*, pp. 100–21.
4. *PD*, p. 67.
5. Nietzsche's relation to negativity is perhaps best summed up in his notion of *sickness*: sickness as a perspective on health. Compare William Burroughs on the 'Human Virus': 'The Sender is not a human individual . . . It is The Human Virus. (All virus are deteriorated cells leading a parasitic existence . . . They have specific affinity for the Mother Cell; thus deteriorated liver cells seek the home place of hepatitis, etc. So every species has a Master Virus: Deteriorated Image of that species).' *Naked Lunch*, p. 168.
6. *PD*, p. 67.
7. Heidegger's critical relation to Husserl does not figure prominently in *Philosophies of Difference*. In general, Husserl is assimilated to the Nietzschean model of Idealism.

8. This new method depends precisely on the difference (and its ambiguity) between *existential* and *existentiell* determinations of *Dasein*. See Martin Heidegger, *Being and Time*, p. 33.
9. Ibid., section 41.
10. Martin Heidegger, *Kant and the Problem of Metaphysics*, p. 211.
11. Ibid., p. 213.
12. Ibid., p. 239.
13. Ibid., p. 236.
14. Ibid., p. 237, in italics in the original.
15. Ibid., pp. 252–3 cited in *PD*, p. 51.
16. *PD*, p. 52.
17. *PD*, p. 37.
18. *PD*, p. 37.
19. *PD*, p. 37.
20. *PD*, p. 55.
21. *PD*, p. 55.
22. *PD*, p. 55.
23. *PD*, p. 55.
24. In the passage from metaphysical to transcendental Finitude, Laruelle proceeds more or less in accord with Reiner Schürmann, who also reads Heidegger 'backward' from the late Heidegger to *Being and Time* in order to understand the earlier work from the outset on the basis of the later elaboration and partial critique it will undergo. See Schürmann, *Heidegger on Being and Acting*, pp. 12–18.
25. *PD*, p. 55.
26. *PD*, p. 68.
27. *PD*, p. 68.
28. The most thorough analysis of this aspect of Heidegger's thought is in Dominique Janicaud, *Powers of the Rational*.
29. The figure of Nietzsche is crucial in setting this internal/external limit for Heidegger. See, for instance, Martin Heidegger, *What is Called Thinking?*, Lecture V, pp. 48–56.
30. *PD*, p. 169.
31. *PD*, p. 169.
32. *PD*, p. 169.
33. *PD*, p. 79.
34. *PD*, pp. 79–80.
35. *PD*, p. 80.
36. See the discussion of the *Kehre* in Laurence Paul Hemming, *Heidegger's Atheism: The Refusal of a Theological Voice*, chs. 3 and 4, especially pp. 87–101.
37. Schürmann's reading of Heidegger in *Heidegger on Being and Acting* uses a methodological reversal of the *ordering* of the early and late Heidegger as a basis for interpreting Heidegger. Besides this, Laruelle's interpretation of Heidegger is in line with Schürmann's on at least the following two points: (1) emphasising the unity and continuity of Heidegger's thought even while

113

taking the Turn as one of its central aspects, and (2) placing the problem of the One at the core of Heidegger's project.

38. Martin Heidegger, 'On the Essence of Truth' in *Basic Writings*, pp. 115–38.
39. Martin Heidegger, *Contributions to Philosophy*, pp. 67–8.
40. Ibid.
41. Ibid.
42. Ibid.
43. Ibid.
44. Cited in Martin Heidegger, *Nietzsche,* vol. II, p. 219.
45. Nietzsche, *Thus Spoke Zarathustra*, 'On the Tarantulas' in *The Portable Nietzsche*, p. 211.
46. Martin Heidegger, *Nietzsche,* vol. II, p. 223.
47. Ibid., pp. 220, 223.
48. Ibid., pp. 224–5.
49. Ibid.
50. Ibid. p. 226.
51. Graham Harman has taken the Heideggerean fourfold as the structural basis for his interesting contemporary ontology in *The Quadruple Object*.
52. For an analysis of the status of the relation between Being and Man in Heidegger's thought, see Michel Haar, *Heidegger and the Essence of Man*, especially chs. 2–4.
53. *PD*, pp. 56–7.
54. *PD*, p. 58.
55. *PD*, p. 69.
56. From Boethius to Pico della Mirandola to Badiou.
57. *PD*, pp. 68–9.
58. *PD*, p. 69.
59. *PD*, pp. 169–70.

5

The Derridean model of Difference:
Differance

Alarming and calming. Sacred and accursed. The conjunction, the *coincidentia oppositorum*, ceaselessly undoes itself in the passage to decision or crisis.
Derrida, 'The Pharmakos' in Dissemination

DIFFERENCE AS DIFFERANCE: GREEK LOGOS/JUDAIC OTHER

Laruelle opens his chapter on Derrida with a quintessentially Nietzschean image, that of the tightrope-walker. Derrida is characterised by Laruelle as being perhaps the most trenchant critic of the Western decision for logocentrism and metaphysics, while nonetheless reinstating that decision despite himself, being unable 'to take the final step':

> Derrida is the thinker who carries philosophical decision to the limit of apo-retic dislocation pure and simple and who yet, through *the virtuosity of the endangered tightrope-walker*, undertakes to seize decision again one last time and to maintain its possibility and truth, refusing to take the final step.[1]

Laruelle appears here to bring to bear against Derrida the same form of criticism that Derrida himself brings to bear against Heidegger in particular, namely that despite his critical acumen, he remains bound within the limits and presuppositions of the tradition he aims to critique. According to this conception, Derrida's deconstruction of metaphysics and logocentrism would be *still* metaphysical, *still* logocentric. Such a characterisation of Laruelle's critique of Derrida is correct within certain limits but needs to be carefully qualified: Laruelle is not simply accusing Derrida of falling into contradiction or of succumbing to the object of his own critique. Above all, Laruelle is *not* claiming that Derrida or Derridean philosophy

115

remains unaware of the situation. If anything, deconstruction is understood to be hyper-aware of its capacity to apply itself to itself, to undergo and withstand its intrinsic self-inhibition. In this regard, Laruelle insists on the philosophical lucidity with which Derrida pursues his deconstructive project. For Laruelle, Derrida *succeeds* at demonstrating consistently (in a strictly performative and no longer directly representational or logocentric way) that philosophy fails finally to ground itself in anything other than the play of *differance*. Most but not all Anglophone reception of Derrida has left *différance* untranslated and therefore includes the French accent on the 'e'. The present text follows the practice of the English translation of *PD* in rendering this key term as 'difference' and distinguishing between 'Differance' as the name of the Derridean model of Difference and 'differance' as the particular concept as it functions in Derrida's work (see *PD*, p. 151, note 1).

What Laruelle will ultimately challenge is the status and range of the very milieu of Derrida's demonstration, the generalised field of thinking in which philosophy is at once defined with respect to its Other(s) and conceived through its resistance to such Other(s). Is what is true specifically of philosophy in the context of this extended field valid for all thinking as such? Is the power and corrosion of deconstruction truly universal? If so, through what (deconstructed/deconstructible) reason? Is there a real Other to and for deconstruction? Can there be a real critique of philosophy that is *other than* deconstructive? Laruelle means to grant to deconstruction everything it wishes to claim of itself. In fact, the maximal coherence and rigour of Derrida's project will be posited by Laruelle from the outset, at least as an initial hypothesis. It will be by taking the deconstructive project seriously as perhaps the ultimate coherent projection of Difference that Laruelle will stitch this third model (Differance) into relation with the previous two (Idealist Difference and Finitude) and thereby bring into relief the most general framework of philosophical Difference all the more clearly.

In effect, in chapter five of *Philosophies of Difference* Laruelle structures his analysis of Derrida within two separate intersecting dualities: on the one hand, within the philosophical opposition of Nietzschean Idealism and Heideggerean Finitude that governs the book as a whole; and on the other hand, within the classical Western opposition born especially from Pauline Christianity and the early Church Fathers between 'Athens' and 'Jerusalem'. Laruelle will take up this latter traditional Western *topos* in terms of the opposition of 'Greek *logos*' and 'Judaic Other'. These two dichotomies, the one a distinctive problematic for contemporary philosophy, the other a long-standing and controversial schema for charting the intellectual and spiritual destinies of 'Europe' and the 'West', intersect and subdivide one another in Laruelle's analysis. The Nietzsche/Heidegger difference crossed by the Greek/Judaic difference – a potent fourfold for the sheltering of deconstruction.

Before engaging these two primary axes of Laruelle's interpretation in detail, it is worth reiterating the broad principle of hermeneutic generosity under which Laruelle's overall critique of Difference alone makes sense. Although Derrida is characterised as failing 'to take the final step', this is not at all because deconstruction would somehow be intellectually deficient or would have failed to understand what it itself is doing. Laruelle is vehemently opposed to what he refers to as the 'Samaritan poison' of a philosophical hermeneutics that would advance by way of claiming 'see how I know the author better than he himself'.[2] Laruelle presumes that the only philosophers worth engaging seriously are those whose thought is rich and robust enough to withstand and throw into insignificance any criticisms of the type 'Look, I found a contradiction!' The philosophers who matter are those who have, if not accomplished fully the tasks they have set themselves, at least provided sufficient indications of a task and means that are worthy of consideration in their own right. The only interesting critiques on this basis are those which take a relatively *successful* philosophical project as their object. This is especially true of the 'philosophers of Difference' since they are understood from the outset to be engaged with the post-Kantian and post-Hegelian problematic of *excessive* difference and a vision of the Real as untotalisable, non-systematic and ungraspable by both representation and reason. If this is true of both Nietzsche and Heidegger, it is valid *a fortiori* for Derrida and deconstruction.

Alluding to Kant's distinction in the first Critique between a transcendental analytic and a transcendental dialectic, Laruelle begins his study of Derrida by claiming that although it 'is fitted into the analytic of Difference', it might equally have been 'placed . . . in the critique or dialectic of Difference'.[3] This claim provides insights into both the overall structure of *Philosophies of Difference* and the specific role played by Derrida in it. In Kant, the transcendental analytic sets forth the constitutive structures of experience as the coordination of the pure manifold given to sensibility with the concepts of the understanding as synthesised and regulated by the categories to organise a unified world of unified objects. It outlines the inner mechanism and correct functioning of the human thought-experience machine. The transcendental dialectic, on the other hand, traces the built-in overreach of this machine, its intrinsic tendency to exceed its proper limits and to take the regulative principles or Ideas of Reason as corresponding to possible objects of experience.[4] The core of Kant's transcendental dialectic is the critical analysis of the antinomies, the separate and mutually exclusive claims that reason is led nonetheless equally to affirm, for example: the universe is finite/the universe is infinite.[5]

By situating Derrida at once in the 'analytic' and the 'critique or dialectic' of Difference, Laruelle puts Derrida in an intermediately critical position with respect to Difference. This becomes important since the distinction then between Laruelle's own critical 'position' and the deconstructive critique of Difference will effectively determine the relation of non-philosophy to Difference. Derrida is in this respect both inside and outside the 'structure' of Difference. As 'inside', Derrida represents a third model relative to those of Nietzsche-Deleuze and Heidegger. As 'outside', Derrida fully completes Difference and by taking it all the way past its limits, all the way to its Other, reveals perhaps a different sort of limit. As Laruelle puts it, on the one hand Derrida 'carries philosophical decision to the limit of aporetic dislocation pure and simple', yet on the other hand it must be '[kept] . . . well in mind' that *'the self-dislocation of philosophical decision is at the same time its becoming-unitary, its self-ensnarement, its intrinsic self-inhibition – its paralysis'*.[6]

Laruelle's analysis orients itself in the densely structured terrain of Derrida's work by treating the general problem of 'writing' in Derrida's sense and his critique of logocentrism in terms of the problem of the relation or non-relation of restricted and general economies. These issues are treated together in an essentially unified way. It is clear that Derrida's distinctive account of writing and his philosophical critique of logocentrism are of a piece. In *Speech and Phenomena* Derrida had already introduced the problem of the *linguistic sign* in terms of a problematic supplementarity whose relative necessity calls into question the possibility of the self-presence of conscious meaning. Every crisis of meaning thus becomes grounded or caught up in the problem of the graphic, material supplement: 'The moment of crisis is always the moment of signs.'[7] In his early work, this critique of presence on the basis of the sign is brought to bear especially against Husserlian phenomenology, but it is also extended to Heidegger and many others.

Throughout these studies, Derrida's theoretical framework for thinking the process of signification is heavily indebted to Saussure and structuralist linguistics. Despite Derrida's own critiques of Saussure, the dyadic relation of signifier-signified remains the basic structure within which deconstruction everywhere develops. Above all, deconstruction will critique the dichotomy of the signifier-signified relation by demonstrating in various ways how the difference between signifier and signified within the sign is always problematised especially on the side of the signified, since the signified never rests in-itself in self-presence but can only be what it is by being for-another, that is, by serving as a signifier for another signified. Contrary to what some interpreters of Derrida assert, Laruelle will argue that there is nothing intrinsically apophatic in Derrida's account at this level that would intrinsically resist formalisation and require 'literary' sophistication or obscurity. We will see further on how this claim emerges, namely by inscribing the otherwise straightforward critique of logocentrism and the signifier–signified relation within the self-enfolding immanent logic of Difference.

More generally, Derrida's critical writings depend upon a distinction between restricted and general economies. These are terms that Derrida himself takes over from Bataille and which he examines explicitly in several places, while the implicit logic of their difference is at work in all his texts. The distinction is roughly that of the difference between closed and open systems in physics: a restricted economy is always in some sense an exchange economy, a system oriented ultimately toward equilibrium or stasis; whereas a general economy involves a unilateral giving or destruction that exceeds all possibility of equality and exchange.[8] This difference between forms of economy serves as a basic framework for Derrida's engagement with the broad questions of philosophical sense and signification. In this respect, along with the distinction between general and restricted economies Derrida takes over from Bataille a certain *impossible mission* within the restricted economy of philosophical discourse: 'how, after having exhausted the discourse of philosophy, can one inscribe in the lexicon and syntax of a language, our language, which was also the language of philosophy, that which nevertheless exceeds the oppositions of concepts governed by this communal logic?'[9] How can restricted means produce unilateral or unexchangeable ends?

On the one hand, the very possibility of such an unrecuperable gift or loss sets an absolute limit to philosophical closure. Derrida writes:

> The blind spot of Hegelianism, *around* which can be organized the represen-tation of meaning, is the *point* at which destruction, suppression, death and sacrifice constitute so irreversible an expenditure, so radical a negativity – here we would have to say an expenditure and a negativity *without reserve* – that they can no longer be determined as negativity in a process or a system.[10]

Yet Derrida maintains that such destructive expenditure, such unreserved negativity, must nevertheless be expressed: 'But we must speak . . . We must find a speech which maintains silence. Necessity of the impossible: to say in language – the language of servility – that which is not servile.'[11] If the means of language are essentially servile, that is, reducible to a restricted economy, language may nonetheless be put to an alternate, per-verse use that opens onto the excessive difference of general economy. Like the Nietzsche/Hegel difference we saw earlier in the context of Deleuze and Klossowski, Derrida takes Bataille/Hegel as the concrete instantiation of this problem:

> Pushing itself toward the nonbasis of negativity and of expenditure, the [Bataillean] experience of the *continuum* is also the experience of absolute

difference, of a difference which would no longer be the one that Hegel had conceived more profoundly than anyone else: the difference in the service of presence, at work for (the) history (of meaning). The difference between Hegel and Bataille is the difference between these two differences.[12]

In this way, Derrida clearly foregrounds the very problem that Laruelle addresses under the heading of Difference. Laruelle will aim to clarify how Derrida's own thought stands with respect to this problem. Although Laruelle's reading of Derrida is meant in this respect to engage Derrida's thought as a whole and indeed to attain the very essence of Deconstruction (to whatever extent this latter exceeds Derrida's own work), Laruelle relies on only two interviews as the textual basis of his argument: 'Between Brackets I' and '*Ja*, or the *faux-bond* II'. Laruelle himself describes this pair of interviews as 'among Derrida's most apparently "theoretical"', suggesting that what is at stake is a theoretical overview or extraction of an essential 'kernel' of deconstruction.[13] Defenders of Derrida will no doubt cry foul at such apparent laxity – is it not Derrida more than any other contemporary thinker who has demonstrated the irreducibility of textual dissemination to abstract condensation or 'summary' that would not involve irrecuperable loss? This is one point where the broadly 'economical' problem of deconstruction's self-presentation and self-conception necessarily emerges. Certainly, any mode of inquiry that has already accepted Derrida's views and internalised his methods will approach Derrida's works in terms of fine-grained textual analysis and the need for a virtuosic reading/writing. But what Laruelle wants especially to call into question is whether a non-trivialising reading of Derrida is possible without necessarily 'ensnaring' oneself in Derrida's own deconstructive practices.[14] Laruelle in effect aims to mount a transcendental analysis of the conditions of possibility of such a non-deconstructive reading of deconstruction.

As oriented toward this end, Laruelle justifies the choice to ground his analysis in only two Derridean texts – and interviews at that – on the basis of the fact that these interviews represent Derrida's own clearest reflections on deconstruction itself as an explicit theme.[15] Laruelle's reading of deconstruction focuses on the uniquely determined *self-relation* of explicitly deconstructive texts and practices. How does deconstruction necessarily stand *with respect to itself*? Even a passing familiarity with Derrida's work will ensure that any such deconstructive self-relation will have to be highly qualified as 'broken', 'non-self-identical', 'differential' and so forth. But it can hardly be denied that deconstruction relates to itself, particularly when it thematises itself. What is at stake between Derrida and Laruelle is whether or to what extent this deconstructive self-relation may be adequately grasped from a theoretical standpoint that would not itself be subject to deconstruction. On deconstruction's own terms, to be subject to deconstruction is to be both positively and negatively conditioned by *différance*, to be always already deconstructive/deconstructed. Without presupposing the correctness of this deconstructive self-interpretation, Laruelle in effect asks: is there a non-deconstructive (for instance, scientific and/or transcendental) mode of access to deconstruction?

A provisional framework for examining Laruelle's reading of Derrida is provided by the following pair of conditional hypotheses:

1) If deconstruction has an 'essence' or 'kernel', then this latter will be most clearly evident in deconstruction's relation to itself (however complex, differential, aporetic, etc., this relation may be).

2) If there exists a theoretically adequate standpoint with respect to deconstruction, then such a standpoint will be distinguished first and foremost through its capacity to relate to deconstruction without thereby reproducing deconstruction's own distinctive self-relation (as specified in (1)).

The first hypothesis is motivated by the insight that although internal/external and self/other differences are both thematised and problematised everywhere deconstruction is at work, these differences are themselves necessarily intensified and re-doubled wherever deconstruction manifestly refers to itself. The second hypothesis is more 'structural'. It depends upon the notion that relations are generally more abstract and translatable than the objects or terms they relate and that, understood as properties, they are more readily marked and theorised. These hypotheses are not fully independent but – as inspection makes clear – the second depends upon the first. Yet this dependence is not simply formal and immediate, but rather builds in additional assumptions and requires additional arguments. Ultimately, Laruelle will want to argue that the second hypothesis does not merely depend upon the first but in fact follows from it. For this reason we should at least indicate as a third (meta-)conditional:

3) $(1) \rightarrow (2)$

This (meta-)hypothesis marks the turning-point in Laruelle's own argument from deconstructive Difference to non-philosophical thinking in–One. Laruelle's specific argument with respect to Derrida is in this way analogous in structure to the overall argument of *Philosophies of Difference* with respect to Difference. At the broadest level, Laruelle asks, is there a science of philosophy as Difference? With respect to Derrida, Laruelle asks, is there a science of deconstruction? The latter question may appear ambiguous: on the one hand it suggests deconstruction *as* science, on the other hand deconstruction as the object *of* a science. Laruelle will aim to clearly separate these two senses. In any case, this question is not external to deconstruction. The early book for which Derrida is perhaps still best known, *Of Grammatology*, orients itself in particular with respect to the question of a possible science of writing, a question that continues to govern Derrida's later work.[16]

Laruelle explains his own argumentative strategy in terms of a twofold movement: (a) from deconstruction to its 'condition of possibility or . . . Greco-occidental *a priori*' and, inversely, (b) 'a Transcendental Deduction of Deconstruction' that would 'derive Deconstruction from Difference'.[17] In other words, there is a (reductive) passage from Differance to Difference on the one hand, and its inverse counterpart, a (genetic or productive) passage from Difference to Differance on the other. The point of this twofold analysis is precisely to demonstrate the way that Derrida may be considered a model of Difference. By including Derrida within Difference, Laruelle will then be able to distinguish his own proposal of non-philosophy from deconstruction and thereby organise a science of the latter. Indeed, it is arguably *only* by distinguishing non-philosophy from Derrida's philosophy in this way that non-philosophy can itself be adequately clarified.

In service of this end, Laruelle introduces yet another distinction into his critical framework. Both the Nietzsche/Heidegger distinction and the Greek/Judaic distinction are inflected or re-doubled or crossed by a basic problematic of the relative and the absolute which Laruelle puts at the very centre of his reading of Derrida. Laruelle describes deconstruction as in this way taking 'the form of a double discourse', and he summarises the essential character of these two discourses in terms of two 'theses' that deconstruction poses with respect to itself and its own functioning:

A) 'a thesis of weakness, of relativitiy, of limited calculation, of micro-economic and tempered vigilance' (restricted economy of deconstruction).

B) 'the insistent thesis, never abandoned, of an effect of absolute difference, of a point of irretrievable loss, of a collapse from which one never recovers, of an incalculable which *still must* finish by being absolute' (general economy of deconstruction).[18]

These two theses are characterised by Laruelle as two 'structural moments' of Deconstruction: on the one hand, a reduction of Differance to the relative continuity of Difference; on the other, 'the requirement of a truly absolute cut-point, of an effect of differance absolutely without return'.[19] It is not Laruelle's intention to examine these two theses independently, since in accordance with their differential and chiasmic intertwining 'it is impossible to separate' them.[20] Instead, what matters for Laruelle's reading of Derrida is to grasp as precisely as possible how their inseparability is maintained both in principle and in fact. Since much of Derrida's work, especially his generalisation of the problem of writing in terms of the structure/non-structure of necessary supplementation, works against the clear distinction between fact and principle, the problem is muddied from the very outset.

Laruelle specifies: 'Their relation alone, the relation of this relativity and this absoluteness of Difference is our object, the delicate point perhaps where Deconstruction itself becomes symptomatic in its turn and must be analysed.'[21] Derrida himself has of course thematised not only his own work, but also the way his work thematises itself (which is not exactly the same thing). At one point he emphasises the difficulty of commenting on his own writings since, as he puts is, 'these texts explain themselves' (a claim that is precisely *not* that of an immediate self-evidence) and further-more 'they explain themselves on the necessity of this gap by which each of them is already placed in relation to itself'.[22]

The key point, again, is that Laruelle's entire analysis is predicated upon conceiving Derrida's enterprise as a coherent one. Somewhat as Kant takes the coherence of Newtonian scientific physics for granted and poses the problem of its conditions of possibility, Laruelle will aim to establish the transcendental conditions (although in a Deleuzean spirit, these would be conditions of reality rather than possibility) of the coherence of Deconstruction. It is important to note, however, that at least in Laruelle's view, this represents a viewpoint other than that which Derrida takes upon himself:

> Apparently, in effect, Deconstruction does not have at its disposal the minimum of internal unity necessary to the coherence of any philosophical project. *Except if, proceeding otherwise, and with the aim of extracting the kernel of real unity, of indivision that renders it autonomous and viable,* one observes that the repulsive and inhibitory alterity, the experience of the cut as absolute is not simply juxtaposed to logocentric immanence, which would be at once absolutely dissolved as such . . ., *but obtained from immanence and through a process of inversion.*[23]

This passage is crucial. What it implies – and this is already an antici-pation of both the method and the conclusion that we will track in what follows – is that on the one hand Derridean Differance is essentially nothing other than Nietzschean immanent Difference; yet on the other hand the 'Otherness effect' Differance continually produces does in fact distinguish it from *both* the Nietzschean and the Heideggerean models we have already examined. This apparent paradox will be resolved by analys-ing Derrida's recourse to the specific operation of 'inversion' that Laruelle insists upon as the unique way deconstruction relates to itself. On its own terms, according to Laruelle, this self-relation breaks with the immanence of Difference through its characteristically intermittent reference to an absolute transcendence or Other. But in Laruelle's view, this recourse to transcendence conceived as an iterated 'break' or 'cut' of the Other within Difference in fact only turns Difference upside down via a purely arbitrary decision, not a real necessity, and thus preserves its syntactical structure even as it alters its manifest philosophical sense. In this way, Derridean Differance as read by Laruelle represents a maximum of the polar opposition of Difference to its own contrary (its 'inversion') that would still be, nonetheless, 'of' or 'within' (that is, structured by) Difference. For Laruelle, the necessity of using such a logic of immanent Difference even to trace the Other from within Difference marks the point at which both the possibility and need for a non-deconstructive analysis of deconstruction are most clearly evident. In order to isolate this 'kernel of real unity' in deconstruction, Laruelle will superimpose two general analytical dichotomies onto the relatively 'restricted' problems of deconstruction's self-interpretation and its explicit/implicit self-relation: Nietzschean Difference/Heideggerean Finitude and Greek *logos*/Judaic Other. The real basis for the non-deconstructive analysis – thinking in-One – will only be fully clarified in Laruelle's final chapter.

DERRIDA BETWEEN NIETZSCHE AND HEIDEGGER

In the 'Instructions for Use', Laruelle sketches his reading of Derrida in terms of how he may be placed with respect to both Nietzsche and Heidegger:

> Derrida is . . . distinguished both from Nietzsche and from Heidegger; he takes over as it were their milieu, borrowing from the former not only the schema or invariant syntax of Difference, but an 'idealist' primacy of the syntax of Difference over its reality; and from the latter the concern for Finitude, which is to say, for an anti-idealist limitation of the primacy of syntax over the real.[24]

In other words, Derrida's philosophy is understood by Laruelle as a complex mixture of Nietzschean and Heideggerean models that is reducible to neither one taken in isolation. Alongside Nietzschean Idealism, Derrida is understood to side with the essentially syntactical or semiotic conception of Being as reversible Difference; yet in accordance with Heideggerean Finitude, Derrida is thought to limit the reach of syntax and to inhibit its claim to grasp the whole. How can this 'playing both sides' be intelligibly understood?

The first stage of Laruelle's analysis of Derrida aims to conceive Derridean Differance as being a variant of Nietzschean Difference. In other words, despite the vigilance with which deconstruction guards itself against metaphysics and seems to restrict itself to a relatively negative, critical function with respect to philosophy, Laruelle will aim to show that deconstruction depends in fact on a positive Nietzschean immanence that is, as we saw earlier, best conceived as a differential Idealism, an identity of philosophical syntax and reality. This result will be especially surprising because of Derrida's seemingly Kantian and Heideggerean emphases on finitude and mortality.[25] The 'reduction' of deconstruction to Difference bears primarily on the Nietzschean ideal infinitude that potentialises Will to Power in and as Eternal Return and thereby forecloses irreducible negativity and real transcendence. Rather than a Heideggerean Finite Real, Derrida on Laruelle's reading only dissimulates such a finitude through an inversion of and not a real cut into the logic of Difference. Thus the finitude in question is ultimately no more than a complex effect of ideal syntax. According to Laruelle, the ultimate schema within which *differance* must be thought is thus Difference and not Finitude, despite an undeniable Heidegger-effect in the textual operations and *pathos* of deconstruction.

As with his engagement of Nietzsche, Laruelle's reading of Derridean deconstruction in *Philosophies of Difference* builds upon a complex engagement in his earlier work carried out across the four closely interconnected books of Philosophy I. We saw already in the analysis of Laruelle's reading of Nietzsche how *Nietzsche contra Heidegger* and *Beyond the Power Principle* together develop a theory of 'machinic materialism' and its correlative 'general hermeneutics'. This problematic serves equally as the focus for his two other main books from Philosophy I, *Textual Machines* and *The Decline of Writing*, both of which engage Derrida directly. In *Textual Machines* Laruelle had already developed his argument that would reduce deconstruction to Nietzschean Difference at some length.

The key point in this early work is to take the Derridean deconstruction of the signifier-signified relation as paradigmatic and to show that the work or effect of deconstruction depends upon the transcendental selection of a potentialised, positively differential sign that infinitises itself in precisely the way Nietzsche needs and posits the Eternal Return of the Same. Laruelle makes this point by showing how, whatever the status of the deconstruction of the signifier-signified relation *in general*, any such operation or event of deconstruction requires an *a priori* potentialisation of the *particular* sign 'sign' itself. Of course, this function may in fact be varied across indefinitely many terms: 'text', 'interpretation', 'signification', '*logos*', 'effect', etc. But the *kind* of terms that are included in this sequence is transcendentally determined and not arbitrary.

Laruelle's point is that the very possibility of deconstruction as an intra-textual event that may be thematised, inhibited, intensified and so forth – in other words, recognised and operated as such – requires the *a priori* selection of a privileged class of terms of this type whose redoubled structure necessarily takes the form of Nietzschean Idealist Difference.

This is not merely a contingent claim about Derrida's idiosyncratic discourse, according to Laruelle, but a transcendental condition for the possibility of anything like deconstruction whatsoever. The deconstruction of signification and signs depends upon a structure of Ideal Difference that regulates the form and meaning of such unavoidable terms as 'the sign "sign"', the 'effect of "effect"' or the 'signification of "signification"'. In *Textual Machines*, Laruelle uses this point to argue for the necessity of a 're-inscription' of the primary textual operators of deconstruction ('sign', 'text', 'signifier', etc.) within the context of a-signifying and a-textual 'desiring-machines'. These latter can only be thought on a Nietzschean and Deleuzean terrain of metaphysical immanence that would be strictly prior to any textuality or signification. They would thus constitute 'an economy or a *transcendental body of writing* as general repetition' that cannot itself be subject to deconstruction.[26]

Laruelle's point may become clearer if we configure it with respect to Hägglund's recent comprehensive reading of Derrida, *Radical Atheism*. Hägglund's *Radical Atheism* offers in several respects a corroboration of Laruelle's account of Derrida, although from a more sympathetic standpoint. Like Laruelle, Hägglund emphasises the systematic unity of Derrida's philosophy. Also like Laruelle, Hägglund locates the unifying principle of Derrida's thought in a certain dialectic of the finite and infinite. For Hägglund, Derrida's definition of *différance* as 'the becoming–space of time and the becoming–time of space' becomes in a sense the canonical Derridean utterance. It serves to ground a view of 'infinite finitude' on the one hand and a philosophy of life as 'the unconditional affirmation of survival' on the other.[27] Hägglund's reading of Derrida depends heavily on the logic of auto-immunity that comes to the fore in Derrida's later work. Hägglund rightly sees this as a rigorously determined structure according to which Derrida's earlier work may be clearly understood. According to the logic of auto-immunity, identity as such can only be determined through its 'contamination' by the other in the very act of endurance or 'survival'. Temporality thus becomes the unsurpassable condition for any being or manifestation whatsoever and the non–self–coincidence of time guarantees that the very act of survival for *any* being will inevitably depend upon an openness to otherness and destruction (the structure of 'hospitality' denuded of its voluntaristic and ethical trappings) that determines that being itself.

Laruelle's point becomes clear when we examine the status of the terms 'ideal purity' and 'contamination' in Hägglund's own analysis. Hägglund is clear that 'deconstruction spells out that there can be no final cure against contamination and that all ideals of purity are untenable, since their "refusal" of contamination equals nothing but death'.[28] Against the quasi-Kantian readings of Derrida that would treat his referrals to 'pure gift' and 'absolute hospitality' as functions on analogy with Kantian regulative Ideas, Hägglund insists that 'contamination is not a privation or a lack of purity – it is the originary possibility for anything to be'.[29] Hägglund argues that, rather than an ideal 'pure gift' that finite worldly gifts might approach as an asymptote, Derrida 'demonstrates why the gift *even in its ideal purity* must be contaminated and why a pure gift is neither thinkable nor desirable as such'.[30] In effect, the basis of Laruelle's analysis asks us to question the status of such terms as 'pure' and 'contamination' in Hägglund's own reconstruction of Derrida. If the unconditional contamination of all purity is the ultimate, unsurpassable horizon for all thinking, how can this contamination itself be thought?[31] Rigorously, there must be a reinsertion of this very difference (purity/contamination) within each of the terms that define the difference. In other words, the canonical structure of Difference as (meta-)Difference reigns as the transcendental condition for Derrida's own transcendental auto-immunity. But this in turn means that what Laruelle has analysed as the Nietzschean immanence of syntax and reality, Idealist Difference, is indeed the structuring principle of Derridean deconstruction through *différance*, trace, arche-writing, auto-immunity and so on.

We pass then to the second stage of Laruelle's analysis. This second stage moves in the opposite direction. It aims to reconstruct Difference from within Difference, to show the mechanism whereby an illusory effect of real Finitude may be produced from within the essentially Nietzschean syntax of ideal, reversible contraries. The point of contention here is first of all Derrida's relation to Heidegger. Laruelle notes: 'In Derrida finitude is an ideal effect of syntax, whereas in Heidegger it is the irreducible transcendence of the real (of the ontic and the One) relative to the syntax (that folds Being and beings).'[32] What does this signify? If in Heidegger the infinitude and reversibility of syntax is delimited and inhibited by an irreducible kernel of the ontic pole of the ontic/ontological difference, in Derrida this delimitation and inhibition are internalised to the syntax of the difference itself. Thus in Derrida, a specific mixture of Nietzsche and Heidegger is concocted as the interiorisation of the Heideggerean 'exterior' of finitude into the play of idealist syntactical or textual differences: a Finite Idealism.

It is crucial to stress the paradoxical nature of this Nietzsche-Heidegger hybrid. For Laruelle, Derrida's thought does not represent a synthesis or reconciliation of Ideal and Finite Difference. Nor, however, does it place these two models of Difference into some new, higher-order dialectical relationship, even one that would be non-synthetic. If according to Laruelle the One is introduced by Heideggerean Finitude into Difference in the mode of an absolute withdrawal prior to Being, the One functions in Derrida within Difference as an absolute cut of the Other, the indivision of a pure non-relation. We might very well ask, the non-relation of *what exactly*? To which the answer is: of 'itself'. In other words, the basic structure of Difference is, in Derrida, assigned to a gap or hiatus in itself that is no longer developed from one pole or side of a less sophisticated (empirical or metaphysical) difference, but is rather the non-relational 'side' of their very discontinuity. Derrida in effect purifies and differentiates the *cut* that is always presupposed by any relation (the difference between the two terms as abstracted from all connection or relation) but which cannot be conceived as an aspect or component of that relation as such.[33] For Laruelle, this assignment of Difference to the cut itself represents a philosophical maximisation of the critical efficacy of Difference with respect to philosophy (and thus equally with respect to itself). This is why Derrida will be placed as much in the 'critique or dialectic' of Difference as in its 'analytic', according to Laruelle.

Thus the Heideggerean role of the Finite transcendence of the ontic 'side' of ontological difference, a transcendence which is Real = One and therefore no longer comprehensible from within the correlation of Being and beings, is in Derrida played by an auto-indexical character of deconstruction and – via generalisation – of all textual difference. This self-indexing may be more or less explicit, but it is always present. In Derrida's own words, as he reflects on his writings up to 1975:

> several of these books, *Glas* or *Dissemination* for example, *explicitly* open onto the concrete question of the *this, here-now*. All of them do so *implicitly*. They do not ask the question; they stage it or overflow this stage in the direction of that element of the scene which exceeds representation.[34]

We have had reason at a number of points to highlight the Nietzsche/Heidegger difference as one of the guiding threads for understanding Laruelle's early work (Philosophy I) as well as the decisive shift to non-philosophy (Philosophy II) of which *Philosophies of Difference* marks an important step. On the one hand, Laruelle reads Derrida as a site of this conflict itself. Derrida's text is, from this point of view, a theoretical and performative amphibology of Nietzsche and Heidegger. Somewhat akin to Luther's Protestant Christian formula *simul iustus et peccator* (at once justified and a sinner), Derrida would be in a philosophical mode *simul* Heideggerean *et* Nietzschean, at once Finite *and* Ideal. This reading is then internally complicated by the fact that it is crossed with a second *simul* . . . *et* . . ., in this case the heavily freighted dichotomy of Greek and Jew. Laruelle's reading puts both of these amphibologies as well as their intersection and mutual overwriting at the heart of Derrida's project.

We might imagine as a kind of thought experiment an attempt by Laruelle to write *Philosophies of Difference* without the inclusion of Derrida; non-philosophy would be presented as a radical alternative to the endless squabble between Nietzschean and Heideggerean modes of philosophy, or more generally between varieties of Idealism and Realism. The risk run by such an argument would be that it would seem by its very form to repeat one of the characteristic gestures of philosophy: to conquer by dividing. 'Neither Nietzsche nor Heidegger' already replicates the basic structure of philosophical Difference, which according to Laruelle is never a simple dualism but always opens up the possibility of a non-dialectical 'third'.

This thought experiment may help us to see the role Derrida plays in the overall argument of *Philosophies of Difference*. In one sense, the two models of Nietzsche-Deleuzean Idealist Difference and Heideggerean Finitude should be sufficient on their own to lay out the field of immanent possibilities – or rather, decisions – available to Difference, in relation to which non-philosophy is meant to offer a theoretical generalisation and real alternative. But in that case an essential ambiguity would still remain: the contrast between two models and all the binary oppositions such a contrast would entail (syntax/reality, reversibility/irreversibility, idealism/finitude, etc.) would appear to suggest the possibility of resolution through the still-philosophical logic of the 'third way' or 'critical' compromise. Derridean deconstruction plays the role in Laruelle's actual text of precisely such a compromise or hybridisation of the two previous models, a complex hybridisation that is neither a synthesis nor a reconciliation, however, because of its unique and essential moment of 'inversion'. By contrasting his own non-philosophical theory of Difference not only with the philosophies of Nietzsche and Heidegger *but also* with that of Derrida, Laruelle thus prevents a potential misinterpretation of his project as yet another philosophical resolution of this type.

How does Derrida stand finally with respect to the Nietzsche/Heidegger conflict? Like Heidegger, Derrida mounts a radical critique of Western metaphysics that would take into account not only the *explicit* manifestations and statements of philosophy regarding the relation of Being and beings, presence and other such key terms but also, and more important, the disavowals, blindsides and absences of those thinkers and their texts. Derrida will take this method of *Destruktion* even further than Heidegger himself, not just to the extent that he will apply it to Heidegger too (this is only a superficial layer) but especially in the way he will give it an intrinsic orientation to the infinite as both affirmation (Nietzschean Eternal Return) and absolute transcendence (Levinas). We will examine the Levinasian 'pole' in the next section, but it should be noted here by way of anticipation that the Nietzschean aspect of Derrida and his Levinasian aspect are, for

Laruelle, placed in a certain manner 'on the same side' to the extent that they are both 'opposed' to Heidegger in an essential way.

So on Laruelle's reading, the relation between Difference and Differance in Derrida mimics and repeats in its own way the differential relation between Nietzschean 'ideal' Difference and Heideggerean Finitude. But emphasis should be placed here on the phrase 'in its own way': Laruelle is by no means reducing Derrida to a mere combination of Nietzsche and Heidegger. On the contrary, Laruelle understands Derrida to represent a genuine and constructive advance within the 'philosophies of Difference'. This advance, despite its initial determination within the polarity of Nietzsche and Heidegger, occurs especially 'through the introduction of a third term – a Judaic component'.[35] This 'Judaic component' produces the effect of the 'inversion' of philosophical (Greek) immanence, in Laruelle's view, that insulates Derridean Differance from being entirely reducible to either Nietzsche or Heidegger on the one hand or to some synthesis of the two models of Idealism and Finitude on the other. It represents at once a guarantee of the relative autonomy of deconstruction and the maximum attenuation of philosophy of which philosophy itself remains capable.

DERRIDA BETWEEN THE GREEK AND THE JUDAIC

Laruelle's reading of Derrida situates deconstruction and Differance not only in relation to Nietzsche and Heidegger but also, in equal measure, to Levinas and the problem of the relation between Greco-Occidental and Judaic modes of thought. In Laruelle's reading of Derrida, there are two complementary absolutes, one immanent and 'Greek' and one transcendent and 'Judaic.' These absolutes function as virtual anchors or attractors with respect to his otherwise unconstrained discourse:

> [Derrida] attempts rigorously a particularly unstable and contradictory combination that he counterbalances *at times* through the 'Nietzschean' recourse to an ideal immanence or to Affirmation, absolute in its own way, and *at times* through a 'Judaic' claim of alterity, itself also absolute, *although in another way*, in relation to the logos.[36]

Derrida, on Laruelle's reading, capitalises on the insistent difference and strategic alignment of these two absolutes in order to guarantee the minimal intelligibility of his discourse on the one hand and to preserve that discourse, on the other hand, from being subsumed within any metaphysical or logocentric closure.

The alternating recourse to one or the other of this pair of absolutes, the one Greek, the other Judaic, 'this oscillation that is neither that of Nietzsche-Difference nor of Heidegger-Difference', structures the fragile

tissue of conditions of intelligibility for Derrida's own texts.[37] As deconstructive, these texts must possess a minimal philosophical sufficiency.
They must have enough coherence and rigour to effect their deconstructive
force. But they must not exhibit *too much* coherence or *thoroughgoing* rigour
on pains of performatively contradicting their critique of logocentrism and
restricted economy. By alternating between two principles, or rather two
absolutes that each in its own way deconstructs the very functioning of
principles, Derrida opens up a textual space within which coherence and
intelligibility themselves become iterative and pulsional, that is, manifest
primarily as *contingent effects* rather than transcendental conditions or
structural invariants.

How is the relative coherence or consistency of these two incommensurable absolutes to be guaranteed? Here, Laruelle introduces an
important element of his critique of Derrida, his insistence upon the total
incommensurability of Greek and Judaic modes of thought. For Laruelle
there cannot be any mediation of the one by the other or the other into the
one without thereby dissolving both of them entirely. The sole recourse
of the Derridean text, then, for Laruelle, in the face of this incommensurability is to that text's own contingent functioning, *its own singular act or
practice* of adjoining Greek and Judaic elements without thereby bringing
them into the unity of a synthesis. On Laruelle's reading, this recourse to
'practical unity' is precisely the aspect of Derrida's discourse that both
'makes Difference stand out with more force' than other forms of 'philosophical decision' *and* highlights to what extent throughout philosophy
such an act of radically contingent decision 'is called or requisitioned
without being elucidated in its possibility and its reality'.[38] It is here, then,
that the intermediate position of Derrida – not between Nietzsche and
Heidegger nor between the Greek and the Judaic but between the 'analytic' and the 'dialectic' of Difference – is most evident. Precisely because
it draws the *decisional* element of philosophy prominently into view by
way of being maximally decisional (and performative) itself, Derrida's
model of Difference – Différance – is already in its own right perhaps the
most powerful immanent critique of Difference still possible from within
philosophy.

It is here that Derrida stands both in closest proximity and sharp-
est contrast with Levinas. With respect to Levinas, it should be said at
the outset that despite the harshness of his rhetoric at times, Laruelle
explicitly points to the Judaic intervention in post-Hegelian French
philosophy as one of its most important and positive developments.[39]
In this context, Derrida is taken by Laruelle to have appropriated the
Levinasian insistence on an absolutely transcendent Other irreducible
to any phenomenological, or more broadly, philosophical conditions of

intelligibility while nonetheless maintaining 'a strategic compromise with the Greco–Occidental'.[40] Derrida still belongs or at least 'co–belongs' to metaphysics. 'Yet Derrida draws a "critical" profit from this belonging, he brings it to its greatest force, revealing it all the better, the transcendence and exteriority, the intimate in–consistency of metaphysics: this is what he calls its deconstruction.'[41]

The clearest distinction with Levinas appears here. For Laruelle, whatever modification and slippage is introduced into Difference by means of the introduction of Judaic transcendence, the basic invariant structure of Difference remains intact. This is 'contrary to what happens with Levinas, whose attempt may be judged at a stroke as strictly *impossible*, really inadmissible, completely devoid of essence and condition of possibility and reposing entirely in the exteriority of a religious tradition that refuses straightaway the minimal conditions of rationality and Occidental intelligibility'.[42] This may sound like an especially sharp criticism of Levinas, but the import of this passage in Laruelle's chapter on Derrida is in fact much closer to the reverse, an affirmation of Levinas's consistency. To judge Levinasian ethics as 'strictly *impossible*, really inadmissible, completely devoid of essence and condition of possibility' is to respect the integrity of a mode of thought that claims explicitly to open itself to a 'persecution by the Other' that cannot be qualified or comprehended by either reflective experience, philosophical reason or fundamental ontology.

To go one step further and to claim that the grounds of Levinasian thought 'repos[e] entirely in the exteriority of a religious tradition' seems perhaps less warranted. It is not at all clear that just because Levinas is not working within the 'Greco–Occidental' framework of the *logos* he must therefore be simply and straightforwardly 'Judaic', unless 'Judaic' functions here as no more than an index or formal indication of 'religious exteriority' as such. The correctness of such an inference would depend upon an exclusive dichotomy (either Greek or Judaic, *tertium non datur*). But this is nowhere supported in Laruelle's text and appears *prima facie* mistaken. It seems much more adequate to Levinas's own writings (at least his non–Talmudic texts) to view them as prophetic yet non–sectarian 'cries in the wilderness'. It may be true that at a fundamental level they reject the minimal conditions of logic and rationality that structure the Western philosophical tradition as such. They do, after all, assert an ethical imperative that is not subject to any rational criteria whatsoever. It is simply an absolute call (thus without being an empirical or ontic instance of some more general structure of calling). Ultimately, Levinasian discourse takes the syntactical form of the pure imperative or command: Do not kill! Be responsible for the Other! Yet this itself does not necessarily make it Judaic, only in principle non–Greek (that is, not philosophical).

At the performative level, Levinas mounts a thoroughly *exterior* critique of Western philosophy – this is at the root of the power and importance of his thought. But that this exteriority is best labelled as 'Judaic' (rather than, say, 'religious' or 'theist' or perhaps 'Abrahamic') seems at best to have only inessential textual markers as evidence. Precisely as *theological*, the essential structure of the Levinasian Other may very well more closely resemble the conceptions of Ockham or Calvin in the Christian tradition or Muslim Hanbalites such as Ibn Taymiyya than the dominant strains of traditional Judaism. This issue is not decided in advance through Levinas's biography.

In any case, Laruelle emphasises 'Levinas's Judaic rigor' as against the Derridean mixture of the Greek and the Judaic.[43] More generally, the language of the 'Judaic' in Laruelle seems to bear at least two primary interpretations. The Judaic can signify a certain relation to the Other (evident most obviously in monotheism, but not restricted to this), or it can indicate something like a Talmudic practice, a particular form of discursivity. To be sure, these two aspects of the 'Judaic' are by no means fully independent. Nevertheless, putting one or the other at the forefront gives a specific character to Laruelle's argument. In either case, however, the Judaic is defined primarily through its difference with the 'Greek' or the 'Greco-Occidental'. This is important because it means that Laruelle's main concern is not some essentialised Judaism, but rather an essentialised dichotomy: the Judaic/Greek. This latter essentialisation certainly has problems in its own right, but the problems it gives rise to and especially the context within which those problems take on concrete significance are distinct from those of the former. Nonetheless, just to ensure that this provisional distinction – (Judaic)/(Judaic/Greek) – is not misinterpreted as a mere easy way out of a genuine problem, we should point out and indeed emphasise that on Laruelle's own terms the very logic of essentialisation must itself be conceived as part of the 'Greek' term or pole of the Judaic/Greek difference. The specific manifestation of the (meta-)Difference problem in this context is precisely the point at which Laruelle will re-inscribe Derrida within the 'Greco-Nietzschean' problematic of Difference. It is with respect to *this* point (which involves the specific (meta-)Difference twist of Differance) that Laruelle will interpret Derrida's critiques of presence and logocentrism as a singular inflection and transformation of a more general Greco-Judaic amphibology in which the Greek side always surreptitiously stacks the deck in advance. The latter, more general concept conforms to the 'metaphysical' level of this problem in Derrida and the former – Derrida's unique transmutation of this Difference into Differance – serves as this problem's 'passage to the transcendental'.

An early work of Levinas, *On Escape*, helps to contextualise. In this text, in a manner quite close to Sartre, Levinas dwells on the 'nausea' of the experience of Being. 'The experience of pure being is at the same time the experience of its internal antagonism and of the escape that foists itself on us.'[44] By the time of *Totality and Infinity*, this same question becomes for Levinas a matter of taking the Neo-Platonic problematic of the *epekeina tes ousias* and thinking it in a new way. For Levinas, the circular trap-like structure of ontology as totality is transcended not by way of escape, but through its being broken or punctured by the face of the Other. The Other's face opens a way 'beyond Being' as a strictly non-appearing (non-phenomenal) address whose ethical call for responsibility is 'heard' (and not 'seen') as a *trace* rather than as an object or even a non-objectivisable being 'in-itself'.

In his early work, Derrida resists Levinas's recourse to transcendence in the strongest possible terms.[45] Yet his career marks an increasing rapprochement with Levinas and the Levinasian Other. One of the more striking aspects of Laruelle's reading of Derrida is that it anticipates in a number of important ways the 'turn' to religious and political themes in Derrida's later work that reflects Derrida's gradual alignment with Levinas. At the time of the writing of *Philosophies of Difference*, several of what are now considered canonical works of the later Derrida had not yet appeared. In retrospect, Laruelle's reading may thus lose some of its initial force; what at the time of the publication of *Philosophies of Difference* was a highly original and provocative set of claims about the implicit reference to a religiously inspired transcendence in Derrida's theoretical writings now appears as a commonplace in Derrida scholarship. Laruelle himself claims that his reading involves 'the highlighting of an element which has hardly, perhaps never, been taken into account . . . a certain Judaic component'.[46] Scholarship on Derrida since the publication of *Philosophies of Difference* in 1986 has undoubtedly 'taken into account' the theological element in Derrida's work to an increasing degree, whether that be taken as evidence of a theism, a negative theology or an unambiguous atheism.

To be sure, the very notion that there is any such 'turn' in the later Derrida remains a matter of some dispute. The question certainly cannot be decided here. Instead, it will be useful simply to highlight Laruelle's claims about the particular relation of the 'Greek' and 'Judaic' tendencies in Derrida's thought with respect to a more recent debate about precisely this aspect of Derrida, namely the debate between John Caputo and Martin Hägglund that arose in the wake of Hägglund's *Radical Atheism*.[47]

Prior to Hägglund's systematic and provocative reading of the Derridean corpus as a thoroughgoing atheism, Caputo had constructed a theological figure of deconstruction as an expression of Derrida's own 'Jewish Augustinianism'.[48] By holding the Levinasian Other and the Augustinian self in closest proximity and yet as irreducibly distinct, Caputo had called in particular for an 'alliance' between Derrida's deconstruction and the Judeo-Christian prophetic tradition:

> The lines of this alliance are traced outside the space of cognition. For Derrida as for the prophets, what is at issue is not a cognitive delineation of some explanatory principle like a *causa prima*, not some being or essence marked off by certain predicative traits, but something, I know not what, that emerges in our prayers and tears, that evokes our prayers and provokes our tears, that seeks us out before we seek it, before we know its name, and disturbs and transforms our lives.[49]

In general, the more theologically oriented readings of Derrida such as Caputo's are able to point especially to the performative and confessional aspects of his later writings, which seem to draw Derrida outside the orbit of Hägglund's more systematic style of reading. These increasingly personal and autobiographical elements of Derrida's writing culminate in the text *Circumfession*, written as a performative response to Geoffrey Bennington's *Derridabase* with the aim of demonstrating the irreducibility of Derrida's own discourse to any anticipatory, systematic programme. This performative and singularly personal dimension of Derrida's work is not neglected by Laruelle. Indeed, Laruelle takes it to its extreme limit, recognising that a philosophical project that grounds itself upon performativity as its condition *sine qua non* and indeed its very principle of determination must ultimately sacrifice the basic conditions of intelligibility. But rather than seeing this, as does Caputo, to be evidence for a religious or quasi-religious confessional stance or like Hägglund to be further confirmation of a consistent atheism, Laruelle takes this dimension of Derrida's writings (though only partly explicit at the time of the writing of *Philosophies of Difference*) to be simply a mark of deconstruction's need to ground itself in its own contingent functioning. In this respect Laruelle himself poses the rhetorical question with respect to the unity and coherence of Derrida's project:

> To what extent does it avoid the risk of passing for heterogeneous, syncretic or inconsistent? And if it is thinkable, or let us say intelligible, neither under Greek or rather 'logocentric' conditions, nor under Jewish conditions, namely as unthinkable, to what extent is it not an enterprise that 'holds' only as a forced yoke, through the genius, that is, the violence of a single man?[50]

DECONSTRUCTION AND THE BODY-WITHOUT-WRITING

The Nietzsche/Heidegger conflict as resolved, or rather relayed, by Differance (the distinctively Derridean model of Difference) will induce a second, more contemporary dichotomy: that of Derrida/Deleuze. This difference or conflict remains mostly implicit in *Philosophies of Difference* (although Laruelle refers to it elsewhere), but it helps to clarify the crucial concept of Body-without-Writing in Laruelle's analysis of Derrida and also helps to sketch some of the details of the implicit critique of Deleuze as it structures Laruelle's overall argument.[51]

The superposed Nietzsche/Heidegger and Greek/Judaic dichotomies are not meant simply to 'situate' or 'position' Derrida, but instead to open up a radical critique of deconstruction that deconstruction's own self-relation forecloses. In the discussion so far, we have implicitly combined the two primary aspects of Laruelle's reading of Derrida: on the one hand, a particular characterisation of Derridean deconstruction (even if this is still Derrida 'in general'), and on the other, a critique of the logic of Deconstruction as a model of Difference. It is now time to carefully tease apart these two aspects, however coordinated and interconnected they may be, and to show how Laruelle's reading of Derrida performs in microcosm, as it were, the overall strategy of *Philosophies of Difference* with respect to Difference as such. To this end, we will examine in detail the concept of 'Body-without-Writing' (BWW) which Laruelle introduces as the unique blind-spot or stumbling-block of deconstruction.

Laruelle puts the relation (and non-relation) of relative and absolute tendencies of deconstruction at the heart of his analysis. His argument overall inclines to the view that to the extent that these may be understood as 'poles' generating a field operative throughout Derrida's work, it is the 'pole' of the relative that is ultimately determinative. In effect, this turns the 'absolute' side of Derrida's discourse into a merely syntactical gesture. It cannot bear the function of 'real critique' that it is called upon to perform. As Laruelle puts it early on in the chapter: 'Deconstruction is an absolute process . . . by dint of relativity; it is not absolute altogether, but relative-absolute.'[52] Laruelle insists on the possibility of clarifying precisely the structure in play. His concept of the BWW as 'a plane of dehiscence' is meant to answer to this more or less technical problem.[53]

How does the BWW allow us to understand the specific inflection of the relative/absolute difference as it appears in Derrida? Laruelle makes extensive use of the notion of the 'double-band' (DB) that Derrida develops in '*Ja*, or the *faux-bond* II'. On the one hand, Derrida wants to be able to distinguish the logic of the 'double-band' from the possibility of an 'unlimited yes' that would remain irreducible to any such logic. But on the other hand, Laruelle argues, there is no way for Derrida to insulate the 'unlimited yes' from the DB in this way. 'The work of the DB is at once "indefatigable" (interminable) and threatened with arrest (terminable); in its own way it obeys the law continuum/cut-continuum, etc., the law of the *et* (cetera). *But this law equally regulates the "unlimited yes": it is everywhere the same scene, that is, the same syntax . . .'*[54] In other words, everywhere that Derrida aims to distinguish an absolute 'moment' in and for deconstruction (such as in his recourse to a Nietzschean infinite affirmation or a Levinasian Other), he unavoidably reintroduces the finite, iterative and thoroughly relative logic of the double band. At most, then, Derrida is able to summon only 'an absolute of alterity that results from a dismemberment or an inversion of the real syntactical conditions of its immanent "production"'.[55]

What this means is that the absolute in Derrida remains at best stipulative. The relativity of textual inscription is established, and then a 'turn' to the absolute is made simply by 'inverting the syntax'. But the inversion of a syntax is still syntactical. This is the point where Heideggerean Finitude reveals its particular strength with respect to Nietzschean Idealism. Heidegger does not invert Nietzschean contraries but instead insists upon an absolute withdrawal of the original, real unity that 'gives' them to be thought. So what Derrida requires is a 'real' supplement or limit to philosophical syntax in the style of Heidegger, but one that is oriented not toward the finitude of ontic beings but instead toward a 'real infinite', that is, what Laruelle will designate as the 'Judaic Other'. The function of this 'real supplement' will be to relativise the finite syntax and to make an unlimited, iterative cut possible. Yet this supplementarity is itself functional by way of guaranteeing the relation between restricted and general economies. It is therefore still syntactical in essence. It repeats, even if in a formidably complex way, the basic structure of Difference as (meta-)Difference. Laruelle introduces the concept of the BWW in order to clarify this structural necessity that allows deconstruction to be at once (relatively) Idealist *and* Finite (in a non-Heideggerean and non-Greek mode).

Laruelle's early critical studies of Derrida from Philosophy I – particularly *Textual Machines* – approach Derrida's work from a broadly Nietzschean and Deleuzean standpoint in order to identify the structural invariants of Derrida's method of deconstruction. Proponents of Derrida will wish to object immediately (this is already an interesting symptom that must be adequately understood) that there is no such 'method', that 'deconstruction' is no more than a potentially misleading name for an intrinsically plural and untotalisable class of practices that in principle cannot be essentialised, mastered or reduced to some methodological kernel. In fact, such readers of Derrida will claim, it is precisely this resistance to any and every disciplinary closure, delimited field of experience or theory, and foundational grounding that most perfectly 'characterises' deconstruction. It seems in this way that Derrida's work cannot be made intelligible without the use of scare-quotes. Indeed, this would be both its weakness and its strength. It indefinitely and unlimitedly complicates any simple definition, dichotomy or unqualified opposition of terms. The enactment of deconstruction – for it 'exists' only *in actu* – therefore always appears to break the idealist reversibility of contraries by forcing the logic of opposition through a moment of radical undecidability. As Derrida puts it in the epigraph from *Dissemination* at the head of the present chapter, 'The conjunction, the *coincidentia oppositorum*, ceaselessly undoes itself in the passage to decision or crisis.'[56]

It is relatively easy to mount an abstract and superficial critique of Derrida along the lines just sketched. This critique would amount to something like the following: Derrida's thought works to unsettle and complicate any simple dichotomy that would function as the organising principle of a philosophical thesis, argument or text (for example: those of ideal/real, transcendental/empirical, form/content, presence/absence, affirmation/negation, writing/speech, genesis/structure, etc.). Yet this very work of complication – of the deconstruction of whatever dichotomy – inevitably introduces a new, higher-order dichotomy between *naive* and *deconstructionist* usages of dichotomous thinking. In other words, dichotomy prevails after all. Again, however, at this the proponents of Derrida will shake their heads: 'No, this misses the point entirely! Deconstruction is not an externally imposed method, but rather a latency and an actuality inherent in textuality as such.' And once again, recourse will be had to scare-quotes around the phrase 'as such' (not to mention 'deconstruction', 'latency', 'actuality' and indeed *every* term in play).

Thus the differend here takes the form of Difference. It does not cut across a single, given region (of whatever degree of concreteness or ideality) so as to split that region into two distinct parts. Instead, it subsists as a milieu *for* any such region; it produces a 'dichotomy' that cannot be stabilised or definitely identified because it always cuts against its own grain. Laruelle's reading of Derrida on this point will be of the utmost importance because it bears directly on the characteristic 'dualism' that will distinguish non-philosophy's mode of thinking in-One from the various modes of thinking structured by Difference. Rather than inhibiting Derrida's claim to radicality (deconstruction as irreducible to traditional metaphysics), it will be in Laruelle's own interest to maximise this claim and to carry it to the 'limit' that still respects deconstruction's own disavowal of fixed or ultimate limits. The radicality of deconstruction, the unsurpassability of its achievement, will serve not to ground or delimit Difference (which would invoke a straightforwardly incoherent syntax) but instead to manifest it in a *thoroughgoing* mode (rather than restricted, on the one hand, or absolute, on the other). The difference between textual objectivity and textual operation will be paramount. Deconstruction treats this difference itself as one of its primary elements of deconstructive fracture and re-inscription. In other words, deconstruction is effected through a destabilisation of this difference as a fixed structure.

Laruelle's reading of Derrida in *Textual Machines* depends heavily on this point. As remarked above, Laruelle emphasises the non-arbitrary nature of the textual 'operators' that are selected to serve as the privileged instruments of deconstruction. Certain terms or 'marks' must necessarily serve a redoubled or 're-inscribed' function that draws upon a fundamentally Nietzschean (and Deleuzean) metaphysics of immanence and repetition that is prior to textuality and signification. Laruelle writes:

> The marks are put in play in a sort of parody of themselves, identifying themselves yet in an identity of the indefinite simulacrum, open and always destabilized [déséquilibrée], with significations that make a chain and network, but not a saturated system. This comedy and mimicry of the sign, that divides it with itself and tears away its identity, one might say that it is 'passive', 'operated' or the 'object' of deconstruction. On the contrary, the operators have a more complex status: according to one of their sides, they enter into the play of the mark, within its textual system, but they cannot be reduced to this passive function of signification as networked and enchained, nor even to their state of sign the two sides of which are indissociable. They contribute to the constitution, ordering, coordinating of the chains.[57]

Laruelle clarifies the point by providing a series of examples. 'For example: metaphor, metonymy, simple assonance (*semen*, seed [sème]) are procedures for constituting certain chains of which they would be the "reason" or the "law".'[58] This double function of sign and law-of-sign would be at once the instantiation and the *a priori* condition for the 're-inscription' of signs. This latter in turn is what makes deconstruction possible. The special operators of re-inscription themselves involve, according to Laruelle, an 'interiorly structured' effect of 'auto-affection' that exceeds signification as such and produces a 'moment of apparent saturation that composes with differance within the general economy of repetition'.[59] This 'saturated moment' is the invariant within deconstruction that will eventually become formalised in *Philosophies of Difference* as the BWW.

The critique is then carried forward through Laruelle's other Nietzsche-based analysis of 'writing' from Philosophy I. In *The Decline of Writing* Laruelle sets up a primary opposition at the heart of his own proposal for a 'machinic materialism', a constructive inflection within the problematics of general textuality on the one hand and interpretation of Heidegger's ontological difference on the other. On one side of this opposition, Laruelle equates 'Differance' with the 'Other' as 'the *ontic* moment of the problematic'.[60] This could be misleading: Laruelle is not equating Difference with the merely empirical here. Rather, this 'ontic' moment is in itself the chiasmic relation between the 'object' of the theory and the 'motor that makes it function as a disposition [*dispositif*] capable of producing theoretical effects'.[61] On the other hand, the *ontological* side or 'moment' of 'machinic materialism' is called by Laruelle the 'Body-of-the-Other [*le Corps-de-l'Autre*], or the plain Body [*le Corps plain*]'.[62]

In *The Decline of Writing* the relation between Differance as Other on the one hand and the plain Body or Body-of-the-Other on the other is conceived as a Nietzschean revision of Heidegger's notion of ontological difference. By substituting (Derridean) Differance for 'beings' and Body-of-the-Other for 'Being' while maintaining the basic form of Difference that at once distinguishes and relates beings and Being, Laruelle intends to revise Heidegger (and Derrida) in light of the 'Nietzschean Cut'. This substitution aims to have 'rendered possible a minoritarian usage of the ontico-ontological function'.[63] What does this mean? This means that here – as generally throughout Philosophy I – Laruelle relatively 'sides with' Nietzsche as against Heidegger (and Derrida). Rather than treating beings as inherently objectified (albeit 'crossed' with the difference between the ready-to-hand and the present-at-hand), that is, precisely as *beings*, Nietzsche – according to Laruelle's reading – substitutes a differential field, an intrinsic relational element of self-surpassing already at the ontic level. Instead of 'beings' or 'entities', there is (*il y a*; *Es gibt*) Will to Power, or the field of differential relations that constitute both the interactions between entities *and* those entities 'in themselves' as already beyond themselves (as structured through differance). Even as ontic, beings amongst themselves in Nietzsche thus already possess the very degree and kind of difference – the unique mutuality of immanence and transcendence – that Heidegger will reserve for the difference between beings and Being. This entails that the ontological pole of the relation for Nietzsche no longer plays the same governing role that it does in Heidegger. Instead, the ontological pole in Nietzsche as Body-of-the-Other is *only* the immanent excess of differentiality that keeps beings from being totalised or reduced to presence (as in Derrida). In this way Nietzsche's Will to Power 'inverts' Heidegger's ontological difference:

> Being as Body or quasi-totality of Differance finds itself at last *in the conditions for* no longer being a dominant totality (presence as *Anwesen*), above all if it is . . . subordinated to Differance, and if this latter no longer contains from its side any subsisting element (such as negativity and contradiction) and thus assures it its minority.[64]

In short, Nietzsche provides the conditions for a minoritarian and revolutionary form of thinking because he fully evacuates the role of objectivity as presence as essential to Difference/Differance. This is for Laruelle in *The Decline of Writing* the basis of a 'libidinal' (that is, *machinic-desiring*) Differance that is finally distinct from Derrida's merely 'textual' Differance (organised ultimately through the priority of the signifier).[65]

In *Philosophies of Difference* the Body-of-the-Other becomes the Body-without-Writing. This shift in terminology corresponds to a subtle shift in emphasis. Conceptually, the two terms represent the same place or function in the analytic 'structure' of deconstruction. But the difference between the two names serves to highlight the 'shift in perspective' that separates non-philosophical from philosophical modes of critique. 'Body-of-the-Other' still marks the unique plane of deconstruction as relative to the operations of writing, relative precisely as 'Other'. 'Body-without-Writing', in contrast, marks a unilateral separation rather than a relation. 'Without' (*sans*) does not here signify any 'lack' or 'exteriority' but simply an 'indifference to. . .'. The 'Body-without-Writing' is not the Other of writing but is what writing itself must presuppose from its side while *it* remains thoroughly indifferent or unaffected by writing from *its* side. Thus, the very idea of two 'sides' in fact only exists from the one 'side' of writing. Yet, importantly and despite appearances, the 'side' of writing is *not* the side taken by the very inscription 'Body-without-Writing'.

This last point is so crucial that it is worth investigating in some detail. The deconstructive *topos* or commonplace is that thinking is constituted by signs that inevitably introduce an element of exteriority or difference into the apparent self-presence of meaning. But the possibility deconstruction cancels in advance (perhaps without sufficient warrant) is the possibility that thought might proceed *from* such an exteriority in a thoroughly simple and direct fashion, without the torsion of re-inscription and deferral. Not only does deconstruction itself not do this (Derrida and Laruelle agree that deconstruction is parasitic in its essence), but more strongly, deconstruction claims on its own terms that such a mode of thought is *strictly impossible*. Deconstruction's mode of access to itself, namely as thoroughly entangled with its parasitic relation to an/the Other, is generalised to the point of enveloping any possible access to anything whatsoever. It is *this* aspect of deconstruction that Laruelle calls fundamentally into question. Derrida states at one point: 'Never all or nothing, that is one simple thing that must be said about access to the text' – and, we might add, by extension, that must be said about access to *the deconstruction of the text*.[66] Deconstruction is quite correct that *on its own terms*, such a modality is impossible. But Laruelle will insist of the relativity of those terms themselves. Deconstruction no doubt legitimates itself and its own functioning. But to be self-legitimating – although it may thereby appear to attain the absolute – is in fact to be self-relative. Why does this matter?

Because it decides in advance the question as to the reality of something 'exterior' to deconstruction that would be not an indeconstructible but an otherwise-than-deconstructible.

In this regard the concept of the BWW marks a distinctively Laruellian mixture of Derrida and Deleuze. This mixture – like the Nietzsche/ Heidegger conflict – becomes one of the privileged instances of non-philosophical 'operation' in *Philosophies of Difference*. Laruelle says much more about Nietzsche/Heidegger, but perhaps that is because the issue is somewhat more straightforward in that case. In terms of contemporary philosophical concerns, however, it may be the direction indicated by the Derrida/Deleuze fusion in the concept of BWW that offers some of the most intriguing avenues for further exploration in non-philosophy. In any case, it is necessary to see how this concept mounts an implicit Deleuzean critique of Derrida in order to grasp Laruelle's overall reading of Derrida and especially to glimpse even at this point the precise way non-philosophy's mode of thought in-One will bring into relief a philosophical 'mechanism' of decision that is more general than logocentrism or the other objects of deconstructive critique.

In Deleuze, the concept of the Body-without-Organs (BwO) – taken over from Artaud and transformed in light of the other major concepts of Deleuze's thought – provides a basis for thinking the self-transcending aspect of Nietzschean Will to Power while still remaining within an imma-nent ontology and ultimately a monist metaphysics. This means that the BwO provides the syntactical role for conceiving an 'immanent excess'. In his collaborations with Guattari, Deleuze's basic Difference of the virtual and the actual is reworked as the interaction between two planes: the plane of consistency and the plane of organisation. To be sure, the distinction between these two planes – no more than the actual/virtual Difference – is not the distinction between two separate regions; it has precisely the complex form of Difference. But in order to maintain the immanence and monism of their ontology, even this Differential structure must be 'flat-tened' or relatively unilateralised. The BwO marks the requisite 'term' that makes the deterritorialising pole of the territorialising/deterritorialis-ing Difference primary or fundamental. It is not enough that there is a chiasmus of the actual and the virtual or of the consistency/organisation planes. The virtual must take priority over the actual (and the plane of consistency take priority over the plane of organisation) in a particular way that itself essentially defines the Deleuzean metaphysical 'system'. The BwO is the transcendental-immanent condition of possibility, or rather the necessary *real* condition, for truly creative lines of deterritorialisation, that is, for 'lines of flight' that would be other than a Heideggerean event of 'appropriation' – that is, an event that would necessarily appear *as* even if not strictly *in* history.[67] In other words – given Laruelle's overall framework of the Nietzsche/Heidegger conflict – it is the role of the BwO to ensure that the Nietzschean system of Will to Power and Eternal Return not be undercut by a 'finite real' of the Heideggerean type. Translated into the context of Derrida, Laruelle asserts in effect that deconstruction requires the positing of an analogous 'plane' in order to ensure that 'writing' in its most general sense remain absolutely open or 'hospitable' to the Other.

For Laruelle, the BWW cannot be secured as such outside of the (broken) circularity of the Derridean 'system' or 'economy' as a whole, even if these are qualified as a (non-)system or (non-)economy that would be broken but nonetheless still circular as the undecidable (meta-)economy of restricted and general economies. Yet like every such system or (non-) system, this remains in essence coordinated with the structure of a *decision*. The 'kernel of real unity, of indivision that renders [deconstruction] autonomous and viable', must be understood, according to Laruelle's argument, not as the BWW itself (a plane of immanence is not a kernel of truth) but as the structural necessity for deconstruction of *positing* such a plane in order to then capitalise on its effects of relative-absolute transcendence which appears then as 'inverted immanence'.

There are thus two levels of decision in play with respect to the BWW. On the one hand, there is the 'passage to decision or crisis' that is explicitly if intermittently marked throughout Derrida's discourse. For Derrida, the aporetic undecidability of philosophy's constitutive oppositions necessitates thought *as* decision. On the other hand, more profoundly, there is the *a priori* decision for a general 'image of thought' that would remain always underdetermined (although only *partially* so) with respect to its Other(s) and thus always structurally and ineluctably in need of decision. Laruelle does not attribute this latter, more profound level *in particular* to Derrida. Rather, it becomes the aspect of philosophy that only a new mode of thinking, a non-Differential thinking in-One, will be capable of adequately describing under the name of *non-thetic transcendence*.

NOTES

1. *PD*, p. 104, emphasis added.
2. *PD*, p. xv.
3. *PD*, p. 104.
4. For a clear and judicious exposition of these basic features of Kant's first *Critique*, see Sebastian Gardner, *Kant and* The Critique of Pure Reason, chs. 6–7.
5. Ibid., pp. 233–7.
6. *PD*, pp. 104, 105.
7. Jacques Derrida, *Speech and Phenomena*, p. 81.

8. See Georges Bataille, *The Accursed Share*, vol. 1, pp. 19–41 and vol. 3, pp. 197–211.
9. Jacques Derrida, *Writing and Difference*, pp. 252–3.
10. Ibid. p. 259.
11. Ibid. p. 262.
12. Ibid. p. 263.
13. *PD*, p. 151, note.
14. Laruelle playfully converts Derrida's own concept of *'paralyse'* into the deconstructive self-relation of *'enlyse*, the self-ensnarement of differance, not by presence but by the unity in progress, the unlimited fusion of differance and presence'. *PD*, p. 146.
15. It should be borne in mind that this claim is made in 1986.
16. See Jacques Derrida, *Of Grammatology*, 'Exergue', pp. 3–5.
17. *PD*, p. 129.
18. *PD*, p. 114. There are interesting contrasts to be drawn here with the 'double reading' of the Nietzschean aphorism discussed earlier.
19. *PD*, p. 134 (in italics in the original).
20. *PD*, p. 114.
21. *PD*, p. 114 (in italics in the original).
22. Jacques Derrida, *Points . . .*, p. 12, which Laruelle cites at *PD*, p. 128.
23. *PD*, p. 112.
24. *PD*, p. xx.
25. Derrida's most detailed theoretical and critical examination of the theme of mortality in Heidegger is found in *Aporias*. Derrida's many writings on remembrance and mourning are also relevant here. See, in particular, the personal and occasional pieces collected in *The Work of Mourning*.
26. François Laruelle, *Textual Machines*, p. 119.
27. Martin Hägglund, *Radical Atheism*, pp. 2–3.
28. Ibid., p. 36.
29. Ibid., p. 37.
30. Ibid.
31. Similar considerations would apply to the other primary deconstructive dichotomies in Derrida's work, such as that of faith and knowledge. Michael Naas has organised a comprehensive reading of the Derridean oeuvre around this thematic. See Naas, *Miracle and Machine*. In principle, *any* of Derrida's terms or dichotomies could serve as such a 'kernel' for an analysis of the entire corpus.
32. *PD*, p. xx.
33. We could say that Derrida takes the formal distinction between essence and *non-existence* as his object, whereas Heidegger remains within the Scotist tradition for which the paradigm of formal distinction is that between essence and existence (even if Heidegger massively reinterprets and even inverts Scotus on this point) – see Ray Brassier, 'Laruelle and the Reality of Abstraction' in John Mullarkey and Anthony Paul Smith, eds, *Laruelle and Non-Philosophy*, pp. 100–22.

34. In Jacques Derrida, *Points . . .*, p. 11.
35. *PD*, p. 106.
36. *PD*, p. 109.
37. *PD*, p. 109.
38. *PD*, p. 109.
39. See François Laruelle, *Future Christ*, pp. 32, 68.
40. *PD*, p. 148.
41. *PD*, p. 148.
42. *PD*, p. 149.
43. *PD*, p. 112.
44. Emmanuel Levinas, *On Escape*, p. 67.
45. See 'Violence and Metaphysics' in Jacques Derrida, *Writing and Difference*.
46. *PD*, p. 107.
47. The details of this debate, more intricate than can be adequately discussed here, may be found in a pair of articles in the *Journal for Cultural and Religious Theory*: John Caputo, 'The Return of Anti-Religion: From Radical Atheism to Radical Theology', *JCRT* 11.2 (2011) and Martin Hägglund, 'The Radical Evil of Deconstruction: A Reply to John Caputo', *JCRT* 11.2 (2011).
48. John D. Caputo, *The Prayers and Tears of Jacques Derrida*, p. 337.
49. Ibid.
50. *PD*, p. 108. If Laruelle is correct on this point, it would go some way in explaining the posture taken by some commentators on Derrida for whom the man himself and his human words become objects of almost religious veneration.
51. Laruelle refers to the Deleuze/Derrida conflict in *PD*, *p.* 188. It is discussed in greater detail in *Textual Machines*.
52. *PD*, p. 114, in italics in the original.
53. *PD*, p. 122.
54. *PD*, p. 135.
55. *PD*, p. 135, in italics in the original.
56. Jacques Derrida, *Dissemination*, p. 133.
57. François Laruelle, *Textual Machines*, pp. 113–14.
58. Ibid.
59. Ibid.
60. François Laruelle, *Decline of Writing*, p. 10.
61. Ibid.
62. Ibid.
63. Ibid., p. 25.
64. Ibid.
65. Ibid., p. 9.
66. In Jacques Derrida, *Points . . .*, p. 175.
67. See Gilles Deleuze and Félix Guattari, *A Thousand Plateaus*, ch. 6.

6

From Difference to vision-in-One

DIFFERENCE AND THE IMMANENCE OF PHILOSOPHY

We noted early in our opening chapter that in *Philosophies of Difference* Laruelle aims to mount a 'critique that would no longer be a complement, a rectification, a deconstruction, a supplement', the object of this critique being philosophy's need 'to think through unifying duality, through the synthesis of contraries, through the One as All or as unity of contraries, through dialectic and difference'.[1] We are now in a position to understand this aim more precisely with respect to the triad of models of Difference represented by Nietzsche-Deleuze, Heidegger and Derrida respectively, as well as the (partially anachronistic) history they compose. It is clear that Heidegger's critique of Nietzsche's metaphysics of the Will to Power and Derrida's critique of Heidegger's own privileging of presence may be understood in broad strokes to stand as 'rectifications', 'deconstructions' and 'supplements' with respect to their critical objects. Perhaps Deleuze's sophisticatedly 'naive' return to Spinozist and Nietzschean metaphysics in the wake of Heidegger may be conceived in this way as well. At any rate, a broadly critical and genealogical approach with respect to the history of philosophy has been part and parcel of continental method for some time. The difficult task that Laruelle has set himself is to define the terms according to which his own critique of Difference would no longer fall under the same description.

Such a 'total critique' clearly cannot proceed by a strategy of divide-and-select, in other words by way of distinguishing within the object of critique an affirmed core versus a rejected remainder. Every such strategy involves a selective identification combined with a partial rejection. In contrast, a total critique must involve a *complete* break with the object of

146

critique, indeed a 'break' so radical that it can no longer be adequately represented even as a discontinuity.[2] The problem is that the metaphor of the 'break' always surreptitiously reintroduces the idea of continuity, even if it does so at a higher level. One cannot break with something without reinstating something else within some ambient 'space' in which the continuity will have been 'broken'. To differ from the object of critique in such a manner is thus already to remain in relation to it. For this reason, a complete or total critique must take the paradoxical form of an undivided identification as well as a thorough separation. Whereas Difference would turn every form of critique into a mode of auto-critique, such an in-Different form of critique would no longer reproduce its object in the very operation it effects. Instead, it would both permeate and exceed the limits of its object without at the same time 'breaking' those limits. At a purely formal level, this helps to explain why non-philosophy should be understood as a generalisation rather than a negation of philosophy. By way of analogy: considering the planar neighbourhood that includes a given geometrical figure 'negates' nothing in the figure itself except the limiting function of its line. What is Laruelle's critical mode and what does it reveal?

In light of Laruelle's analysis, the three models of Difference come into sharper focus as complementary mixtures of immanence and transcendence. These distinct mixtures are then generalised for Laruelle as variations on the core distinction of philosophy: ideality (or syntax) and reality. With Nietzsche-Deleuzean Difference, philosophy attains what in retrospect appears from its point of view as philosophy's very essence: immanence *in critical opposition to* transcendence. In Deleuze's *Expressionism in Philosophy*, the study of Spinoza that appeared simultaneously with *Difference and Repetition* and *The Logic of Sense*, Deleuze identifies the mark of Spinozist immanence: not only that thought would be made immanent, but that this immanence would no longer be immanent *to* something else. Instead, philosophical immanence would be immanent only to itself. Laruelle does not challenge this claim to philosophical immanence. He essentially grants that the philosophies of Difference have achieved their respective aims. Immanence in Difference (at least in the Nietzsche-Deleuzean model) is thus conceived as really immanent to itself and not to something other than itself.

Indeed, this notion of an immanence that would be immanent only to itself provides a clear way to distinguish the more general differences that in fact define the three models as models rather than merely instances of Difference. Once philosophy is identified with immanence-to-immanence, the problem unavoidably arises as to what is then properly *non*-philosophical (not in Laruelle's sense of non-philosophy, but in the now clearly delimited sense of what, if anything, is *not* immanent-to-immanence).

147

Here then, the ordinary or naive idea of negation appears to take its inevitable revenge. Even after the philosophies of Difference have worked so hard to distinguish a nuanced, sophisticated, even 'positive' notion of the negative, this very effort raises the question of how this more nuanced conception precisely is *not* equivalent to the naive or empirical sense of 'not'. Or, to place the problem in the register of immanence and transcendence, once immanence-to-immanence has been achieved – in whatever manner and by whatever means – how, from the perspective thus realised, can transcendence appear otherwise than as a simple negation or a 'mutilated idea' (Spinoza)?

On Laruelle's reading, Nietzsche-Deleuze remains rather on the side of 'pure' immanence, which is to say that transcendence is understood always as a reactive mechanism, an alienation and self-abasement. We already saw how with Nietzsche this problematic is the essentially structuring element of the relation between active and reactive willing. While the struggle of active and reactive wills necessarily structures any concrete historical situation, from the singular perspective of the Eternal Return, reactivity and transcendence are in fact *absolutely* overcome. With respect to Deleuze's Spinozism, things are perhaps even clearer. For Spinoza, there is no problem of reactive wills at all. There are only relatively inadequate or 'mutilated' ideas. Interestingly, this basically 'privative' understanding of transcendence ends up looking quite similar to the traditional Neo-Platonic and Augustinian notion of evil as the mere privation of the Good.

On this basis, the stakes of the Nietzsche/Heidegger difference then come into clearer focus as well. If for Nietzsche, transcendence is *absolutely* overcome (although this absoluteness is itself still relative to the 'noon' of Eternal Return), for Heidegger the residue of transcendence as the non-objectivisable finite essence of beings is taken to mark the uneffaceable register of every possible metaphysics. Rather than a metaphysics of Finitude, Heidegger thus posits metaphysics as itself Finite. From this point of view, Heidegger does not himself 'break' with metaphysics but effects precisely its immanent 'turning' in and as One.[3] The complexity of this 'thesis' is such that the 'turning' of Heidegger and its concomitant division of Heidegger I from Heidegger II becomes not just an accidental biographical fact, but an essential component of what-is-to-be-thought in Heidegger. If 'immanence' in Heidegger marks above all the tautological form of the withdrawal of the Real, this entails a corresponding inhibition of philosophical pretensions – but an inhibition that still needs philosophy in order to weaken and 'turn' philosophy.

Finally in Derrida, then, the lucid recognition of this problematic in its full generality and its essential irresolvability becomes the basis for a singular 'inversion' of the syntax of immanence-to-immanence. It is not that Derrida gives up the basic achievement designated by this syntax. Rather, he intensifies or absolutises not the 'relatively positive' pole (as in Nietzsche) nor the 'relatively negative' pole (as in Heidegger) – although of course each of these 'polar' characterisations requires qualification and reinterpretation on its own terms through Difference – but instead induces a 'new' pole of absolute transcendence, the Other. This 'pole' of the Other as absolute transcendence necessarily 'appears' as an eerie and uncanny doppelganger of immanence-to-immanence. The Other *as such* must 'appear' as immanent-to-itself. Derrida thus marks the last form of theological transcendence left when such transcendence is neither the transcendence of a 'highest being' nor even that of a 'beyond being', but instead an absolute hospitality to the Other of and within immanence. At this point, the substance of the dispute between Hägglund and Caputo, and more generally, the differend of Derrida's atheism and/or theological inclinations, is thoroughly dissolved from the standpoint of any real, non-self-presupposing locus. Only the dispute itself remains as 'its own' substance. 'Absolute hospitality' becomes the host of its own interminable conflict: between Hägglund and Caputo, *Derrida* wins.

With the three models taken together, what this means in effect is that '*Difference, in thinking itself, thinks everything that it is possible to think of Being as soon as one no longer wishes to think it onto-theologically. On the other hand it thinks next to nothing of the One and is content merely to make it "function".*'[4] In these two sentences Laruelle's critical position with respect to Difference is crystallised. The positive aspect of Laruelle's reading is evident in the first sentence of the citation. Difference, Laruelle says, is able to think *everything* thinkable of Being once Being is no longer thought in terms of onto-theology. For Laruelle this is true equally (although not identically) of Nietzsche, Deleuze, Heidegger and Derrida.

Here already there is an important difference between Laruelle's critical position and those of Heidegger and Derrida at least with respect to *their* predecessors. For Heidegger and Derrida it is always a matter of delimiting the sphere of metaphysics as onto-theology and then showing that the predecessor in question (Nietzsche and Heidegger respectively) remains at least partially confined within that sphere. To be sure, Heidegger and Derrida are perfectly aware of the situation and do not hesitate to include themselves in the same partial confinement. Laruelle, in contrast, is willing to grant the philosophies of Difference relative success in their aim of escaping transcendence or onto-theology in their respective manners. Difference in each case for Laruelle attains all the immanence (or, if it so wishes, all the complex mixture of immanence and transcendence) *of which philosophy is really capable in that case*. Indeed, one of the strengths of Laruelle's reading of Difference is to have shown how the 'logic' of

Difference is able to accomplish this in various ways without thereby contradicting itself.

The second sentence in the citation marks the key distinction between the philosophies of Difference themselves and the mode of non--philosophical thinking Laruelle brings to bear upon them. It says that Difference *uses* the One, but does not *think* the One. What does this mean? The insistent theme throughout Laruelle's text of 'Difference's requisition of the One' is the exact point of contention that separates Difference from non-philosophy. Difference needs self-relation in order to function, but it cannot remain Difference without conceiving such self-relation as Differential. The critical force of Laruelle's thought of the One is thus directed at an aspect of Difference that it itself spontaneously rejects. Yet, if this point is one of which Difference itself remains unaware in its spontaneity, then the 'contention' of Difference and non-philosophy is not a contest between two sides. A different set of stakes are in fact at stake in the two projects.

In one way or another, all the philosophies of Difference aim at an overcoming of some form of transcendence via some mode of immanence (either positive: Eternal Return, negative: tautological withdrawal, or undecidable: differance). What Laruelle's analysis aims to show by isolating the structure of Difference instantiated differently in the three models is that the immanence posited in each case *depends upon its opposition and hence its relation to the form of transcendence it rejects.*[5] It remains in this respect a second-order, self-scaling transcendence and necessarily reinstates, despite itself, what Laruelle identifies as the core Platonic metaphor of Western philosophy: a reciprocally determined hierarchy of ascent and descent, a movement out of and back into the Cave, a polarised Great Circle of decisional souls, a harmonised disharmony of the One and the Indefinite Dyad, a system of the One/Multiple – in short, Difference.[6] The genius of Nietzsche, Heidegger, Derrida and Deleuze, on Laruelle's account, has been in each case to lift this highly problematic metaphysical dualism at the heart of Western philosophy into a new, relatively purified mode – precisely its passage in each case to the transcendental – and thereby to inaugurate new ways of philosophising capable of escaping the traps and limits of representation, binarism, *ressentiment* and so on.

Nevertheless from the stance of non-philosophy, Difference and its avatars remain finally unable to fulfil their aims of overcoming traditional metaphysics as such. The philosophers of Difference effect partial cures that alleviate some of the symptoms of metaphysics, but they cannot help but reinstate subtle variants on the form of metaphysical dualism within the relative immanence of Difference itself. As Laruelle summarises his basic claim:

The thesis undertaken here against Difference, in Heidegger and others, is that it does not save itself from the meta-physical in general as it would propose, but saves only the metaphysical itself from its most reified, inferior forms (Representation, Logocentrism) and thereby carries it back to its essence as scission or transcendence. Far from destroying metaphysics, Difference remains content merely to purify its essence, just as it purifies and safeguards the essence of Representation against its most empirical forms: by sacrificing the essence of the One.[7]

In this way, Difference would 'consist . . . [i]n the combination, each time, of an immanence and a transcendence, of an ideality and a supposed real'.[8] We have seen three distinct ways that this mixture occurs. In none of these does it appear as a simple binarism, but in each as a complex, differential composite. Is there any way to decide among the three models? Which is right? Which is best? For Laruelle there is no need for decision here. What Laruelle wishes us to see is simply that even as Difference, philosophy remains philosophy. Indeed, the purification of Difference goes far in this respect in exhibiting according to Laruelle the very *essence* of philosophy.

GENERALISING DIFFERENCE

There is a point of view from which philosophical Difference, in order to be what it is, must be understood not only to *tolerate* but positively to *require* its proliferation in various 'concrete' philosophical models. From this perspective, Nietzsche *needs* Heidegger, as well as the reverse, just as both need Derrida and Derrida needs them. The 'need' in each case differentially articulates its terms *between* conjunction and disjunction, as if the two binary operators 'either/or' and 'both/and' were to be introduced chiasmically into the general (meta-)Difference schema and crossed with one another in unlimited permutations. Yet the need itself in each and every case takes this *same unlimited shape*. This, then, is the indivisible core of Difference that Laruelle's analysis may claim to have brought to light. It is the infinitely supple and variable structure of a purely differential relation that does not depend upon any prior identity, object or material upon which to operate. Yet this in turn implies that when it *does* operate, it can do so only on and through itself. It is immanence-to-immanence or self-without-self – in short, the One *as* Difference. Laruelle takes this usage-through-occlusion of the One to define philosophical thinking as such.

Recall the first two of the three theses sketched earlier in chapter two: T1 and T2. First of all, a common structure of Difference is said to be evident in Nietzsche, Heidegger, Deleuze, Derrida (T1). Secondly, it is claimed, this structure is not restricted to these thinkers alone, but in fact expresses an underlying 'logic' that allows the unity of the otherwise diverse traditions, epochs and schools of Western philosophy to become evident (T2). Once Difference has been analysed and defined with respect to the intersecting problematics that link and discriminate Nietzsche, Deleuze, Derrida and Heidegger (with Kant and Hegel always hovering in the background), it is thus a question of assigning this structure retrospectively to Western philosophy as a whole. Difference then becomes the essence of philosophy, the 'invariant' that cuts across all of the differences among philosophy's epochs, schools and systems.

On the face of it, this latter thesis would seem to be a rather grandiose, even outrageous claim, one that appears to fall into precisely the trap of overreach and hasty totalisation that Laruelle otherwise seems at pains to criticise. But better sense can be made of it if we follow Laruelle and allow the distinction between a 'general' and a 'restricted' sense of Difference: the former would designate the 'empirico-transcendental parallelism' whose basic structure would '[render] a consistent account of the greater part of Occidental thinking', while the latter would represent the specific 'Greco-Nietzschean' metaphysics which serves as 'the principal mode' of the former.[9] In other words, the standard or base model of Nietzschean Difference that we analysed in chapter three and whose variations or mutations in Heidegger and Derrida occupied us in chapters four and five is conceived here as itself a condensation or intensification of a more general Difference that would envelop all of philosophy to the extent that philosophy uses its difference and relation (transcendence and immanence) with respect to the Real as leverage for thinking the Real.

This more general structure is what Laruelle calls 'empirico-transcendental parallelism'. Nietzschean Difference in particular *clarifies* the empirico-transcendental parallelism through its very intensification. In Nietzsche we see the structure of empirico-transcendental parallelism 'writ large' by way of being brought close, indeed brought into the interior heart of the identity of beings via his immanent metaphysics. In this way the 'restricted' model appears in fact as the generalisation in a sense of the 'general' model! By now, however, we should be familiar with this kind of chiasmic inversion, this turning-inside-out and reciprocal mutability of concepts, their referents and their inevitable paradoxes of self-reference. If indeed we have become somewhat desensitised to the effect of surprise and sudden vertigo, the 'shock and awe' of this sort of conceptual manoeuvre, it is perhaps because we have begun to see how much philosophy (especially in the philosophies of Difference) depends upon the production of this effect/affect and also in what light it may appear as more or less banal and unsurprising. But this latter mode of 'vision' seems to take place from somewhere other than philosophy. Philosophy may very well, as Plato and

Aristotle already agreed, begin in the experience of wonder (*thaumazein*). But what if philosophy were no longer to be a source of its own wonder at itself (*thaumazein* = Difference) for those who think it?

After having passed through the fire of the analyses of the philosophies of Difference, it now becomes possible to return to Laruelle's introduction and to rehearse his brief discussion there of 'the oldest concrete philosophical matrix, a matrix of the empirico-transcendental parallelism and/ or circle'.[10] In this regard, Laruelle had himself already referred to the 'canonical enunciation' of the Pre-Socratics: '*Everything is (Water, Earth, Fire, etc.).*'[11] The form of this utterance is now taken as constitutive for philosophy as such: philosophy aims at the authoritative determination of all things.

What does this determinative structure that opens the Western tradition have to do with Kant's transcendental turn, or Hegel's Great Circle of Spirit, or Husserlian phenomenology? Laruelle asserts the common basis of philosophy as follows:

> It is to think the real as all (*the* all: not only the universal, but an absolute or unifying universal) and thus, inversely, the *all* of the real as still an element of the real, indeed as Other: *it is ontico-ontological 'difference' in its broadest sense*, in the sense that Being is here definitively affected by the beings that it conditions.[12]

This general correlative structure becomes for Laruelle the core thesis of philosophy as such (though perhaps only becoming fully explicit in the philosophies of Difference), namely the 'position' (Greek *thēsis*) of a decisional stance with respect to the Real: *the Real may/must be decided by thought*. Paradigmatically, thought would decide the Real by determining everything in advance as part or element of an All, even where this All itself is understood to be open, horizonal or self-differed.

This general 'position' is conceived precisely as philosophy's constitutive *self*-position, which is what the mechanism raising Difference from the metaphysical to the transcendental makes particularly evident. One of the main conclusions of Laruelle's analysis of the Nietzschean, Heideggerean and Derridean models of Difference, then, is that in each case Difference produces its own differential self-relation as an essential determination of the Real. In other words, despite the various critiques of identity, objectivity, representation and presence that characterise the philosophies of Difference, in each case Difference is in fact compelled to relate itself to itself by means of itself (that is, to solicit the One in its synthetic or unifying function) as it produces its own distinctive philosophical mixture of immanence and transcendence. Indeed, this is for each model of Difference how it 'becomes what it is' singularly and irreducibly to the other models.

153

Laruelle then takes this specific conclusion concerning Difference and the philosophies of Difference and generalises it across the entirety of the Western tradition by conceiving the self-relating/self-differing structure of Difference to be the intrinsic condition of possibility for philosophy's many and various 'empirico-transcendental' decisions, which are in each case philosophically self-determining. In every such philosophical decision Difference *requires* the One, and yet requires it in the form of functional *opposition* and/or *interiorisation* (that is, the very form of Difference).

Laruelle's claim that Difference generalises across Western philosophy and pinpoints its essence as a tradition is in this way not meant to be inductive but transcendental. In any case, T2 can hardly be justified through recourse to textual and historical evidence. The empirical scope of the term 'philosophy' is simply too vast. The only possible legitimation for Laruelle's claim that Difference is more than just one episode in philosophy, that Difference is indeed the intrinsic structure of all philosophical thinking, must come ultimately from the very vision of philosophy it effects. In this respect, the justification of T2 depends in an important sense on the soundness of T3, the assertion that a non-philosophical mode of thought is possible. It is the new way philosophy itself appears from within the stance of non-philosophy that will at once legitimate T3 and in turn lend credence to T2.

THE PROBLEM OF INDIVIDUALS AND MULTIPLICITIES

With the problem of Laruelle's generalisation of Difference thus clearly in view, we return to the question of authoritarianism and resistance. The primary dynamic at work throughout Laruelle's text leads to the notion of a *separation of two principles* that would themselves no longer be distinguishable or relatable through Difference. This dynamic, if successful, serves to realise the critique of Difference *as* an instance of non-philosophy. There would then be two modes of thinking at work simultaneously and yet separately: philosophy as structured through Difference; non-philosophy as realised in-One.

We have followed Laruelle's argument up to this point along two parallel tracks: the general critique of Difference and the critical analysis of the three dominant models of Difference. Although this two-track project indeed takes up the bulk of *Philosophies of Difference*, it remains strictly preparatory to Laruelle's primary concern, which is to initiate a new, non-Differential form of thought that would no longer reproduce philosophical authoritarianism. Since, as we have seen, the philosophies of Difference are conceived by Laruelle not as merely particular instances of philosophy but rather as expressive clarifications of the very essence of 'Greco-Occidental' philosophy taken as a whole, non-Differential thought – if such a thing indeed proves to be possible – will, by the same token, be equally *non-philosophical* thought. Philosophy's authority cannot reach and thus will not have governed a thoroughly non-philosophical critique of philosophy.

In this sense the actual *content* of Laruelle's most basic claim is none other than the *form* of his critique of Difference, or rather the theoretical 'stance' in which that critique itself can be made coherent. In this respect, the text of *Philosophies of Difference* possesses the somewhat 'monstrous' form of an extended preface (chapters one through six) followed by a relatively terse and seemingly underdeveloped argument proper (chapter seven). Yet this apparent monstrousness is perhaps better understood on analogy with the form of a difficult mathematical proof in which a long series of preparatory constructions and apparently unrelated partial results attains its conclusion almost anti-climactically in a relatively simple and straightforward lemma, the sense and power of which, however, would depend entirely upon having worked through the step-by-step progress of the preceding series. Laruelle's method is in this way essentially distinct from both Hegelian philosophical recapitulation and Nietzschean philosophical break with respect to being and history. Non-philosophical vision is a kind of *result* on analogy with a mathematical result or a result in experimental physics; it is not a historical product or an untimely creation. Philosophy, it seems, always *needs* the history that prepares it (either positively or negatively). By contrast, a scientific result does not *need* but simply *is* its strictly scientific demonstration.

Chapter six of *Philosophies of Difference* gathers the results of the previous studies of Nietzsche, Deleuze, Heidegger and Derrida and consolidates them in a unified critique of Difference. The ultimate stakes of this critique become clear in its final section, 'The Powerlessness to Think Individuals and Multiplicities'. In his first chapter, Laruelle had already explained that the aim of *Philosophies of Difference* is not to resolve the long-standing philosophical 'aporias of Unity and Multiplicity, the Universal and the Singular' but instead 'to awaken philosophers to a problem, to an experience rather, that is non-philosophical but that is capable of founding a rigorous science of philosophy'.[13] If Laruelle, then, does not claim to have resolved finally the philosophical problem of the One and the Multiple, he does nonetheless claim to have relativised this problem itself to the 'side' of the principle of Difference and thereby to have shown that it is not a problem at all for or from the 'side' of the One itself.

'The Powerlessness to Think Individuals and Multiplicities' thus functions as an important hinge between the two main parts of the text. The contrast of non-philosophy to philosophy naturally gives rise to its expression in terms of binary oppositions, especially that of Difference as opposed to the One. However, the notion of non-philosophy as a generalisation of philosophy and not merely its negation depends upon a separate kind of distinction. The non-philosophical One is not opposed to philosophical Difference in the way philosophy has traditionally opposed (and then related, dialecticised, mixed, etc.) the One and the Multiple. Rather, Difference is here relativised with respect to *both* poles of the traditional philosophical relation of the One and the Multiple. Laruelle writes:

> The reason prohibiting Difference from acceding to the One is the same that prohibits it from acceding to the essence of multiplicities. It is its manner of thinking the One and the multiple through 'difference' that causes it to take these once again in their 'in-between' and constrains it to take this 'in-between' at times for a thinking of the One, at times for a thinking of multiplicities, whereas it in fact thinks neither this one nor these others.[14]

In other words, the failure of Difference is not found in its 'falling short' of the One as if the One were something to be aimed at, a goal or target one either hits or misses. It is found rather in its insistence on thinking both the One and the Multiple (or multiplicities) in terms of a *relation* that would hold *a priori* between these two 'poles' as such (a relation whose inner structure would be the transcendent-immanent mixture of Difference). Thus, Difference in fact must think the One and multiplicities *as* differential poles (thus through itself) and never possibly as thoroughly 'separate' terms whose separation would be unthinkable as any operation, polarity or relation.

Clarification of this point is of the highest importance because it not only provides the basis for the proper 'distinguishing' of non-philosophy from philosophy but also clarifies the motivations underlying the non-philosophical project in the first place. This new inflection of the old question of the One and the Multiple (or multiplicities) is not simply one instance or example of how Laruelle holds Difference and the non-philosophical One to be distinct. It strikes at the heart of why Laruelle makes this distinction in the first place. Non-philosophy is a defence of the real multiple and in particular real human multiplicities, as well as real individuals and in particular real human individuals. Here the 'ethical' and 'political' impetus of Laruelle's work – which might otherwise tend to be overlooked at this stage – is clearly manifest as being at stake in even its most seemingly abstract and technical engagements.

In this respect, the final section of chapter six of *Philosophies of Difference* may be understood as revisiting the fundamental problem addressed in Laruelle's *The Minority Principle*, namely how to conceive of individuals and multiplicities without reducing one to the other. For Laruelle, when individuals are reduced to multiplicities, precisely their *indivision* is lost. They are understood as irreducible swarms or manifolds at best, or at worst as compositions of lower-order elements. Instead of genuine individuals, one then has only relational singularities or deposited remainders of processes of individuation. On the other hand, when multiplicities are reduced to individuals, beings tend to be reduced to their merely objectivised forms. They are 'counted as One' by a subjective consciousness or the objective 'logic' of a world. Real dispersion and difference are thereby denied, and the One appears in the conquering guise of 'unity' and 'totality'.

Laruelle inflects this problem through his analysis of the philosophers of Difference in order to show in effect how Difference governs the spontaneous philosophical understanding of *relations*. Philosophy always conceives at least *manifest* multiplicities as embroiled necessarily in a web or tissue of relations. The Kantian synthesis of the sensible manifold under the categories of the understanding is perhaps the clearest instance of this general structure. But even when Heidegger 'ontologises' the Kantian in-itself and allows the relatively 'negative' determinations of inauthenticity, untruth, forgetting and so on to destabilise somewhat the coherent network of worldly relations, it remains the case that the multiplicity of real beings is only thinkable *as* a multiplicity with respect to the Being/beings correlation that 'worlds' them. Equally, when Levinas critiques the 'totality' of Heideggerean ontology in favour of the 'infinity' of the Other, he too nonetheless retains the notion of actual multiplicity as inherently relational and thus as a limit or restriction on the absolute ethical transcendence of the (singular) Other. For example, Levinas writes:

> How is it that one can punish and repress? How is it that there is justice? I answer that it is the fact of the multiplicity of men and the presence of someone else next to the Other, which condition the laws and establish justice. If I am alone with the Other, I owe him everything; *but there is someone else*. Do I know what my neighbor is in relation to someone else? Do I know if someone else has an understanding with him or his victim? Who is my neighbor? It is consequently necessary to weigh, to think, to judge, in comparing the incomparable. The interpersonal relation I establish with the Other, *I must also establish with other men*; there is thus a necessity to moderate this privilege of the Other; from whence comes justice.[15]

What Laruelle may appear to aim at vis-à-vis these three cases (and the sequence they compose) is to think immediately from the 'side' of the pre-manifest and pre-relational term in each instance, as if Laruelle were attempting to think simultaneously from the Kantian sensible manifold itself (prior to its synthesis by the understanding), from the depths of the Heideggerean Earth (before its 'rift' with the World), and from the height of the Levinasian Other (as yet unmet by its qualification and remediation in justice and the 'third'). In this way, 'multiplicity' as thought by non-philosophy would amount to the rejection if not precisely the negation of the philosophical moment of experiential synthesis and conceptual reflection (more generally, the introduction of relationality into the 'matter' of thinking).

This way of conceiving Laruelle's project may serve a broadly indicative or heuristic purpose in certain respects, but it is ultimately incorrect, even fundamentally so. To the extent that it would have any value at all, it would be as a kind of Wittgensteinian ladder that one ascends only to discard afterwards. Yet a key aspect of Laruelle's approach is to throw into relief how all such methodological scaffolding that would orient itself either toward the critique of or the escape from philosophy necessarily reproduces and relays the whole of its object. Such philosophical modesty is always false modesty, and an entirely different way of proceeding is needed. On the present point, Laruelle will insist as contrasted with every philosophical privileging of the multiple, multiplicity, difference, etc., that the only real thought of multiplicity is multiplicity thought in-One and thus neither *for* nor *against* manifestation, synthesis, relation and so on.

Rather than the Differential problem of syntax and reality on this point, Laruelle poses a new problem of the transcendental conditions for Difference itself. Laruelle writes:

> The One and the multiplicities proper to the One thus form a peculiar *a priori*, purely 'transcendental' and not 'metaphysical' or universal, since they precede every species of universality and are the *a priori* not only of experience, as is traditionally the case, but of the universal forms themselves, consequently also of Difference.[16]

How are we to understand 'the One' here as well as 'the multiplicities proper to the One'? It is Laruelle's concept of the *(non-)One* that serves to clarify these terms and to resolve their apparent contradiction.

FROM DIFFERENCE TO THE (NON-)ONE

Laruelle's entire argument, but particularly the extended critical discussion of Heideggerean Finitude, reaches its climax in a pair of related concepts: the *(non-)One* and *non-thetic transcendence* (NTT). These concepts themselves depend upon the new stance of non-philosophy and its mode of thinking 'in-One'. As concepts, the (non-)One and NTT are themselves 'effectuated' within the material of the problem of individuals and multiplicities. In other words, these concepts emerge naturally as soon as this general philosophical problem is viewed 'in-One'. We will examine these one at a time, noting at the outset that the second concept, non-thetic transcendence, is itself a specification or restricted perspective on the (non-) One.

The (non-)One is essentially the aspect in which diversity or multiplicity appears when it is no longer structured through Difference, in other words when multiplicity or diversity is no longer conceived in terms of any *necessary relation* between the multiple and the One (whether an asymmetrical relation in which one term dominates the other, or a mutual one in which both terms are chiasmically intertwined).[17] It is thus a kind of suspension of Difference with respect to or according to the One. However, it is important to be careful here. Difference as such is not suspended; only the apparent second-order necessity that Difference would *also* structure every mode of access to Difference. The (non-)One, then, is not the One 'itself' but is what of Difference remains, or rather the newly restricted aspect in which it appears, when the stance of non-philosophy is taken. What remains is 'a diversity which is the residue of the unary destruction of Difference and which is neither ontic nor ontological'.[18]

It is important to distinguish the diversity or multiplicity at issue here from any and every diversity that is posited, requisitioned, deduced and so forth by one or another version of Difference. The diversity of the (non-) One cannot be subject to any intrinsic relation whatsoever, in particular to any relation with ideality (no matter how differentiating or disseminating or atomic). In this respect the parentheses around the 'non-' in (non-)One are meant to signify that the diversity at issue here is not really distinguished from the One or from the character of being thought in-One. It is *real* diversity, or diversity *as* real rather than *some given* diversity, which would presume the diversity as merely one component of a more extensive structure, for example of possibility, virtuality or general economy.

Laruelle identifies the One and the Real. In the history of philosophy, the Real has been conceived in two predominant forms: a) as *independence*, and b) as *authenticity*. The former conception, the Real as what exists independently of thought, is the predominant one throughout the history of philosophy. On a common-sense view, the granite block is real because it exists as what it is whether or not anyone perceives it, thinks about it, or refers to it via language. This notion depends upon an *a priori* transcendence of reality with respect to ideality, a relative transcendence or cut which Laruelle designates as the philosophical distinction of syntax and reality. The latter conception, the Real as what exists in accordance with its true essence, is in some respects more nuanced and variable. It allows for degrees of reality, since a given existent may be more or less in accordance with its essence and essences themselves may be gradated. Of course, this general conception itself depends nonetheless upon an *a priori* coordination of essence and existence. It thus tends to appear on Laruelle's terms as a relatively immanent difference within syntax itself, a relation rather than a cut.

One thing to note about both independence and authenticity, however, is that they both serve as qualifications on what exists. The Real is, in this sense, always a species or property of (genuine) existence. It is what *ultimately* exists, or what exists *most*. In contrast, when Laruelle identifies the One and the Real, it is in order to detach the Real from any determination through Being. Yet Laruelle's One must equally be distinguished from the 'Absolute' as it functions variously in the systems, for instance, of German Idealism. To the extent that 'One' is introduced as a term at all by Laruelle, it is as a strictly determinate and finite representational 'object'. It is simply 'the One' as one might say 'the apple' or 'the West'. It is not, as is the Absolute for Fichte or Schelling or Hegel, a term with respect to which all other terms must be ordered and relativised. There is thus for Laruelle no dialectical or differential problem of the 'appearance' or 'manifestation' of the One.[19] One way to formulate this would be to say that even if the One for Laruelle is in some sense absolute, it is not *the* Absolute. The One is by virtue of its essence absolved from all relation, but this does not entail that it is some quasi-theological Other or ground of Being. It is not in any way *opposed* to relations. It is thus not the absolved-from-relation *of* manifest beings, and it neither governs nor escapes Being. It is just simply and non-mysteriously the One, indifferent. Yet if the One in this way has simply nothing at all to do (or not do) with the world and its relations, what does the world have to do with it?

To repeat: the One is not the Absolute. This does not mean, however, that the 'One' is not special, even supremely special in certain respects. After all, just because it may be treated as 'only' another object does not necessarily entail that it is thereby subsumed in its reality under some *a priori* schema of objectivity. The status of such a schema is precisely what is in question. What is especially interesting about the One when it is taken in this naive way is the definitive self-indexing of its own meaning and being. Just because it is not self-*problematising* does not mean it is not self-*participating* in its own unique way (precisely as One). There is in addition to this special feature an immediate effect such indexical-taking-hold-of-itself has on all other objects and modalities of experience in their very multiplicity. Let us unpack this key notion.

If the One is in fact transcendental, that is, if it indeed (at least) conditions every possible form of existence and object of experience, it is nonetheless the only transcendental that is in no manner compromised by being *also* a perfectly determinate, even finite, 'object'. Not only is 'One', like 'Being', not a predicate, it is not even a difference or the ground of a difference! But this does not make it unthinkable or mysterious or God-like, according to Laruelle. It simply must be thought in a separate fashion from the more conventional thinking of beings or even of Being. The One is neither Same, Difference, nor Other, although it excludes none of these. So how then do we see it, know it, 'get' it? In our Kantian/post-Kantian age, it is fair game to ask with respect to any object of experience or discourse, 'What is the proper mode of access to X?' This remains true even (and especially) for objects or terms that are purported to be immediately or self-evidently given as well as, on the other hand, given as transcendently Other. This broadly Kantian problematic of access is not merely a matter of the prioritisation of epistemology over ontology. It is equally the problem, as we have seen in Heidegger, of existential-phenomenological conditions for manifestation and relationality as such, irrespective of any question of representation or knowledge.[20] From a name to its referent as from *Dasein* to Being: *relation to reality* is for philosophy an inescapable milieu. It is a real problem, the problem *of* the Real.

How does Laruelle mean in effect to outflank this question of relational access? By taking as the object of his discourse the One understood as the in-One of 'immediate givens' as such. There is not then some particular or even general content (experience, objects, beings, ego, consciousness, etc.) conceived as *given immediately*. The various philosophical criticisms of the 'myth(s) of the given' remain in place and are perfectly valid here.[21] Rather, the 'object' at stake for Laruelle just is the 'in-One' as 'the immediate' or, more precisely, the 'given-without-givenness' simply and straightforwardly, no longer even *as such* ('as such' cannot but imply a distinction).[22] There is no *objective content* here, nor any *logical form* that could in principle be 'filled' with some such content. There is only, on the one hand, a *determinate finite mode*, that is, the One as a strictly determined modality of itself and thus a finitude limited by itself alone: One-in-One. And then, on the other hand, there is – indivisible from this – the immediate transformation of the appearance of all forms of relation and correlation and, more generally, Difference in light of this peculiar, strictly separate finitude. These latter all appear themselves in-One, yet without thereby losing their relational, correlational or differential structure. They are (non-)One.

There is in this way an immediate transmission or contagion of the in-One since no exterior limit or division can mark it. The modality of the 'in-One' limits nothing other than itself, it *excludes* nothing. It thus becomes a simple analytic truth that there is no problem of access to this determinate 'object' and its effects. It is not only *everywhere*, but equally *anywhere* and *anyhow*. Immediate givens-without-givenness are not – by definition – given with (any) givenness. They are simply in-One. But this does not limit, exclude or deny givenness of any sort. On the contrary – or is this a contrary? – everything that is given through some mode of given-ness must *also* be 'given' simultaneously or super-positionally in-One. This would be true not only for *what is given* but for every *mode of givenness* as well, indiscriminately. The One thus allows for a truly unlimited pro-liferation of givens and modes of givenness, without in any way producing or 'emanating' these. The One is not *related* to anything in any way, by definition, but by the same token it is unreservedly and immediately 'open' to any things in all ways. 'In-One' is in this respect the non-exclusively unique 'term' that would transcendentally determine the question of access to any given or givens whatsoever without being determined in turn by this very question.[23] It is just such a thoroughly unidirectional conditionality that licenses Laruelle's description of the One as at once *transcendental* and *real*.

Like Kant, Laruelle inquires into transcendental conditions, but instead of transcendental conditions of experience (how are self-consistent and law-like empirical structures possible?) Laruelle asks into the tran-scendental conditions of Difference (how are the non-self-consistent and indeterminate forms of Difference possible?). The concept of (non-)One represents the way in which the 'hiatus between the empirical and the ideal' – the traditional philosophical distinction which the philosophies of Difference had themselves in one fashion or another finessed or com-plicated – becomes 'definitively re-opened' and thereby 'lets *a new kind of gap* be glimpsed'. This 'is the gap that the unary real itself straightaway imposes upon what is not it, upon this relation as such that is philosophical decision'.[24]

Since for Laruelle the One is interchangeable with the Real, to speak of a *real* diversity or multiplicity is immediately to speak of the One, or rather of an immediately given diversity in-One.

> It is no longer a matter of an idealized diversity in general, but a diversity of the contingency that refuses itself absolutely to any idealization whatsoever, that is rather the presupposition of every idealization by philosophy in general and by Difference in particular. Diversity *'in itself' and non-thetic (of) itself, more profound than the 'Thing in itself' and testifying to an absolute contingency of Difference, even 'finite' Difference.*[25]

Thus, Laruelle, like Heidegger, mounts a defence of the Real as against any and all forms of philosophical idealism. How, then, is this distinct from Heideggerean Finitude? It seems that Laruelle's (non-)One and Heidegger's pre-ontological, finite essence of Being share certain basic characteristics. Both relativise the metaphysical (and even ontological) cor-relations of Being and beings and thereby escape the logic of objectivisa-tion, even as this appears in its most subtle, non-representationalist forms.

The distinction between them is marked, however, by the most general framework within which each mode of thinking is 'situated'.

For Heidegger, the finite, non-objectivisable real is precisely *pre*-ontological. It serves a *necessary* function with respect to Being. It is both a real and a non-contingent transcendence. While real finitude for Heidegger certainly produces manifest effects within the 'fold' of Being and beings, these effects cannot by definition be identical to the essence of their Being but only symptoms or indications of the absolute withdrawal of the in-itself (ultimately the One as Event of Beyng or withdrawal-of-withdrawal). This withdrawal is itself conceived as the real and necessary abyssal ground of Being.

For Laruelle on the contrary the One is simply in-One by its very essence (which from its standpoint is in no way distinguished from any being or existence that at any rate it would in no way require). It neither 'withdraws' (Heidegger) nor 'emanates' (Neo-Platonism) nor 'immanates' (Spinoza-Deleuze) nor 'differs/defers' (Derrida). The (non-)One is thus not an effect or product of the One, but simply the way whatever is taken *not* to be the One – paradigmatically, multiplicities, relations and terms of relations – registers as already transcendentally given in-One *if* any such appear. This is the way every form of relation, diversity or multiplicity becomes manifest when the philosophical difference between syntax and reality is no longer operative for thought.[26] The transcendence and difference involved in such relations and multiplicities are in no manner negated by the One, but they are rendered thoroughly contingent. *If and when* transcendence and difference are manifest then they can only register as (non-)One, but such manifestation in no way marks a 'break' with the One from its own standpoint, much less some necessary and inevitable fracture *within* it.

How does this stand with the triad of Nietzsche-Deleuze, Heidegger and Derrida? First of all, it should be clear that the traditional conceptions of the Real as outlined above do not obviously or neatly accord with any of them. Nietzsche's rejection of Platonism and ultimately of truth itself takes traditional conceptions of the Real out of play. If anything, in Nietzsche to think the Real as Will to Power is nothing other than to resolve upon the evacuation of notions of independent being ('everything is perspectival') *and* of authenticity ('there are no subjects, only masks'). In a similar way, in Deleuze the appropriation of Bergson's concept of the virtual serves the function of guaranteeing the possibility of something being 'real without being actual, ideal without being abstract'. In Heidegger, 'authenticity' is certainly a key term in *Being and Time*, but the later work moves away from this earlier conception. Even in *Being and Time*, authenticity is not correspondence to some pre-given essence, but is rather the resolution with which human *Dasein* may act *in the face of* its own essentially finite possibilities. And of course 'truth' as *aletheia* in the late Heidegger is never grounded in an independent state of affairs but is rather effected as pure, event-ful upsurge. Finally in Derrida, the critique of presence on the basis of the irreducibility of differance universalises non-self-identity not as unlimited becoming but as irreducible trace of the Other. Yet even across this inversion or restriction/supplementation of Nietzsche via Heidegger, the basically Nietzschean rejection of truth and authenticity remains unaltered.

So it might appear that by rejecting the coordination of the Real with (some part of) what exists, Laruelle is only proceeding in a manner already clearly marked out by the philosophers of Difference. Indeed, Difference itself as Laruelle conceives it *just is* the lifting of the *différence* between the empirical on the one hand and the metaphysical or ideal on the other to the level of the (presumed) transcendental or Real. Difference, on Laruelle's own account, puts the very split between the real naively understood as the merely actual (the empirical or concrete) and the real as other-than-actual (as virtual, or as thing-in-itself, or as Other) at the heart of the Real as such.[27] It is this invariant structure that clothes itself variously in the philosophies of Difference at issue. It remains to be considered, then, how the conception of multiplicities given in-One applies in particular to that complex and rich multiplicity called philosophy, that peculiar multiplicity which understands itself to govern – via the synthesis, divergence or identity of thought and being – *all* relations, terms, singularities and multiples.

NON-THETIC TRANSCENDENCE (NTT) AND PHILOSOPHICAL DECISION

What Laruelle calls 'non-thetic transcendence' or NTT is conceived as a 'mode' or specification of the (non-)One. It is in fact the core thesis of philosophy as seen in-One. As such, it represents 'the real kernel of transcendence that is the basis of every philosophical decision'.[28] For Laruelle, the philosophical interpretation of transcendence is in effect a transcendental usage by philosophy of the 'difference' between the One and the (non-)One (a difference which is itself a mode of the (non-)One) for the purpose of redefining the One from the standpoint of this very difference itself. Of course, for Laruelle such a 'difference' between One and (non-)One exists *only* from the Differential standpoint of philosophy. An *image of transcendence* thus becomes philosophy's constitutive 'transcendental illusion' of the One as seen unavoidably from philosophy's own standpoint, that is, by means of Difference. Difference, which sees itself and everything else in-Difference and not in-One, can only interpret the One in terms of transcendence. It then makes, as Laruelle points out with regard to Heidegger in particular, a twofold error: 1) the transcendence it wrongly ascribes to the One is interpreted as Real; and 2) the Real, in turn, is conceived solely in terms of such transcendence.[29] In this way, the One appears to philosophy either as *the transcendent* (the Absolute) or, more subtly, as a general *operation of transcendence* (for example, as Heideggerean *ek-stasis* or the Badiousian 'count-as-One').

NTT designates the way the forms of this transcendental illusion of Difference appear when they are themselves 'seen' from the non-philosophical stance of the One, that is, seen in-One. Viewed in this way, they appear as arbitrary and self-legitimising as rejecting the One outside themselves simply on their own authority or decision. Yet in doing so they are nonetheless in no way distinct from the One as seen from its 'side'. Thus, the concept of NTT serves to ground Laruelle's theory of philosophical decision as the pure, ungrounded contingency of Difference. According to Laruelle, it is precisely this concept of philosophy's own radical contingency that philosophy *as such* remains incapable of grasping, since Difference will necessarily interpret itself on the basis of Difference and thus will inevitably interpret the One as a transcendence relative to this immanence of Difference.[30] Laruelle thus does not in any way *deny* the reality of transcendence; he only rejects the philosophical interpretation of transcendence as somehow *related* to the Real (and therefore as structured by Difference).

On the basis of the 'system' formed by the (non-)One and NTT, then, a non-philosophical theory of philosophical decision becomes possible. Perhaps an intuition of the structure invoked by Laruelle here can be given by taking the instance of fractal geometry or the concept of 'fractal' in general and then tracking the transformation this latter undergoes when it is applied to or fused with the concept of the One. A fractal is any curve that is 'self-similar', that is, a curve that reproduces its own form at varying levels of magnification. It is as if a fractal is in some way 'proto-intentional' or even 'proto-philosophical': it is, in a somewhat vague but intuitively powerful sense, a form that is *about itself*. It is clear that not all shapes are fractals, but it is also clear after some reflection that many if not all common non-fractal shapes have fractal analogues. However, these latter can be no more than analogues. The self-relating *itself* of the fractal is not some external supplement – a tacked-on self-indexing – but is rather an intrinsic determination of the fractal's form. The strangeness of this situation bears considerable thought: a shape becomes *self*-relating (fractalises) only by being modified through its own self-reflection. Yet this modification is not modification by way of external determination but instead through a self-deepening or self-enrichment of its own structure. The analogy here, if we take this geometrical metaphor as a representation of philosophy and in particular of Difference, would be the following: just as a 'simple' shape purifies and intensifies itself (that is, fractalises) by relating to itself only by modifying itself, the Real would purify and relate to itself only through its modification by philosophy, which would not alter the Real from some exterior position but would be rather the abstract function of self-mirroring or infinitisation as applied by the Real within the Real as such.

How then does the analogy treat the relation of non-philosophy to philosophy? Consider the special case of the One, understood in a straight-forward manner as the form of the simple, or the without-form (a form is a relation of parts, and the One by definition has no parts). The One's 'simple' essence is *also already* its self-similar or fractalised form. To draw out the analogy, the distinction and relation between fractal and non-fractal forms would correspond to philosophy's distinction and relation between itself and the Real. The unique indifference of the One to the distinction fractal/non-fractal would correspond then to non-philosophy's generalisa-tion of philosophy. The 'form' of the One in no way annuls the distinction between fractal and non-fractal forms, but it renders that distinction itself relative and contingent.

Laruelle himself proffers the 'Nietzsche-Heidegger conflict' as a kind of test-case for his theory of philosophical decision. From the standpoint of the One, both Idealist Difference and Difference as Finitude are equally arbitrary interpretations of non-thetic transcendence. They are philosoph-ical self-interpretations that as such equally *mis*-interpret the 'real kernel of transcendence' that in fact makes them both possible and real. As seen in-One, the strategy of Heideggerean Finitude on the one side inevitably misjudges its own critique of philosophical idealism since

> it is always possible to draw out the thesis of real Finitude from its naïvete and to reduce it to being still a philosophical thesis but one of a new style, forming *with* the restricted philosophy that it grounds a new space but one the real unity of which is beyond it, in a non-thetic, absolute and contingent decision.[31]

'Inversely', as Laruelle puts it, Nietzschean Idealism fares no better. From *its* side,

> the *a priori* reduction of all inauthenticity and the expulsion of the principle of the in itself beyond the essence of truth, is solely – in this still classical type of philosophy – the denial of a presupposition, a denial that it is always possible to re-introduce into this system of the idealizing usage of Difference in order to reconstitute an absolute decision.[32]

Seen from this standpoint, there is no need to decide between Nietzsche and Heidegger, since there is no sense in deciding among hallucinations.

These hallucinations 'decide for themselves' by treating the non-thetic transcendence that they *are* in each case as a thematic Difference to which they must each *relate*.[33]

What principle would justify this indifference to Nietzschean and Heideggerean decision? For Laruelle, the final criterion of all philosophical decision and its groundless absurdity is the human individual as understood in the new non-philosophical sense, and therefore no longer in terms of any essential definition such as 'rational animal', 'transcendental subjectivity', '*Dasein*', or 'Will to Power'. In the face of this irreducible, non-philosophical human identity (human-in-One), all philosophies become effectively interchangeable, not in terms of their content (which is clearly different in each case) but in terms of their common form of decision:

> measured against finite or 'individual' man who precedes philosophical decision, who affects it with a stronger contingency, there is neither more nor less absurdity in one choice than in another, but an equal absurdity, an equal absence of sufficient reason for the choice, an 'absence' that is the true 'sufficient reason' of philosophical decision and of the war philosophical decision wages against itself.[34]

Thus, not only in the case of Nietzsche and Heidegger but *in general* 'we must posit the equivalence of philosophical decisions'.[35] Not an abstract principle, then, but the ordinary human Real throws the contingent, decisional essence of philosophy into relief.

Is this simply the rejection by *theory* of (decisional) *practice*? In the context of reflecting on the differences among the schools of ancient philosophy, Pierre Hadot offers a fine metaphor for the relation between the theoretical aspect of philosophy in general and the particular choice of one philosophical school among others. Hadot likens the relationship between philosophical practice as a determinate way of life and philosophical theory as a systematic interpretation of the world to the feedback loop constituted by a bicycle's forward motion through dark streets and the visibility made possible by the bicycle's headlight as powered by that motion.[36] Even if this system as such takes the form of a kind of reciprocally determined circuit (motion produces illumination; illumination ensures continued motion), the proper functioning of the circuit as a whole depends upon an initial propulsion that is entirely one-sided. Even if only for an instant, one must move (or choose) in the dark prior to any guidance by a theory that would guide that motion (or choice). One can only leap blindly into the choice of *a* philosophy, for Hadot, which is not to say that philosophies themselves are blind, only that there is an irreducible priority of act or will to reflection or theory, even if this priority is infinitesimal.

Difference itself already problematises any clear distinction between the practical and the theoretical, just as it blurs any distinction that would not be lifted or transversalised so as to cut across itself and re-divide itself. Yet the one distinction that Difference will not be capable of blurring in this way is the only distinction it remains incapable of tolerating because it is the only one that would relativise this very process and reiteration of lifting and transversalisation, of Difference as such: the distinction-without-difference imposed by the One. So if Hadot's metaphor cannot apply to Difference at the level of any clear and absolute distinction between the theoretical and the practical, it may indeed apply at a level that is no longer a level at all, on the 'level' of the veritable One-Real, which may no longer be characterised through any difference whatsoever, even an infinitesimal one. In general, philosophy tends to consider the Real as a kind of 'first push' or 'initial ground', when it is not simply identified with the internal structures of ideal syntax. In other words, for philosophy the Real functions essentially as a *condition*. As a condition, it then serves in principle as the basis of theoretical or practical decisions. For Laruelle, in contrast, the Real is not a condition but rather a transcendental determination *as distinct from any and all conditions*, even the 'immanent' conditions of Difference.

This is what Laruelle means by his syntax of 'determination-in-the-last-instance'.[37] X as determined-in-the-last-instance refers to nothing other than the real determination of X as separate from every determination through conditions and conditioning. This means directly that determination-in-the-last-instance cannot be used to generate causal consequences or logical entailments of any kind. It is neither a specification nor a grounding. What 'purpose' then does it serve? None whatsoever. But this purposelessness in turn relativises every purposeful structure of specification, deduction, entailment, generalisation or grounding, even through Difference. It 'unlatches' but does not 'break' or 'throw open' such determinations themselves. The key here is to recognise a priority that is *only* a 'secondarisation' or 'relativisation' of its 'other term' and thus one that does not split itself off from that 'second' term.

What then is the 'decision' of Difference? It is not the decision for one or another philosophy, although some such decision is always a necessary consequence of the decision for Difference. The decision of Difference is the decision for philosophy as such. Here, then, is Laruelle's fully elaborated answer to the question of how Difference is generalised across Western philosophy as a whole. Difference is not a genus that would subsume all the diverse, specific philosophies that span such a massive braiding and syncretism of traditions that no community of inquiry, much less any particular scholar, could possibly survey and produce exhaustive judgements about them. Difference is not a genus or schema but the very form of philosophical decision, *the* decision for philosophy. However, this identity of Difference and decision is constitutively inaccessible from within Difference itself. It is not only that Difference does not view itself as 'just one more philosophy' and thus does not interpret itself as a decision – this it shares with every philosophy more or less. What makes Difference so general is precisely the power with which it occludes its own decisive nature from itself. Not just for external reasons, but for the most consistent and rigorous of reasons internal to its own functioning, Difference *denies* decision. Why? Because *if* a philosophy conceives of itself as simply the result of an act of decision, it immediately negates itself *as philosophy*. At a minimum, philosophy involves a commitment to the constraining force of determination (by Truth, Being, One, Ego, Real, etc.). For this reason, philosophy may accept an *element* of decision as one factor within its internal workings, but it cannot – on pain of self-contradiction – understand itself as *wholly* decisional, as decisional through and through. Philosophy as such *begins* with the rejection of the wholly arbitrary. It *needs* the Real in one form or another as determining constraint (as Same or Other) in order to leverage itself into the position of arbiter of judgement or real co-determinant. The significant accomplishment of Difference is to have brought this need fully into itself philosophically and to have made of it a principle of immanent determination. Difference enables philosophy to need *itself* as Real.

Nietzsche and Deleuze select selection as the moment of philosophical decision, Being determined as Will to Power and creative desire. For Heidegger decisive existence as resolute authenticity in the early work is softened by the letting-be of the later work. In Derrida, decision becomes the paradigm of the unique mixture of the necessary and impossible that defines his own project. Thus for all three models, decision is an essential component of Difference. But for none of them is the very belonging of decision to Difference a matter of decision. In each case, decision is only thinkable as relative to the constraint of its necessity. Decision forms a couple with the undecided and undecidable or, more strongly, identifies the undecidability between decision and indecision as the ineluctable crisis of thought, 'the mixture of Difference as "un?decidable" decision'.[38]

What then of non-philosophy? If it brings the decisional nature of Difference and, by extension, of philosophy as such to light, what positive characterisation remains for the stance of non-philosophy other than being merely 'non-decisional'?

Thinking that is none other than 'unary' is in a state of poverty that is practically absolute, it is stripped of all operation, all technique, all power. It is content with a description without intervention, a contemplation without decision. The One has need of neither repetition, nor reduction and suspension, nor turning, it clasps nothing of Being, contenting itself with unclasping Being or de-clutching Difference.[39]

An adequate understanding of this passage clearly depends upon being able to distinguish rigorously between a philosophical 'reduction' or 'suspension' on the one hand and a non-philosophical 'unclasping' or 'de-clutching' on the other. What exactly is the difference?

It is the essence of truth that is determined differently in the two cases. From the non-philosophical standpoint, there is no pre-given field of any type whatsoever no matter what degree of generality or horizonality (neither Being, nor experience, nor beings, nor ideas . . .) toward which the question of truth would be directed. Instead, non-philosophy 'no longer has need of a *metaphysical a priori* in general, of a *universal transcendental field* of experience or of the Unity of experience, which always forms a system with the thesis that there will have been presuppositions that must be analysed, divided, reduced'.[40]

In effect, all such co-ordinations of one region or term with respect to some other region or term, every possible model of thought structured by essential correlation, is relativised as an inessential characterisation of truth: 'The empirico-transcendental mixture of truth and appearance, this inalienable alienation posited by the unitary tradition, if in effect it even exists, no longer co-belongs to the essence of the truth and has no more legitimation, in the last instance, than that of its real contingency upon the One.'[41] The emphasis here on 'legitimation' is paramount. Laruelle's point is not that Difference is incoherent. It is that the structure of its legitimation ultimately requires *both* itself *and* the One, whereas there is a way of thinking that finds 'legitimation' *only* in-One (without thereby *denying* the double legitimatisation strategy of Difference). It is not that Difference is *reducible* to the One; it is rather that the autonomy of Difference is at best a relative autonomy that cannot do without the One. Whereas the One by its essence has no need of Difference, even to think 'itself'. It is this latter claim that Difference contests.

Clearly, Laruelle *in fact* uses philosophical Difference to think the One – this is undeniable. What Laruelle does deny is that such usage is constitutive for thinking the One in the sense of serving as a necessary and essential condition. Or, more precisely, he relativises this necessity to the restricted essence of Difference itself and reserves a more comprehensive notion of essence – essence as unilateral, transcendental and real – for the One. It may be true as a banal, merely empirical fact that we, as human beings, think 'in Difference'. Philosophy on Laruelle's account would lift this empirical fact to the status of a transcendental essence of thinking as such. The structure of Laruelle's argument allows him to respect the former fact within its proper limits, but nonetheless to reject the latter 'lifting' to the transcendental.

Difference is not the simple negation of or opposition to the One – the entire philosophical innovation of Difference is to think difference as prior to identity, as the 'difference of difference' or difference-in-itself. But in order to differ from 'itself' the syntax of Difference requires the One as the transcendental condition of a self-relation (a Same) in the most general sense that would include non-identical repetition and differentiation. What exactly, then, is to be criticised in Difference? Laruelle's argument here is to show that Difference entails an inevitable moment of decision within philosophy – a decision of and for a philosophy from among philosophies – but that it cannot provide any principle or criterion that would be adequate for determining which decision should be made. In other words, Difference requires a distinction – a difference – between the real or correct philosophy from among possible philosophical models, but every choice of a suitable criterion is equivalent (or reducible) to the choice of one of the philosophical models themselves.

> Do we have a *real* criterion for deciding between Hegel and Heidegger? Nietzsche and Heidegger? Heidegger and Derrida? Is Finitude a criterion, and of what kind, capable of constraining us to the choice against absolute Idealism? etc. It is not a matter of knowing empirically or even ideally why we choose such and such a philosophy, the criterion must be transcendental or real and possess a power that would be at least that of a sufficient reason for philosophical decision.[42]

In other words, Laruelle is pursuing a kind of transcendental deduction of philosophy. He is not concerned to find structures governing possible experience (causality, substance, etc.) that would be necessary for experience *a priori* and which therefore would not themselves be derivable from experience. Rather, he is concerned to find a criterion governing the choice among possible philosophies that would be *real* and which therefore cannot itself be derived from any philosophical choice. In one sense, Laruelle is simply posing the question: *If* a real criterion among philosophies were to be found, what characteristics would it necessarily possess? His answer is that only the Real itself would suffice as the criterion. But now we feel the incipient swoon of philosophy confronted by the vicious circle of its reasoning. The Real is of course precisely the point of contention among philosophies.

Philosophers are likely not to disagree with Laruelle here but only to point out his apparent naivety. *To be sure* the Real is at once the prize to be won and the standard of judgement for its winning. The whole problem is that of the correct or best or least restrictive interpretation of the Real.

This is precisely the point at which the philosophies of Difference appear to offer a genuine philosophical advance. All of these philosophers are in agreement that the classical conception of truth as correspondence and the natural understanding of thought as representation are one-sided, falsifying and in need of critique. Already in Hegel philosophy comes into the fullness of its maturity that promises never to return to such ordinariness and lack of sophistication. The core structure of Difference involves a twist of all hierarchies and a self-inclusion.

If the philosophies of Difference are in agreement with one another on this point, what exactly is the object of their contest? Nietzsche-Deleuze, Heidegger and Derrida should not be compared as mutually exterior points of view or incompatible theses. The importance of Laruelle's conceiving of these three models as models of Difference rests in how this very 'reduction' remains internal to Difference. There is no line of demarcation between Nietzsche and Heidegger, for example, or between Heidegger and Derrida, that would not already be internal to each of the two sides. This is a consequence of Laruelle's hermeneutics of generosity: it is impossible to situate oneself (or anyone else) outside of the philosophy of any of the thinkers at issue. There is no point of exterior critique to any of them, and certainly no Archimedean point of neutral critique relative to them all. Does this mean that these philosophies have been placed beyond the possibility of any critique whatsoever? Not at all. It only means that any critique must be understood (at least potentially) as a *self*-critique, an auto-inhibition. It follows as an immediate consequence of Difference = (meta-)Difference that not only is every philosophy of Difference in excess of itself, unlimitedly 'beyond' itself and everywhere conjoined with its Outside but also that every exterior critique, every counter-example or alternate position is posited in advance as relatively interior to its complement. Does this then mean that by being subsumed into Difference the distinct models of Difference may find a common peace? No, because their differences are real with respect to Difference. Instead of peace, Difference manifests a self-contested immanence of war.

For Laruelle the Real is not an object of contestation but the indisputable 'immediate givens in-One'. Laruelle defines the 'Transcendental Illusion' of Difference as the reflexive and uncritical conception of 'its own interpretation of its work, of the real that it posits and works upon, of its historicity and its decisions', in short, of its own *self*-interpretation as the sole, universal Real.[43] In other words, at a first level and in a very clear and almost common-sense manner, Laruelle claims of Difference that it succumbs to the same form of error that is common in other domains to egoism and to ideology, that is, the error that takes the particular for the universal: 'My concerns are (or should be) everyone's concerns'; '*Our*

values are (or should be) *real* values.' The 'specific difference' of Laruelle's
critique is that he applies this form of criticism to what would otherwise
appear as the most general and open model of thought as such. The 'self'
of Difference is the most pluralistic and non-identitarian 'self' that is possible for philosophical thought. Difference is *already in itself* the maximum
philosophical critique of ideology as the opposition of a narrowly conceived
partiality to the true universal. Every false totality and limited perspective
is *already* exploded by Difference. Of course, Difference is not an algo-
rithmic program that would somehow take ideological views or statements
as input and automatically output critical *différance*. But Difference as
the generic syntax modelled by Nietzsche, Heidegger and Derrida is rich
enough and flexible enough in principle to support *any* critical procedure.
Its two 'sides' of infinite potentialisation and critical self-inhibition are
both maximal in their own right.

So how does the non-philosophical critique of Difference proceed? The
critique of Difference follows as 'a simple effect' from the conception of the
Real that does not accept the premises of Difference, the very conception
that is the transcendental condition for deciding among various philosophies.[44] In other words, if Difference is going to do what it claims it needs
to do – namely, to *decide* philosophy – then it will require something *other
than Difference* to do this: 'If the real is by definition the Unconstituted, the
Unproduced, the Undecidable, every theory of decision would from the
very beginning have to install itself in this problematic of the real and its
"undecidable" essence.'[45] It suffices to demonstrate that there is a mode of
thinking that does not *need* Difference.

THE VISION-IN-ONE AND NON-PHILOSOPHICAL DUALISM

The conceptual apparatus of (non-)One and NTT is meant to make the
difference between the non-philosophical 'dual' and the philosophical
'duel' intelligible. In other words, the critique of the decisional nature of
philosophy is at the same time a clarification of the distinction between
(A) the 'duality' between the One and Difference on the one hand and (B)
the 'duel' inherent to Difference on the other. Since this new distinction
A/B is claimed to itself become visible only from the standpoint of (A),
Laruelle appears to incorporate the generic form of Difference as against
Difference. Finally, then, we must examine the notion of 'dualism' that
Laruelle develops in the final section of chapter seven in order to explain
the precise relation (or lack of relation) that holds between philosophy and
non-philosophy.

Laruelle invokes dualism not in terms of its Cartesian connotations of
a two-sided metaphysics of mind and body but rather through the sense it

takes on in Gnostic speculation of a radical (and soteriological) *separation* of the subject of *gnosis* with respect to the apparently all-enveloping world. Non-philosophical thinking is thus conceived as a form of individual experience conjoined with neither world nor object. This experience is taken to underlie and yet to be occluded by the philosophical experience(s) of being, world and truth. According to Laruelle, non-philosophical 'dualism' in fact provides the basis in this way for 'retrieving the irreducible "mystic" condition of every philosophy'.[46]

In this regard, Laruelle distinguishes three generic claims to the experience of the immediate as designated by three terms – the *mystic*, the *mystical*, and *mysticism* – in the following way:

The mystic: 'the immediate givenness of the One, as well as of the Other *in* this radical immanence of the One, the givenness of Indivision as such and as separate from the All'.

The mystical: 'the immediate givenness of the Other in what remains here despite everything a theological transcendence'.

Mysticism: 'the immediate givenness of Being or the All of reality'.

Laruelle claims, 'The "mystic" such as we understand it here is the token or guarantee of the radical autonomy of the most "individual" thinking and, through this, of philosophy with regard to what is not philosophy.'[47] This would be 'not a matter of claiming to dissolve or to destroy Difference, for example into two principles, but of thinking the technology of Difference from its real essence, precisely what Difference on its own account has never been able to do.'[48] As distinct from the 'mystical' and 'mysticism', then, the 'mystic' does not depend upon any *unifying* function of the One. It is neither a union with the transcendent Other nor an identification with the totalised All. Instead, the dualist 'mystic' is an instance of thought as individual *gnosis*. This means above all that there is no need to ratchet oneself free of Difference by means of Difference or even by means of the One. The One is not a means, except for philosophy (a means of unification, of transcendence, of totalisation or the escape from totality). For Laruelle, the 'mystic condition of every philosophy' entails that 'it is perhaps possible, if not to "exit" from metaphysics, and from Heidegger as well, by "entering back" into the One, at least to comprehend that we need not enter metaphysics in the first place and that gnosis is what, of itself, separates the principles'.[49] In other words, non-philosophical dualism, rather than marking the means for an *escape* from the world via some synthesis or identification with the One, simply allows the world and the principle of philosophical Difference that governs it to separate itself off from an indifference that the individual subject *already is*.

There is an easy and yet powerfully tenacious objection to Laruelle's entire enterprise that emerges most clearly at this 'final' level. Does it not enact an obvious performative contradiction?[50] Philosophers are familiar with the logical fallacy of *tu quoque* ('you too'), that is, the mistaken inference from a performative contradiction of some kind, particularly from some given speaker's criticism applying to the act or person of the speaker him/herself (or, conversely, some positive claim or asserted criterion failing to be satisfied by the speaker), to the falsity, senselessness or inapplicability of the criticism (or claim) as such. A simple example would be found in the following – of course, highly contrived – exchange:

Mary: 'Tom, you shouldn't be judgemental.'

Tom: 'Mary, your very utterance is itself a judgement against me and thus contradicts its own essential content. You can't possibly judge my being judgemental without being judgemental yourself. Thus, I needn't take your self-contradictory judgement seriously. I am free to be as judgemental as I please.'

What supposedly renders Tom's reasoning fallacious is precisely his failure to recognise the independence of the truth or falsity of Mary's statement from its particular conditions of utterance. Whether or not it is in fact the case that Tom should not be judgemental (or even that people in general should not be judgemental), the judgemental nature of Mary's own act of stating this very fact is thought to have no bearing on the truth-value of what Mary says.

Now, it is clear that the independence of truth from the conditions of its utterance is at best a relative matter. Indeed the very idea of such independence has served as one of the presumptions of modern philosophy in particular upon which various strains of post-Enlightenment critique (including those of the philosophies of Difference) have brought special critical scrutiny to bear. In general, the fallacious nature of any particular instance of *tu quoque* dissolves or is at the very least rendered questionable when either 1) the content of the statement at issue refers either directly or indirectly to the speaker him or herself or to some class in which the speaker is included; or 2) the statement at issue concerns a claim about the structure or function of utterance in general. In the former case, the potential logical relevance of the *tu quoque* charge comes from the inclusion of the given speaker within the field of the semantic range of the claim. In effect, the speaker becomes part of the referent of the assertion and various problems and paradoxes of self-reference may ensue. In the latter case, language speaks about itself and thus includes its own operations in the domain of that of which it speaks. Here, the possibility of a different kind of self-referential paradox emerges, one grounded in the strange and impersonal 'reference of "reference"'. To clarify the distinction, consider the difference between two scenarios: 1) A Cretan says 'All Cretans are liars'; and 2) A Cretan says 'Language always lies'. Both of these may be understood as variants or specifications of the 'paradox of self-reference'. The fact that this 'paradox' itself admits of variation and specification points to the complexity of the issue of the self-relation it involves.

This more general logical issue is relevant here because it speaks to the core of the 'problem' which Laruelle has set himself in terms of articulating the *real* and *radically dualist* thinking of individuals and multiplicities. A similar problem has traditionally plagued philosophies of radical scepticism on the one hand and mystical, absolute and non-dual philosophies on the other.[51] In particular, non-philosophy shares with such modes of thought the problem of apparent performative contradiction: in the case of scepticism, to *claim* the ungroundedness of all claims; in the case of mysticism, to *speak* of the unspeakable.

In fact, the charge of *tu quoque* may be turned on its head to reveal the peculiar theoretical rigour of non-philosophy. The non-philosophical stance of vision-in-One deactivates the charge of *tu quoque* in advance by radically reinterpreting the general relation of enunciation and meaning from within this stance itself. In particular, the vision-in-One *simplifies* any chiasmus between the two kinds of self-reference just discussed. Instead of the negative critique of *tu quoque*, non-philosophy would instigate a strangely critical *affirmation*. Rather than charging the 'opponent' with a contradiction between what is said and what is done, non-philosophy would itself axiomatically assign an identity of utterance as sense and as act. The result is a radical simplification of the event of meaning. Instead of meaning as generated within a correlation between the immediate context of utterance and the general structure of sense (roughly, *parole* and *langue* or *enunciation* and *enunciated*), meaning would occur as a simple index of the identity of its utterance: *this*.[52] To grasp what is at stake in this 'this', imagine a participant in a dialogue, say, Mary, who decides to interpret every utterance of her interlocutor, Tom, as an *M-truth* assertion that *he is in fact saying what it is that he is saying*. In other words, when Tom says X, Mary will understand Tom to be affirming the *M-truth* 'I am saying "X".' If Tom utters the words 'Let's eat', Mary will understand him to be making the *M-truth*-claim 'I, Tom, am saying "Let's eat".'

Three results immediately follow. First, no matter what statement Tom utters, Mary will be able to affirm – on her own terms – the *M-truth* of what he says, and she will be able to do this *a priori*. Mary's mode of interpretation thus converts Tom into an *a priori* event of performative consistency, an unconditional *M-truth*-speaker. Second, Mary will be able to apply the same interpretative framework to her own utterances without introducing any contradiction or paradox. In other words, the generalisation of Mary's interpretative strategy does not (and cannot) produce a performative contradiction. Third, as bizarre as Mary's mode of interpretation may seem, it in no way interferes in principle with the normal functioning of ordinary discourse. If Mary understands Tom to be saying 'I, Tom, am saying "Let's eat"', there is nothing in this understanding that would inhibit her from joining Tom for a bite.

Interestingly, this particular case suggests the possibility of other modes of interpretation with analogous structure. For instance, utterances might be interpreted in terms of the schema '"X" is understood as "the physical conditions of the present utterance are as *so*"' with an implied indexing of the local environment around the utterance of X. Or, '"X" is understood as "the sociological and historical contexts enabling the present event of meaning are *these*"' with a characteristic indexing of the relevant conditions. There are infinite possible variations. If we gather all such interpretative schemata into a common class, a sort of generalisation of the principle of *nota notae*, we have a useful indication of the *kind* of 'interpretation' that non-philosophy makes of philosophy, namely, that of a *generalised indexicality* according to which any and all distinctions of level or hierarchy are rendered inoperative (though not invisible).

There is something quite close here to the method of phenomenological reduction, but with two important differences: one, this is not only a mode of *reception*, but equally a field of possible production; and two, there is no longer a natural *opposition* of the ordinary and the reflective. Phenomenology produces an insistent and perhaps ultimately insolvable problem once the standpoint of reduction is meant at the same time to 'reduce' or overcome the 'natural attitude' on the one hand and to take the 'lived experience' of and within the 'natural attitude' as the object of its investigation on the other. Either one gives up the natural attitude entirely (Husserl), in which case the object of phenomenology can only be something like a field of Platonic *eidai* and thus cannot grasp the lived *as such*, or one brings both the act of reduction *and* its inevitable failure and incompleteness into the structure of lived experience itself (Heidegger).

Still, even if Laruelle is correct that (T3) there is a form of thought that does not proceed according to Difference and its associated patterns of organisation, is it not the case that *our* access to the very idea of thinking the One in-One depends upon conceptualisation, syntax, etc., and hence philosophy? Does the status of the One as 'transcendental' not lead to a repetition in its own way of the long-standing interpretation of the Kantian transcendental as *a priori* conditions of experience *that would be inconceivable in themselves independently of the* fact *of experience*? Is Laruelle's insistence on the status of the One as both transcendental *and* real anything other than merely stipulative? In this regard, at the close of *Philosophies of Difference* Laruelle does appear to concede that the entire critical analysis has taken place within the (non-)One and thus can be no more than an indication from within Difference itself of a separate practice of thought.[53] It seems thus to remain impossible for Laruelle to claim to have 'done' non-philosophy, only to have demonstrated its 'internal consistency' or sheer possibility.

In this respect, *Philosophies of Difference* perhaps concludes in a kind of theoretical deadlock. This deadlock, however, is a productive one. It sets forth a clear problem and organises a definite theoretical agenda. It is the solution to this problem that Laruelle aims to formulate in his work subsequent to Philosophy II. In this prolific extension and refinement of the core ideas of non-philosophy, two main strategies or proposed solutions become discernible: (1) the generalised (non-)phenomenological approach that culminates in *Principles of Non-philosophy* and (2) the more recent generic philosophy/science matrix via idempotent and complex algebras, set forth more or less comprehensively in *Non-Standard Philosophy*. *Philosophies of Difference* and its fellow texts from Philosophy II may be seen as the 'first wave' that diffracts into this pair of later systematic specifications of non-philosophy. Perhaps without them, *Philosophies of Difference* would have to be judged an incomplete work. But considered together with these two later projects in particular, it may be said to be one key component of a richly realised theoretical enterprise.

In order to see in–One, it is necessary to have thought through the philosophical problem of the One and the Many to the point of recognising it almost viscerally in nearly every branch and question of philosophy. The general question of the One, the Many and the form of their relation(s) serves as an essential framework for ethics, politics, epistemology, ontology and aesthetics, not to mention logic. The motivation for non-philosophy and the vision-in-One stems from reflection on the authoritarian presuppositions built into simply posing philosophical problems in such terms. This is why the philosophies of Difference represent a natural point of entry into non-philosophy.

How does the vision-in-One respond to the traditional, indeed constitutive, philosophical question of ideality and reality? Rather than providing a new and different answer to this perennial problem, non-philosophy as introduced in *Philosophies of Difference* provides a new strategy for understanding it *as* a problem. This strategy consists of placing oneself, as a thinker, within a stance that sees the problem as simply an effect of using thought that orients itself ultimately within Difference (of course thought *may* always do so, but it *need* not). That is, it notes the problem as merely an instance of philosophy. Seen in this way, the problem of how to think the Real appears as no more than an index of philosophy's self-granted charge to dominate and determine the Real by differing from it or being identical to it. Non-philosophy rethinks the traditional philosophical problem of ideality and reality in such a way that the authoritarian presuppositions built into this problem come to light. Laruelle's proposal is distinct from familiar modes of philosophical critique in that it separates itself fully (in-One) from these presuppositions themselves. In other words, Laruelle's non-philosophy marks a critique of philosophy that is not also by the same token a *self*-critique.

Does this not risk reintroducing the worst authoritarian tendencies of the philosophical tradition, namely the claims to modernist sovereignty and epistemological universality that the philosophies of Difference and those following in their wake have criticised with such good reason? This is the crux of the matter. Does non-philosophy mark a mere regression to pre-Differential arrogance? Or does non-philosophy provide instead a way of understanding the authoritarian tendencies still operative within the philosophies of Difference but to which they themselves may remain blind? How could such questions be decided? Are they perhaps already decided as determined by the Real prior to any possible decision? In any event, what could a radical critique of authoritarianism be, if not the immediate taking up of a stance with respect to authority that would already be Other to the very problem and possibility of authority?[54] But what, then, is such an Other, if not the real human individual who exists prior to any interpretation through worldly categories or principles, who lives in-One and not by-Difference? The non-philosophical vision-in-One is neither pie in the sky nor blind luminosity. It is how we human beings see if and when we acknowledge honestly that we are real and yet no longer bolster that acknowledgement with any foundation, ground or authority: World, Logic, History, Power, Matter, Reality, Self, Truth, Philosophy, God, One.

Is Difference the best *philosophical* strategy available for contesting philosophical authoritarianism? Probably. But it always runs a twofold risk. On the one hand, it threatens to take upon itself too much of the power of authority in marshalling its forces against authority. Nietzsche and Deleuze confront this problem head-on, valiantly, and each probably succumbs in his own way. On the other hand, Difference may risk curtailing authority as no more than a limit with respect to some inaccessible Real. This tends from its side to idealise authority itself as Other and only a god can save us then. If the victims of authoritarianisms of all kinds are always singular and real human beings irreducible to any kind of object and other than any philosophical form of the subject, then only a mode of thought that thinks *from* rather than *of* the human Real truly takes its stand with and for such victims. It does so by taking a stance radically Other than every authority that would or could dominate them. This is to see in-One.

NOTES

1. *PD*, p. xxii.
2. This problem is posed and discussed in the context of Deleuze's philosophy in Iain MacKenzie, *The Idea of Pure Critique*.
3. See Gianni Vattimo on *Verwindung* and *Uberwindung* in *The End of Modernity*.
4. *PD*, p. 174.
5. The 'meta-' constitutive of Difference = (meta-)Difference depends upon its exclusion (or at least its difference from) the *epekeina* of transcendence (the *philosophical* One).
6. See Laruelle's phantasmagoric imaging of the 'strangely Platonizing spectacle' of contemporary, ostensibly anti-Platonic, philosophy: *PD*, p. 179.
7. *PD*, p. 175.
8. *PD*, p. 15.
9. *PD*, p. 105.
10. *PD*, p. 16.
11. *PD*, p. 16.
12. *PD*, p. 16.
13. *PD*, p. 15.
14. *PD*, p. 188.
15. Emmanuel Levinas, *Ethics and Infinity*, pp. 89–90, emphasis added.
16. *PD*, p. 195.
17. The way the (non-)One functions in *Philosophies of Difference* is itself developed from the pair of concepts '(non-)One' and 'non(-One)' in *A Biography of Ordinary Man*, and its distinction of an 'ordinary mystics' from an 'ordinary pragmatics'. See especially François Laruelle, *A Biography of Ordinary Man*, pp. 113–15.
18. *PD*, p. 200.
19. Compare Slavoj Žižek's very clear exposition of Fichte in *Less than Nothing*, ch. 3.
20. 'Object-oriented' approaches ultimately founder on this Kantian reef. To admit the question as such is already the devastation of their position. So it seems the best they can do is to hope for the withering away of the question. But the simple turning away from a question is not itself a successful argument.
21. See Wilfred Sellars, *Empiricism and the Philosophy of Mind*.
22. Laruelle's insistent use of the notion of 'unilaterality' should be understood on this basis. It is not a matter of 'counting the number of sides' but of grasping the simplicity of an un-gainsayable 'movement without return'.
23. The mathematically adventurous may want to consider in the context of category theory how Laruelle's project in this respect corresponds structurally to the role of the initial object 0 (the unique category with no objects and no arrows) in William Lawvere's 2-category, CAT. See Saunders Mac Lane, *Categories for the Working Mathematician*, pp. 272–9.
24. *PD*, p. 198.

25. *PD*, pp. 200–1.
26. This diversity may be compared to contemporary work such as Quentin Meillassoux's *After Finitude* and Dan Barber's *On Diaspora*.
27. In this respect Laruelle's analysis of Difference is in fundamental accord with Žižek's proposal for a very general synthesis of Hegel and Lacan as the essential *topos* of contemporary philosophy. See, for instance, Slavoj Žižek, *Less than Nothing*, chs. 7–8.
28. *PD*, p. 202.
29. *PD*, p. 213.
30. In later works, especially *Principles of Non-philosophy*, Laruelle develops the concept of non-thetic transcendence more fully and unpacks what remains in *Philosophies of Difference* a more or less gnomic indication of a theoretical solution rather than a fully fledged conception. In particular, the broadly 'methodological' implications of NTT, that is, the consequences that it must be deployed 'from' or 'according to' the One in a way that calls to mind the dense fabric of methodological issues surrounding *reduction* in phenomenology, are taken into account through the closely linked concepts of 'cloning' (*clonage*) and 'dualysis' (*dualyse*).
31. *PD*, p. 208.
32. Ibid.
33. As Laruelle writes: 'precisely because it is a matter of a relation, transcendent inasmuch as relation, it cannot emerge globally, comprehending its terms, except through a gesture that is, itself, straightaway contingent and "finite" to the extent that nothing could ever sublate or idealize this contingency in any "transcendental necessity"' (*PD*, p. 209). On this basis, Laruelle concludes: 'Metaphysics is not contingent as a empirical fact, nor even as an *a priori* fact; it is absolutely contingent and absurd beyond every historical insertion, every historical or perceptual model of contingency: it is not necessary except for itself and at the interior of its hallucination of the real' (*PD*, p. 210).
34. *PD*, p. 211.
35. *PD*, p. 211, in italics in the original.
36. Pierre Hadot, *The Present Alone is Our Happiness*, p. 104.
37. See *PD*, pp. 221–2. This key concept is more fully unpacked in François Laruelle, *The Minority Principle*, pp. 93–7 and François Laruelle, *A Biography of Ordinary Man*, pp. 139–41.
38. *PD*, p. 209.
39. *PD*, p. 218.
40. *PD*, pp. 218–19.
41. *PD*, p. 219.
42. *PD*, pp. 196–7.
43. *PD*, p. 197.
44. *PD*, p. 197.
45. *PD*, p. 197.
46. *PD*, p. 154.
47. *PD*, p. 154.

48. *PD*, pp. 154–5.
49. *PD*, p. 159.
50. In a long footnote to *Heidegger on Being and Acting* Reiner Schürmann puts his finger on the very point at issue. The note begins: 'Heidegger makes his own the results Nietzsche had already reached in his deconstruction of epochs (although in a different idiom), only then to label Nietzsche the last metaphysician. It seems that today [in 1982 – RG] Jacques Derrida is engaged in a similar game with Heidegger.' What Schürmann suggests is that the three-term sequence Nietzsche-Heidegger-Derrida may be understood as the three-fold iteration of a single strategy: situate the predecessor at the limit of (and thus partially within) the history of metaphysics and then initiate a mode of thought that would exploit this internal difference of the predecessor in a way that remains inaccessible for that predecessor himself, in other words, appropriate what has come before and at the same time objectify it. Nietzsche: truth against truth. Heidegger: Nietzsche against Nietzsche. Derrida: Heidegger against Heidegger. To point this out does not in any way negate the differences among the three thinkers. In fact, the reiteration of the strategy not only does not exclude differences among each iteration; it positively *requires* them.
51. For the rigorous defence of ancient scepticism, see Sextus Empiricus, *Against the Logicians*. For the most influential Buddhist position of ultimate non-dual emptiness, see Nāgārjuna, *The Fundamental Wisdom of the Middle Way*. One of the outstanding tasks for non-philosophy and its critical reception remains the precise analysis of how the two 'extreme' philosophical models – sceptical and mystical – such thinkers instantiate in fact relate to non-philosophy.
52. An excellent historical and technical framework for understanding this position in Kantian and speech-act theoretical terms is given in Isabelle Thomas-Fogiel, *The Death of Philosophy*. Although Thomas-Fogiel's conclusions differ in important respects from those proposed here (above all in the distinction between the 'congruence' and the 'indexical identity' of a statement and its enunciation), this text in general offers many latent and potentially productive connections with non-philosophy.
53. See *PD*, pp. 222–3.
54. This question arguably organises the entirety of Laruelle's thought, from the political materialism of Philosophy I to his most recent *General Theory of Victims*.

Bibliography

Allison, David B., ed., *The New Nietzsche: Contemporary Styles of Interpretation*. London and Cambridge, MA: MIT Press, 1985 [1977].

Althusser, Louis, *Philosophy and the Spontaneous Philosophy of the Scientists and Other Essays*, ed. Gregory Elliott, trans. Ben Brewster et al. London and New York: Verso, 1990 [1974].

Badiou, Alain, *Being and Event*, trans. Oliver Feltham. New York and London: Continuum, 2006 [1988].

Badiou, Alain, *Deleuze: The Clamor of Being*, trans. Louise Burchill. Minneapolis and London: University of Minnesota Press, 2000 [1997].

Badiou, Alain, *The Concept of Model: An Introduction to the Materialist Epistemology of Mathematics*, ed. and trans. Zachary Luke Fraser and Tzuchien Tho. Melbourne: re.press, 2007 [1969].

Badiou, Alain, *Theory of the Subject*, trans. Bruno Bosteels. New York and London: Continuum, 2009 [1982].

Barber, Daniel Colucciello, *On Diaspora: Christianity, Religion and Secularity*. Eugene, OR: Cascade Books, 2011.

Bataille, Georges, *The Accursed Share: An Essay on General Economy*, 3 vols, trans. Robert Hurley. New York: Zone Books, 1989–91 [1967–76].

Brandom, Robert, *Between Saying and Doing: Towards an Analytic Pragmatism*. Oxford and New York: Oxford University Press, 2008.

Brassier, Ray, *Nihil Unbound: Enlightenment and Extinction*. Basingstoke and New York: Palgrave Macmillan, 2007.

Braver, Lee, *A Thing of This World: A History of Continental Anti-Realism*. Evanston: Northwestern University Press, 2007.

Bryant, Levi, Nick Srnicek and Graham Harman, *The Speculative Turn: Continental Materialism and Realism*. Melbourne: re.press, 2011.

Burroughs, William, *Naked Lunch*. New York: Ballantine, 1973 [1959].

Caputo, John D., *The Prayers and Tears of Jacques Derrida: Religion without Religion*. Bloomington and Indianapolis: Indiana University Press, 1997.

Caputo, John D., 'The Return of Anti-Religion: From Radical Atheism to Radical Theology', *Journal for Cultural and Religious Theory*, 11:2 (2011).

Deleuze, Gilles, *Bergsonism*, trans. Hugh Tomlinson and Barbara Habberjam. New York: Zone Books, 1988 [1966].

Deleuze, Gilles, *Difference and Repetition*, trans. Paul Patton. New York: Columbia University Press, 1994 [1968].

Deleuze, Gilles, *The Logic of Sense*, ed. Constantin V. Boundas, trans. Mark Lester and Charles Stivale. New York: Columbia University Press, 1990 [1969].

Deleuze, Gilles, *Nietzsche and Philosophy*, trans. Hugh Tomlinson. New York: Columbia University Press, 1983 [1962].

Deleuze, Gilles and Félix Guattari, *A Thousand Plateaus: Capitalism and Schizophrenia*, trans. Brian Massumi. Minneapolis: University of Minnesota Press, 1987 (1980).

Derrida, Jacques, *Aporias*, trans. Thomas Dutoit. Stanford: Stanford University Press, 1993.

Derrida, Jacques, *Dissemination*, trans. Barbara Johnson. Chicago: University of Chicago Press, 1981 [1972].

Derrida, Jacques, *Of Grammatology*, trans. Gayatri Chakravorty Spivak, corrected edn. Baltimore and London: Johns Hopkins University Press, 1997 [1967].

Derrida, Jacques, *Points . . . Interviews, 1974–1994*, ed. Elisabeth Weber, trans. Peggy Kamuf et al. Stanford: Stanford University Press, 1995 [1992].

Derrida, Jacques, *Positions*, trans. Alan Bass. Chicago: University of Chicago Press, 1981 [1972].

Derrida, Jacques, *Speech and Phenomena and Other Essays on Husserl's Theory of Signs*, trans. David B. Allison. Evanston: Northwestern University Press, 1973 [1967].

Derrida, Jacques, *Spurs: Nietzsche's Styles*, trans. Barbara Harlow. Chicago and London: University of Chicago Press, 1979 [1978].

Derrida, Jacques, *The Work of Mourning*, ed. Pascale-Anne Brault and Michael Naas, various translators. Chicago and London: University of Chicago Press, 2001.

Derrida, Jacques, *Writing and Difference*, trans. Alan Bass. Chicago and London: University of Chicago Press, 1978 [1967].

de Vries, Hent, *Minimal Theologies: Critiques of Secular Reason in Adorno and Levinas*, trans. Geoffrey Hale. Baltimore and London: Johns Hopkins University Press, 2005 [1989].

Dufrenne, Mikel, *The Notion of the A Priori*, trans. Edward S. Casey. Evanston: Northwestern University Press, 1966 [1959].

Duméry, Henry, *The Problem of God in Philosophy of Religion: A critical examination of the category of the Absolute and the scheme of transcendence*, trans. Charles Courtney. Evanston: Northwestern University Press, 1964 [1957].

Euclid, *Elements*, trans. Thomas L. Heath. Sante Fe, NM: Green Lion Press, 2002.

Flaxman, Gregory, *Gilles Deleuze and the Fabulation of Philosophy: The Powers of the False, Volume 1*. Minneapolis: University of Minnesota Press, 2011.

Gardner, Sebastian, *Kant and the* Critique of Pure Reason. Abingdon and New York: Routledge, 1999.

Geroulanos, Stefanos, *An Atheism that is Not Humanist Emerges in French Thought*. Stanford: Stanford University Press, 2010.

Haar, Michel, *Heidegger and the Essence of Man*, trans. William McNeill. Albany, NY: SUNY Press, 1993.

Hadot, Pierre, *The Present Alone is Our Happiness*, trans. Marc Djaballah. Stanford: Stanford University Press, 2009.

Hägglund, Martin, *Radical Atheism: Derrida and the Time of Life*. Stanford: Stanford University Press, 2008.

Hägglund, Martin, 'The Radical Evil of Deconstruction: A Reply to John Caputo', *Journal for Cultural and Religious Theory*, 11:2 (2011).

Hallward, Peter, *Out of this World: Deleuze and the Philosophy of Creation*. London and New York: Verso, 2006.

Harman, Graham, *The Quadruple Object*. Winchester, UK and Washington: Zero Books, 2011.

Heidegger, Martin, *Basic Writings: from* Being and Time *to* The Task of Thinking, ed. and trans. David Farrell Krell. New York: Harper Collins, 1993 [1927–1964].

Heidegger, Martin, *Being and Time*, trans. John Macquarrie and Edward Robinson. New York: Harper and Row, 1962 [1927].

Heidegger, Martin, *Contributions to Philosophy (of the Event)*, trans. Richard Rojcewicz and Daniela Vallega-Neu. Bloomington and Indianapolis: Indiana University Press, 2012 [1989].

Heidegger, Martin, *Kant and the Problem of Metaphysics*, trans. James S. Churchill. Bloomington and London: Indiana University, 1962 [1929].

Heidegger, Martin, *Nietzsche*, 4 volumes, trans. David Farrell Krell. San Francisco: Harper Collins, 1979–82 [1954–61].

Heidegger, Martin, *What is Called Thinking?*, trans. J. Glenn Gray. New York: Harper and Row, 1968 [1954].

Hemming, Laurence Paul, *Heidegger's Atheism: The Refusal of a Theological Voice*. Notre Dame: Notre Dame University Press, 2002.

Hofstadter, Douglas, *I am a Strange Loop*. New York: Basic Books, 2007.

Hyppolite, Jean, *Genesis and Structure of Hegel's* Phenomenology of Spirit, trans. Samuel Cherniak and John Heckman. Evanston: Northwestern University Press, 1974 [1946].

Hyppolite, Jean, *Logic and Existence*, trans. Leonard Lawlor and Amit Sen. Albany, NY: SUNY Press, 1997 [1953].

Janicaud, Dominique, *Powers of the Rational: Science, Technology, and the Future of Thought*, trans. Peg Birmingham and Elizabeth Birmingham. Bloomington and Indianapolis: Indiana University Press, 1994 [1985].

Kerslake, Christian, *Immanence and the Vertigo of Philosophy: From Kant to Deleuze*. Edinburgh: Edinburgh University Press, 2009.

Klossowski, Pierre, *Nietzsche and the Vicious Circle*, trans. Daniel W. Smith. Chicago: University of Chicago Press, 1997 [1969].

Kojève, Alexandre, *Introduction to the Reading of Hegel: Lectures on the Phenomenology of Spirit*, trans. James H. Nichols, Jr., ed. Allan Bloom. Ithaca and London: Cornell University Press, 1980 [1947].

Land, Nick, *Fanged Noumena: Collected Writings 1987–2007*. New York and Falmouth: Urbanomic/Sequence, 2011.

Laruelle, François, *Anti-Badiou: Sur l'introduction du Maoïsme dans la philosophie*. [Anti-Badiou: The Introduction of Maoism into Philosophy]. Paris: Kimé, 2011.

Laruelle, François, *Au-delà du principe de pouvoir* [*Beyond the Power Principle*]. Paris: Payot, 1978.

Laruelle, François, *Une biographie de l'homme ordinaire: des Autorités et des Minorités* [*A Biography of Ordinary Man: Of Authorities and Minorities*]. Paris: Aubier Montaigne, 1985.

Laruelle, François, *Le déclin de l'écriture* [*The Decline of Writing*]. Paris: Aubier Flammarion, 1977.

Laruelle, François, *Future Christ: A Lesson in Heresy*, trans. Anthony Paul Smith. New York and London: Continuum, 2010 [2002].

Laruelle, François, *Introduction aux sciences génériques* [*Introduction to Generic Sciences*]. Paris: Petra, 2008.

Laruelle, François, *Machines textuelles: Déconstruction et libido d'écriture* [*Textual Machines: Deconstruction and the Libido of Writing*]. Paris: Seuil, 1976.

Laruelle, François, *Mystique non-philosophique à l'usage des contemporains* [*Non-philosophical Mysticism for Contemporary Use*]. Paris: L'Harmattan, 2007.

Laruelle, François, *Nietzsche contre Heidegger: Thèses pour une politique nietzschéenne* [*Nietzsche contra Heidegger*]. Paris: Payot, 1977.

Laruelle, François, *The Non-Philosophy Project: Essays by Francois Laruelle*, Gabriel Alkon and Boris Gunjevic, eds. Candor, NY: Telos, 2012.

Laruelle, François, *Phénomène et Différence: Essai sur l'ontologie de Ravaisson* [*Phenomenon and Difference: Essay on the Ontology of Ravaisson*]. Paris: Klincksieck, 1971.

Laruelle, François, *Les philosophies de la différence: introduction critique*. Paris: PUF, 1986.

Laruelle, François, *Philosophies of Difference: A Critical Introduction to Non-philosophy*, trans. Rocco Gangle. New York and London: Continuum, 2010 [1986].

Laruelle, François, *Philosophie Non-standard: générique, quantique, philo-fiction* [*Non-Standard Philosophy: Generic, Quantic, Philo-Fiction*]. Paris: Kimé, 2010.

Laruelle, François, *Le principe de minorité* [*The Minority Principle*]. Paris: Aubier Montaigne, 1981.

Laruelle, François, *Principes de la non-philosophie* [*Principles of Non-philosophy*]. Paris: PUF, 1996.

Laruelle, François, *Théorie des Identités* [Theory of Identities]. Paris: PUF, 1992.

Legay, Jean-Marie and Anne-Françoise Schmid, *Philosophie de l'interdisciplinarité. Correspondance (1999–2004) sur la recherche scientifique, la modélisation et les objets complexes*. Paris: Pétra, 2004.

Levinas, Emmanuel, *Ethics and Infinity: Conversations with Philippe Nemo*, trans. Richard A. Cohen. Pittsburgh: Duquesne University Press, 1985 [1982].

Levinas, Emmanuel, *On Escape: De l'évasion*, trans. Bettina Bergo. Stanford: Stanford University Press, 2003 [1982].

Levinas, Emmanuel, *The Theory of Intuition in Husserl's Phenomenology*, 2nd edn, trans. André Orianne. Evanston: Northwestern University Press, 1995 [1930].

Lord, Beth, *Kant and Spinozism: Transcendental Idealism and Immanence from Jacobi to Deleuze*. Basingstoke and New York: Palgrave-Macmillan, 2011.

Luhmann, Niklas, *Social Systems*, trans. John Bednarz, Jr. and Dirk Baecker. Stanford: Stanford University Press, 1995 [1984].

MacKenzie, Iain, *The Idea of Pure Critique*. London and New York: Continuum, 2004.

Mac Lane, Saunders, *Categories for the Working Mathematician*, 2nd edn. New York: Springer-Verlag, 1998.

Meillassoux, Quentin, *After Finitude: An Essay on the Necessity of Contingency*, trans. Ray Brassier. New York and London: Continuum, 2008 [2006].

Merleau-Ponty, Maurice, *The Visible and the Invisible*, trans. Alphonso Lingis, ed. Claude Lefort. Evanston: Northwestern University Press, 1968 [1964].

Milbank, John, *Theology and Social Theory: Beyond Secular Reason*. Malden, MA and Oxford: Blackwell, 1990.

Mullarkey, John, *Post-Continental Philosophy: An Outline*. London and New York: Continuum, 2006.

Mullarkey, John and Anthony Paul Smith, eds, *Laruelle and Non-philosophy*. Edinburgh: Edinburgh University Press, 2012.

Naas, Michael, *Miracle and Machine: Jacques Derrida and the Two Sources of Religion, Science, and the Media*. New York: Fordham University Press, 2012.

Nāgārjuna, *The Fundamental Wisdom of the Middle Way*, trans. Jay L. Garfield. New York and Oxford: Oxford University Press, 1995.

Nietzsche, Friedrich, *Beyond Good and Evil: Prelude to a Philosophy of the Future*, ed. Rolf-Peter Horstmann, trans. Judith Norman. Cambridge and New York: Cambridge University Press, 2002 [1886].

Nietzsche, Friedrich, *The Portable Nietzsche*, ed. and trans. Walter Kaufmann. New York: Viking, 1954.

Nietzsche, Friedrich, *The Will to Power*, trans. Walter Kaufmann and R. J. Hollingdale, ed. Walter Kaufmann. New York: Vintage, 1968 [1901].

Non-philosophie, Le Collectif, *La Non-philosophie des Contemporains*. Paris: Kimé, 1995.

Peirce, Charles Sanders, *Reasoning and the Logic of Things: The Cambridge Conferences Lectures of 1898*, ed. Kenneth Laine Ketner. Cambridge, MA and London: Harvard University Press, 1992.

Priest, Graham, *Beyond the Limits of Thought*, 2nd edn. Oxford and New York: Oxford University Press, 2002.

Rajan, Tilottama, *Deconstruction and the Remainders of Phenomenology: Sartre, Derrida, Foucault, Baudrillard*. Stanford: Stanford University Press, 2002.

187

Ramey, Joshua, *The Hermetic Deleuze: Philosophy and Spiritual Ordeal*. Durham, NC and London: Duke University Press, 2012.

Richardson, William J., *Heidegger: Through Phenomenology to Thought*. Dordrecht: Martinus Nijhoff, 1963.

Ricoeur, Paul, *Husserl: An Analysis of His Phenomenology*, trans. Edward G. Ballard and Lester E. Embree. Evanston: Northwestern University Press, 1967 [1949–1957].

Schürmann, Reiner, *Broken Hegemonies*, trans. Reginald Lilly. Bloomington and Indianapolis: Indiana University Press, 2003 [1996].

Schürmann, Reiner, *Heidegger on Being and Acting: From Principles to Anarchy*, trans. Christine-Marie Gros. Bloomington: Indiana University Press, 1987 [1982].

Sellars, Wilfrid, *Empiricism and the Philosophy of Mind*, Cambridge, MA and London: Harvard University Press, 1997 [1956].

Sextus Empiricus, *Against the Logicians*, trans. Richard Bett. New York and Cambridge: Cambridge University Press, 2005.

Spencer Brown, G., *Laws of Form*. New York: Bantam, 1973 [1969].

Smith, Gregory Bruce, *Nietzsche, Heidegger and the Transition to Postmodernity*. Chicago and London: University of Chicago Press, 1996.

Thomas-Fogiel, Isabelle, *The Death of Philosophy: Reference and Self-Reference in Contemporary Thought*, trans. Richard A. Lynch. New York: Columbia University Press, 2011 [2005].

Toscano, Alberto, *The Theatre of Production: Philosophy and Individuation Between Kant and Deleuze*. Houndmills, Basingstoke and New York: Palgrave-Macmillan, 2006.

Vattimo, Gianni, *Dialogue with Nietzsche*, trans. William McCuaig. New York: Columbia University Press, 2006 [2000].

Vattimo, Gianni, *The End of Modernity*, trans. Jon R. Snyder. Baltimore: Johns Hopkins University Press, 1988 [1985].

Willatt, Edward, *Kant, Deleuze, and Architectonics*. New York and London: Continuum, 2012

Williamson, Timothy, *The Philosophy of Philosophy*. Malden, MA and Oxford: Blackwell, 2007.

Žižek, Slavoj, *Less Than Nothing: Hegel and the Shadow of Dialectical Materialism*. London and New York: Verso, 2012.

Zupančič, Alenka, *The Shortest Shadow: Nietzsche's Philosophy of the Two*. London and Cambridge, MA: MIT Press, 2003.

Index

Heidegger, Martin *see* Finitude
Husserl, Edmund, 8, 10, 12, 19, 40, 41, 94, 118, 177

Idealism (Nietzsche-Deleuzean model of Difference), 47–8, 58–85
as contrasted with Hegel, 59
Deleuze's role in, 60–1, 65–6, 79–85
and reversibility of contraries, 59–61, 72
immanence *see* Difference

Kant, Immanuel, 8, 10, 12, 39–41, 47, 65, 78–9, 90, 92, 93–9, 103, 109, 117, 157, 161–2, 177
Klossowski, Pierre, 62, 70–2, 75, 119
Kojève, Alexandre, 9–10, 70

Laruelle, François *see* non-philosophy
Levinas, Emmanuel, 11–12, 14, 19, 129, 130–57
Lobachevsky, Nikolai *see* Euclidean and non-Euclidean geometries

(meta-)Difference, 32–3, 35–6, 127
in Greek/Judaic distinction, 133
in metaphysical/transcendental distinction, 41–2
metaphysical/transcendental distinction, 39–44, 47–8, 150, 153
in Derridean Difference, 133
in Nietzschean Difference, 63–8
in Heideggerean Finitude, 96–9, 108–9
model theory, 50–3
mystic/mystical/mysticism, 174

Nietzsche, Friedrich *see* Idealism
Nietzsche/Heidegger conflict, 16, 48–9, 76–9, 92, 98, 111, 148, 166–7
in Derrida, 116, 128–9
(non-)One, 158–64
non-philosophy
as critique of philosophy, 4, 9, 31–2, 117–18, 146–7, 179

as generalisation of philosophy, 51–3, 147
history and development of (Philosophy I –V), 15–20
as science, 21, 33–4, 46, 121
non-thetic transcendence (NTT) 143, 158–9, 164–5

One, 17, 34–9, 159–66, 170–1; *see also* Difference

phenomenology, 19, 118
in French thought, 8–10
reduction, 177
theological turn in, 14
philosophical decision, 153–4, 164–71

Real *see* One
reality *see* syntax/reality distinction
relations, logic of, 5, 35, 156–8
in Derrida, 128
in Heidegger, 99
in Nietzsche-Deleuze, 60–1
representation, critique of, 9, 11, 33, 45, 150–1
Riemann, Bernhard *see* Euclidean and non-Euclidean geometries

self-reference, 32–3, 175–7
of Differance/deconstruction, 116, 120–1
see also (meta-)Difference
speculative realism, 14–15
structuralism, 8–10, 118
syntax/reality distinction, 21, 22, 44–7, 48, 92
in Finitude, 110–11
in Idealism, 68–76

tautology
in Heidegger, 96–8
in Nietzsche, 77–8
transcendental *see* metaphysical/transcendental distinction

vision-in-One, 178–9